THE CHEMICAL CHOIR

Frontispiece: A list of alchemical signs and their meanings. It begins (third line) with gold, gold filings and silver, and ends with symbols for days, nights, hours, and a day and a night.

The Chemical Choir

P. G. Maxwell-Stuart

continuum

Hambledon Continuum is an imprint of Continuum Books
Continuum UK, The Tower Building, 11 York Road, London SE1 7NX
Continuum US, 80 Maiden Lane, Suite 704, New York, NY 10038

www.continuumbooks.com

First published 2008
British Library Cataloguing-in-Publication Data
A catalogue record for this book is available from the British Library.

ISBN 978 1 84725 148 0

Typeset by Pindar NZ (Egan Reid), Auckland, New Zealand
Printed and bound by MPG Books Ltd, Cornwall, Great Britain

Contents

For David Stewart

Illustrations

Introduction

In 1675 Johann Joachim Becher, physician, metallurgist, economic theorist, adviser to the Elector of Bavaria and alchemist, transmuted lead into silver from which he made a commemorative medal. During the same year Wenceslas Seiler, an Augustinian monk and later officer of the Bohemian Mint, went one better and transmuted copper and tin into gold. Then in 1677, on the saint's day of the Holy Roman Emperor, Leopold I, he transmuted a large medallion, over a foot wide, from silver into gold. Both transmuted artefacts can be seen in the Kunstshistorisches Museum in Vienna, along with another similar medal struck from gold which had been transmuted in the presence of Karl Philip, Count Palatine of the Rhineland on the last day of December 1716. These alchemical displays were by no means unusual – indeed, they were encouraged at the Imperial Court, partly as diversions, partly as demonstrations that God was favouring the Habsburgs with these signs of His pleasure and approval – and we must put aside the conventional image of the alchemist as a threadbare, etiolated individual, filthy and stinking from sulphurous smoke and half-poisoned by mercury, and picture a well-dressed, articulate man surrounded by noble men and women in a vaulted chamber of a castle or imperial palace, lecturing deferentially to people who almost certainly well understood what he was talking about and who had examined his equipment thoroughly beforehand to obviate any chances of fraud. Demonstrations by members of the Académie des Sciences in the presence of Louis XIV, or by Fellows of the Royal Society of London before Charles II, provide close parallels, the demonstrators being some of the foremost scientists of their day.

But beyond these refined and elevated circles there did indeed exist thousands of poor alchemists who spent their inheritances, their substance and their future prospects, not to mention the money of any patrons they might acquire in the course of their researches, in pursuit of what all too often turned out to be an elusive goal. Nor was the phenomenon confined to Europe. The Far East, India and the Middle East housed thousands of alchemists in their turn – before Europe, in fact – and while it is often assumed that alchemy was largely replaced by chemistry during the eighteenth century and relegated to those dark corners of history in which failed or superseded beliefs are supposed to lurk, the truth is that at this present time alchemy has never been more vigorous or more widely practised, especially in the homelands of science and rationality. When we look at the history of alchemy, therefore, we are observing a living, not a dead, science, and questions about what it is and what alchemists do are, in consequence, both pertinent and relevant to modern enquirers.

Alchemy is a branch of knowledge that deals with the possibility of changing one metal into another more 'noble' or more 'evolved', and of making an elixir that will cure intractable illnesses and prolong active life even to the point where an individual can become immortal. To this should be added its role as a catalyst to induce or aid spiritual transformation in the alchemist him- or herself, a role which has been present from the start, although it has gone through several stages of expression during the last 2,500 years. Like all intellectual and practical disciplines, alchemy developed a jargon of its own, specialized vocabulary, symbols and images which often render alchemical texts more or less impenetrable. The jargon, however, is not so peculiar nor the images and symbols so obscure that they cannot be interpreted, as long as one realizes that often words we think we recognize do not actually mean what we think they mean. Most notorious of these are 'mercury', 'sulphur' and 'salt'. They appear constantly in every alchemical work, but, as several writers subtly warn us, they do not refer to ordinary mercury, sulphur or salt, and when such writers call them 'our mercury' or 'our sulphur', it is a sure indication we have entered the realm of jargon and that therefore we must not take literally what we are reading.

But why should anyone think that one metal can be changed into another? The notion rests upon the belief that everything consists of specific elements – the irreducible constituents of material things – in different proportions. If this is so, then reducing a piece of matter to its elements, separating those elements, and altering their proportions relative to each other, will result in a fundamental change of the matter itself. One substance can quite literally become another. It was also thought that metals grow in the ground, just like plants, and that while they grow they gradually mutate from one metallic form to another 'better' or 'more perfect'; and since gold is the most noble and most perfect form any metal can take – it does not rust or deteriorate in any way – all metals are in fact striving to become gold. What the alchemist does in the laboratory is merely an imitation of Nature. He or she goes through each process used by Nature in her ordinary course, but speeds it up, so that what takes Nature hundreds or thousands of years is reduced to a matter of months or a year or two.

What makes this process so quick is the insertion of a catalyst, the philosopher's stone, not so much a stone as a reddish powder, which has an almost miraculous effect on the transformation taking place in the alchemist's crucible. The alchemist's goal was thus the production of this powder, not the gold-making itself, and in order to produce it he or she had to begin with the correct basic material, called the *prima materia*, whose identity was one of alchemy's best-kept secrets. Confusion was added by some alchemists who maintained that there were three different 'stones', one animal, one vegetable and one mineral, each of which fulfilled a different purpose: curing illness, stimulating growth and transmuting metals. Was the *prima materia* different for each of these? It is difficult to tell. What is clear, however, is that the laboratory process went through specific stages, and that these stages indicated their success or failure by the colours which appeared as they completed each stage. First the matter being used to produce the *prima materia* had to be broken down into its constituent parts. 'Calcination' reduced it to an ash, 'purification' saw it washed by waters, acids, salts, or such liquids as urine or vinegar. Black in the vessel indicated that the requisite breaking down was taking place. The stuff which survived this process was made volatile by 'sublimation' and 'distillation', which converted a solid to vapour, and was then fixed by 'congelation' so as to render the volatile solid again. The solid was sometimes referred to as the 'body' of the material, and the vapour as its 'spirit'. Black gave way to white and grey and then a brilliant flashing white, indicating the achievement of the white stone or elixir, a substance which would change metal into silver. Further processes in the crucible saw its contents change to a burst of colours usually called 'the peacock's tail', followed by a yellow-red which told the alchemist that he or she had produced the red stone, the red elixir, the philosopher's stone whose properties were such that any metal touched by it would turn into gold, and anyone who ingested it would recover health and youth in an instant.

Is any of this a real possibility? Has it actually been achieved? During the 1920s, a hectic period of alchemical experimentation, Dr Irvine Masson told the *Daily Mail* newspaper, 'So far no definite transmutation of an element by building up heavy atoms of gold from lighter metals has been achieved. On the other hand, Sir Ernest Rutherford has disintegrated certain of the lighter elements into one still lighter. While one cannot say it is impossible, there seems to be no reason why gold should be specially singled out by Nature to be the ultimate product of a building-up or breaking-down process'. In other words, 'let's wait and see', a wise injunction, because during the succeeding 80 years many more claims to have achieved this particular goal have been made, and sooner or later one of them would prove to be genuine. For in the 1960s, Judith Temperley, a physicist at Edgewood Arsenal in Maryland, bombarded mercury with high-energy neutrons and destroyed one of its 80 protons by a process known as 'electron capture'. What was left was an atom with only 79 protons, and that is an atom of gold. In essence, therefore, the transmutation had succeeded and the claim of alchemists that such a change could take place was finally justified.

Making gold, however, as we shall see, was never the primary aim of many alchemists. For them, as for their patrons, the creation of youth-giving elixirs was far more important and far more desirable. Even more important, however, was the growing belief that what had begun as a set of laboratory techniques was at bottom little more than an extended set of metaphors for parallel changes in the soul of the alchemist him- or herself. 'The sun and moon are two magical principles, the one active, the other passive, this masculine, that feminine,' wrote the seventeenth-century alchemist Thomas Vaughan in his *Anthroposophia Theomagica*. 'As they move, so move the wheels of corruption and generation. They mutually dissolve and compound, but properly the moon is *organum transmutationis inferioris materiae*. There is not a compound in all Nature but hath in it a little sun and a little moon.' Humankind was a mirror image of Creation itself, a microcosm to the macrocosm. Hence, whatever happened in the latter had its effect in or on the former – a perception not far removed from that of the modern physicist who says that the experiment which takes place in a test tube is affected by the presence of the experimenter. Alchemy thus resonates and echoes across the centuries.

China: The Golden Road to Immortality

Beginnings are often contentious and it is a moot point whether alchemy began in China or India. Did it filter through to China from India – or even Egypt – during the second or third centuries BC; was it of Chinese origin and carried thence by traders to India, to the Middle East, and finally to the West; or are we to think that it arose independently in several different places from a combination of metallurgical experimentation and philosophical observation of change and transformation in Nature? If we go by etymology, there seems little doubt that 'alchemy' is a mongrel term originating in Chinese *kim* or *chim* meaning 'aurifaction' – the theoretical possibility that gold can be manufactured. It is then possible to suggest that the various techniques involved in this process, along with their blanket name, trickled into the Mediterranean world where *kim* was transliterated into the Greek of Egypt as *khemeia*, to which later still, perhaps under the influence of Syria, was added the Arabic definite article *al*, and that thus was produced the form *alchimia* adopted by Latin and Western vernaculars. But let us put these aside for the moment and accept, for the sake of argument, China's pre-eminence in the origin of this group of activities.

The word *kim* seems to relate Chinese alchemy to a process whereby gold may be produced from the application of certain protracted laboratory techniques to natural metals or minerals, and thus to refer to the same kind of alchemy with which we are familiar in the West. But making gold is merely one part of this complex and extensive science, because Chinese alchemy differs from its Western counterpart in at least one fundamental respect. For while the manufacture of gold was certainly one aim of its practitioners, a more important one concerned the effort to produce an elixir or pill of immortality – that is, a substance which could be ingested and, by acting on key organs of the body, alter it so that the individual was enabled to live many hundreds of years beyond the normal span, or even become immortal and thus join the ranks of divine or semi-divine beings. Such a goal was never the principal aim in the mediaeval or early modern West, although it is possible to see its modern counterpart in Western hopes that medical techniques such as genetic manipulation may lengthen human life considerably.[1]

In Chinese alchemy, then, we are dealing not only with a science whose main features differ in many ways from that in the West, but also a mindset which is different, too. Three questions need to be asked immediately. Why was gold considered to be so important? Does 'gold' in alchemical texts necessarily refer to what a modern metallurgist means by 'gold'? When the Chinese looked for longevity or immortality, what did they think or believe these were?

Gold was well known in China from ancient times. Coins were made from it, emperors were presented with large quantities of it, and references were made to it in several of the early classics such as the fourth-century BC *Book of Changes* (*I Ching*) and its contemporary *Historical Classic* (*Shu Ching*). The fact that gold does not rust or lose its colour or tarnish will almost inevitably link it with notions of that state in which everything is perfect and lasts for ever – by definition a state which is not encountered in this material world but belongs to another superior realm of existence. Wearing gold, using vessels made from it, even ingesting gold must surely, it was thought, cause something of that innate virtue in gold to impart itself to human beings, and in consequence gold was conceived to have a value far beyond that of mere exchange in buying and selling. Indeed, one development of alchemical opinion maintained that 'in a well-ordered society, all gold would be thrown away in the mountains' because the time and effort spent in searching for it distracted people from a more profitable use of their allotted years.[2]

Nevertheless, the practical advantages of manufacturing gold were well understood and by no means ignored by everyone. Gold-working artisans had early acquired the skills of cupellation, for example, the procedure whereby precious metal is refined and then assayed, and thus were able not only to detect pure gold but also to make that wide variety of metallic substances which could pass or be mistaken for gold by those without such expertise. Indeed, by 144 BC making artificial gold had become so common that the Emperor Ching Ti was obliged to issue an edict against it, and thereafter anyone who wished to practise this form of alchemy needed an imperial licence to do so. Fiscal considerations apart, it may be that this kind of alchemy had become too closely associated with magic to allow the authorities to view it with equanimity. Only 31 years after Ching Ti's edict, Luan Ta, a magician and pharmacist, was presented to the Emperor. 'My master', he said, 'maintained that yellow gold can be produced [artificially], that the breach in the Yellow River can be closed, that the herb of immortality can be found, and that the *hsien* can be made to appear.' It was a bold proclamation of his interests, considering that the Emperor had recently put to death an imperial magician; but fortunately for Luan Ta the Emperor now regretted doing so and was feeling gracious. So Luan Ta was permitted to give a demonstration of his magical abilities. The way was now open again to ask for licences to pursue the arts of aurifaction and, as such a promising way of replenishing imperial treasure could scarcely be passed by, the practice of alchemy picked up again. Indeed, in the eleventh century, we are told, an alchemist made gold from iron in such quantities that the Emperor was able to have several hundred tortoises and medals made out of it, artefacts he either distributed among his officials or used as talismans to protect two of the imperial palaces; while in the twelfth, we learn of silver made from mercury and gold from iron by another alchemist whose final products the author links with potable medicines.[3]

The alchemical term 'gold', then, was not necessarily confined to the dense, bright yellow, lustrous metal whose chemical symbol is *Au*. Mediaeval Chinese texts list various kinds of gold (and indeed silver) which clearly include other metals which have either been gilded, tinged with sulphides, or coated with gold, or were themselves yellowish, such as the cuprous or brassy alloys, or were actually ores of other metals such as chalcopyrite or bornite. So we must be prepared to find that alchemical gold may have been a substance which strove after the condition of gold (*Au*) inasmuch as the alchemist was endeavouring in his laboratory to hasten what he conceived as a change which took place in Nature as one metal 'grew' into another; or to work with a metal or alloy which could be made to take on the appearance of gold. Consequently, when we find that an alchemist claims to have produced gold artificially, we are not entitled to dismiss out of hand what he is saying, nor to assume that there must have been any intent to deceive. As Arthur Waley observed:

> In China ... the attempt to make gold went on simultaneously with the attempt to make artificially pearls, jade, and other 'talismanic' substances, and this combination of speeding up what were conceived as natural processes and a theoretical approach to the alchemical treatment of substances, which relied on extracting their vital 'essences' – essences which were not the same as the physical substance itself, but were its innermost reality and therefore just as much 'gold' or 'mercury' or 'cinnabar' as the material substance – meant that alchemists could legitimately call their artificial products 'gold' or 'silver' without any sense of falsehood.

It is also worth observing that certain Chinese writers were suspicious of natural, unrefined gold. 'It wards off evil influences,' wrote Thao Hung-Ching in c.AD 500, 'but it also contains poison which, if the metal is ingested in the unpurified state, can kill.' Alchemical gold, on the other hand, had been subjected to a large number of refining processes before it emerged in its final form. It followed, therefore, that it was superior to natural gold as an ingredient in elixirs or pills which were to be taken internally.[4]

The growth of minerals, ores and metals in the ground was a theory common to both Chinese and Western thought. *The Book of Huai Nan* (c. second century BC), for example, describes how, after 500 years, the mineral *chüeh* (perhaps realgar) gives birth to yellow mercury which in turn, after another 500 years, produces gold, while azurite or malachite takes 800 years to give birth to green mercury and green mercury another 800 to produce a blue metal which was probably lead. Similarly, Liu An observed, 'Gold grows in the earth by a slow process and is evolved from the immaterial principle underlying the universe, passing from one form to another up to silver, and then from silver to gold.' Minerals, then, matured within the earth which acted as a kind of womb for their growth, and were subject to those cyclical rhythms of birth, growth, maturity and death, which could be observed in everything else. But not only did they grow, they also decayed – all except gold which seemed to be immune to natural corrosion – so the speculation arose, if Nature takes so long to achieve her ends, can the process she employs be speeded up? Hence experimentation in the alchemical laboratory.

Experimentation of such a kind and scale, however, represents human in-trusion into forces normally well beyond human control, since birth, growth, decay and death are processes subject to the will of the Divine, no matter how that Divine may be envisaged. As Nathan Sivin has remarked, 'an alchemist who set out to fabricate an elixir in a few months or a year was creating an opportunity to witness the cyclical sweep of universal change.'[5] Yet in doing so, he or she was not merely an observer but an active and powerful player, intruding upon the realms of both religion and magic, the former because, as an alchemist, one is challenging the power and will of the Divine by seeking to alter its settled will, the latter because, so extraordinary is the process whereby Nature is bent to the wishes of a human operator, the resulting gold or elixir will be capable of producing effects which are beyond the usual or, indeed, 'natural', effects one can normally employ for one's own advantage. Thus, for example, we are told by the great Chinese alchemist Ko Hung that past adepts and alchemists could disappear at will, or cause cloud and mist to appear, or make water flow backwards and similar occult feats. Magic, he said, was essential to protect the alchemist against natural or even preternatural dangers, and therefore an alchemist ought to know which amulets he must wear or carry in order to ward off dangerous animals and evil spirits. We may also note the common term for 'alchemist' – *fang shih*, which means 'magician-technician'.

Preparations for working the science and making an elixir were complex, involving astrology so that one might be sure the time was propitious for undertaking such work, abstinence from certain foods as part of a more general purification of the body in order to prepare the alchemist psychologically for the awful importance of the experiments he was about to make, and withdrawal from town or village into the fastness and solitude of a mountain retreat where concentration could be complete and uninterrupted. Maintaining a balance of male and female, too, was important and so the alchemist's wife, or at least a female assistant, often played a crucial role in the progress of the work. Consequently we find that alchemy was an operation practised by women as well as men. From the *Records of Strange Magician-Technicians* (Chiang Huai I Jen Lu), written in c.AD 975, we are told about a female alchemist, Keng hsien-seng, who was not only a mistress of the 'art of the yellow and the white' (i.e. alchemy), but also of many other techniques ranging from distillation of perfumes to conjuring tricks; the twelfth-century poet Hsü Yen-Chou recorded the sad story of Li Shao-Yün who spent many years trying to concoct an elixir from cinnabar – one of the many key ingredients in Chinese alchemy – but died without achieving her aim; and Ko Hung, whose wife was also an alchemist, relates a well-known anecdote about Chheng Wei who, purportedly, lived in the first century BC. He tried to manufacture gold according to instructions laid down in a book by the second-century BC alchemist Liu An, but without success:

> One day his wife went to see him just as he was fanning the charcoal to increase the heating of a reaction-vessel in which there was mercury. She said, 'Let me show you what I can do', and, taking a small amount of some substance from her pouch, she threw it into the vessel. After about the space of time in which a man could take a meal, she opened the vessel, and they saw that the contents had all turned to silver. Chheng Wei was amazed and asked his wife how it was that she could achieve a successful projection. She replied, 'It cannot be gained unless one has the right destiny'.[6]

Now, it will have been noted that while Chheng Wei and his wife were experimenting with the creation of a precious metal, Li Shao-Yün was trying to make an elixir. Over time, Chinese alchemy developed more than one branch of itself and its pursuit of an elixir of immortality could be followed in one or two ways, *wei tan* which made it out of mineral or inorganic substances, or *nei tan* which used bodily tissues and secretions such as saliva or semen or blood, extracting from them their primary vitalities, their 'essences', in forms which could then be incorporated into ingestible or potable concretions. One clear difference between the two methods, however, is obvious. *Wei tan* produced elixirs which proved time and again to be poisonous. It is not possible to eat or drink compounds of mercury, lead, cinnabar and a host of other minerals or metals, no matter how refined or distilled, without succumbing to their lethal effects. A sixth-century AD text, *Records in the Rock Chamber* (Thai Chhing Shih Pi Chi), describes how the ingester might feel:

> After taking an elixir, if your face and body itch as though insects were crawling over them, if your hands and feet swell dropsically, if you cannot stand the smell of food and bring it up after you have eaten it, if you feel as though you were going to be sick most of the time, if you experience weakness in the four limbs, if you have to go often to the latrine, or if your head or stomach violently ache – do not be alarmed or disturbed. All these effects are merely proofs that the elixir you are taking is successfully dispelling your latent disorders.

Alas, on the contrary, as Needham points out, these are actually symptoms characteristic of metallic poisoning, something which was candidly admitted about two centuries later by the author of the *Mirror of the Alchemical Laboratory*, Tan Fan Ching Yuan: 'When people use mercury and cinnabar to fabricate [gold] vessels, it is a technique to make private profit, and this [material] should not be taken internally, for it contains the poisonous *chhi* of [this] metal'.[7]

Why, then, did people continue to manufacture and use these dangerous elixirs? The answer lies in the goal at which they were aiming: longevity or immortality. Chinese concepts of longevity and the afterlife are radically different from those in the West. Mahayana Buddhist notions in particular provide a multiplicity of hells and heavens, with reincarnated spirits ascending and descending through an immense range of possibilities including life as an incarnated human. Indigenous Chinese ideas, on the other hand, were firmly rooted in this world, this corporeal existence, and so the goal of *longevity* was one at which people found it easy and natural to aim. Drugs of various kinds, coupled with breathing and sexual exercises, not only rejuvenated the body here and now but prolonged its existence far into the future; while remarkable preservation techniques enabled even a corpse to retain its plasticity, apparently incorruptible, as the famous case of the Lady of Tai illustrates. Rarefication of the body through ingestion of herbs or herbal concoctions could transform it from its grossly material form into something rather less human like and rather more spirit-like – the *hsien* of technical Taoist vocabulary.

The author of *Kinship of the Three* (Tshan Thung Chhi) in the second century AD expressed it thus:

> Even if the herb chü-sheng can make one live longer,
> Why not try putting the Elixir into the mouth?
> Gold by nature does not rot or decay;
> Therefore it is of all things most precious.
> When [the alchemist] includes it in his diet
> The duration of his life becomes everlasting . . .
> When the golden powder enters the five entrails,
> A fog is dispelled, like rain-clouds scattered by the wind.
> Fragrant exhalations pervade the four limbs;
> The countenance beams with well-being and joy.
> Hairs that were white all turn to black;
> Teeth that had fallen grow in their former place.
> The old dotard is again a lusty youth;
> The decrepit crone is again a young girl.
> He whose form is changed and has escaped the perils of life,
> Has for his title the name of [Purified] Man.[8]

Immortality, however, as opposed to longevity, is a different matter. At first it was an attribute of the Divine, but with the advent of Taoism as a philosophical and religious system this began to alter. *Tao* is the immanent order of Nature and thus inextricably linked with the notion that life is of paramount importance. But 'life' in this philosophy is not merely a generalized concept but one applied to each individual part of creation. As the second-century AD Taoist *Canon of the Great Peace* (Thai Phing Ching) explains it, 'what Heaven stresses and values is the succession of life. Therefore the four seasons, following the teachings of the Heavenly Way, carry on and help to complete the development of life in an endless process so that all kinds of things can grow. So Heaven is known as the Father, the Life Producer and Earth is known as the Mother, the Life Fosterer.' The notion of extending the individual life endlessly seems to have developed in around the eighth century BC when people began to pray not only to escape old age but also to avoid the experience of death; and from this came the hope that one might be able to leave this world altogether and live as a *hsien* in some spiritual domain. The *wei tan* and *nei tan* forms of alchemy offered elixirs or pills for this purpose, and these were pursued eagerly not only in pre-Chhin times (before the third century BC) but afterwards, when rulers intensified their searches for what were called 'drugs of no death', an eagerness which was sometimes dampened by the inevitable deaths attendant upon ingesting such substances, but which revived from time to time in later centuries.[9]

At this point it may be wise to pause and ask ourselves about the evidence on which this narrative of alchemy is based. There is a remarkable variety of sources on which to draw: folklore, poetry, fiction, medical and encyclopaedic literature, alchemical treatises in large number, most of which have still not been translated, historical records and archaeology. The material is therefore both plentiful and rich. Many legends, for example, tell us about the amazing abilities and feats of those who have become *hsien*, such as the Eight Immortals including Chung-li Ch'üan, who became a Taoist wanderer and alchemist who discovered the secret of immortality during meditation; Lü Tung-pin, his pupil – a real individual whose dates are uncertain but who may have lived in the eighth, tenth or even eleventh century – who became famous as an adept and an alchemist, and has as his attribute a two-edged sword which confers invisibility; and Han Hsiang Tzu who bent his alchemical efforts to finding an elixir, and was killed when he fell from the peach tree of immortality, only to be transfigured and reappear as a Taoist priest. Stories about historical figures abound. The most famous, which bears repetition in spite of its celebrity, is told of the alchemist Wei Po-Yang and his dog. One day he retreated into the mountains, as was recommended by Taoist writers on the subject, in order to have no distractions from the work of preparing elixirs. He took with him his dog and three pupils, two of whom he distrusted because he had the feeling that they lacked a full and sincere belief in what he and they were doing. So he finally made his elixir and then decided to test them. 'Let us administer the elixir to the dog,' he said. 'If it survives and is able to fly, then we shall know if it is safe for humans to drink. If, on the other hand, the dog dies, we shall know not to take it.' The dog was fed the elixir and immediately collapsed and died. Whereupon Wei Po-Yang turned to his pupils and said, 'I'm afraid there was something wrong with the elixir. Since it has killed the dog, it is clear our understanding of the theory behind the process is faulty, and if we ingest the elixir we shall go the same way as the dog. What do you think we should do?' His pupils replied by asking Wei Po-Yang if he would be daring enough to take it himself, to which Wei Po-Yang answered that he would be ashamed to return to his family and friends a failure, and that death by the elixir would be no worse than living with disappointment and loss of face. So he took the elixir and died. The one pupil Wei Po-Yang trusted did likewise, leaving the two untrustworthy students to decide they wanted to cling to this life a few decades longer. So off they went down the mountain to arrange the burial of their master and their friend. Meanwhile, Wei Po-Yang revived, administered a restorative to his faithful student and his dog, and all three became *hsien*.[10]

Such legends should not necessarily be dismissed as entirely imaginative, of course, for in common with folklore there may well be remnants of fact underlying their surface or lurking in the details. Thus, the Wei Po-Yang anecdote bears witness not only to the possible practice of animal experimentation in the fourth century AD, but also reminds us of the lethal nature of so many of the compounds manufactured, used and administered by these early alchemists. Arsenic, mercury, lead, gold, digitalis, aconite, hemp – these are merely a few of the ingredients we can identify, and they raise the question, posed also by the Wei Po-Yang story, of whether such elixirs were not deliberately concocted so as to produce either death itself or a period of profound insensibility mimicking death, on the grounds that physical death is the gate to immortality.

Similarly, verse frequently records evidence of possible or actual alchemical activity. Thus, Pai Chü-I, a ninth-century AD alchemist, borrowed a book on alchemy, set up a laboratory and conducted a series of experiments with both mineral and metallic substances, his aim being to create an elixir of immortality. In spite of his best efforts, however, he failed and recorded his failure and his disappointment in a poem:

> I bade a lofty farewell to the world of men;
> All my hopes were set on the silence of the hills.
> My platform of brick was accurately squared,
> Compasses showed that my aludel [*alchemical pot*] was round.
> At the very first motion of the furnace-bellows
> A red glow augured that all was well;

> I purified my heart and sat in solitary awe.
> In the middle of the night I stole a furtive glance,
> The Yin and Yang ingredients were in conjunction
> Manifesting an aspect I had not foreseen,
> Locked together in the posture of man and wife
> Intertwined like dragons, coil upon coil . . .
> [*But the experiment did not work*].
> It seems that the dust was not yet washed from my heart;
> The stages of the firing had gone all astray.
> A pinch of elixir would have meant eternal life;
> A hair's-breadth wrong, and all my labours lost.[11]

That such failures and disappointments were not uncommon can be guessed from another poem, this time of the second century AD:

> Even with the Yellow Emperor to build the furnace,
> And Great Oneness himself to attend the firing,
> The Eight Lords to pound down the material
> And Huai Nan to stir them together;
> If you set up a High Altar
> Under cover, with white jade steps,
> And unicorn and phoenix meats offered up,
> With many lengthy prostrations,
> Prayers to the earth spirits,
> Wailing pleas to the ghosts and sprites,
> If you bathe, fast and abstain,
> Hoping for that so long hoped for;
> Even then, like mixing glue to repair a pot,
> Or sal ammoniac daubed on a sore,
> Adding ice to get rid of cold,
> Or using hot water to do away with heat,
> A flying tortoise or dancing snake
> Would be equally unreasonable.[12]

Historical records, too, preserve for us the names and often the experiments of alchemists from the second century BC down more or less to the present, the golden period (so to speak) of the science being the 400 years between AD 400 and 800, followed by a slightly less active five centuries to c.AD 1300. Perhaps the earliest such passage comes from the *History* of Ssu-ma Ch'ien and is datable to the first century AD:

[The wizard Li] Shao-chün said to the Emperor, 'Sacrifice to the stove and you will be able to summon [spirits]. Summon spirits and you will be able to change cinnabar powder into yellow gold. With this yellow gold you may make vessels to eat and drink out of. You will then increase your span of life. Having increased your span of life, you will be able to see the *hsien* of P'eng-lai that is in the midst of the sea. Then you may perform the sacrifices *feng* and *shan* and escape death.'[13]

Here we have a remarkably succinct summary of various key aspects of both the aurifactional and the spiritual goals of Chinese alchemy: ritual magic, preternatural help, making gold, longevity and immortality. Sacrificing to the stove meant that the alchemist was seeking help from its tutelary god in achieving a successful transmutation; but it was only one of a battery of assistances he or she might feel obliged to search out one way or another. Rendering him- or herself fit for the exercise of alchemy and achieving physical longevity in the process frequently involved respiratory exercises, a dietary regime in which, for example, one refrained from eating cereals, meditational techniques, and the use of sex either through Tantric control of the various stages of the sexual act itself, or through deliberate celibacy. Such efforts were necessary for someone intending or hoping so to manipulate the processes of Nature that its vital energy (*chhi*) would flow in the directions he or she desired, its five elements come under his or her command, and its two complementary balancing powers (*yang* and *yin*) follow the new, accelerated paths into which the alchemist was endeavouring to force them. The laboratory, therefore, became a working model of the cosmic order (Tao). As Nathan Sivin has expressed it, 'The laboratory was oriented to the cardinal points of the compass, the furnace centred in it, and the reaction vessel centred in the furnace to make it the axial point of change. The designs of furnaces and vessels were precisely specified to make them concrete metaphors for sky and earth, with the work of man centred between the two and in perfect accord with both.'[14]

If these multifarious operations of the alchemist were adumbrated in Ssu-ma Ch'ien's *History*, they can be seen at much greater length in the life and work of the so-called father of alchemy, Wei Po-Yang. His *Kinship of the Three* (*Tshan Thing Chhi*), was written in c.AD 120 or 142. Little is known for certain about Wei's life, but according to a later alchemist, Ko Hung, he came from one of the magician-technician families of the ancient kingdom of Wu in the east of China – partly Kiangsu, partly Chekiang – consisting for the most part of the marshy delta lands of the Yangtse River. After serving for a while as a provincial administrator, he resigned his post in c.AD 150 to devote himself to the study of the Tao. The *Kinship of the Three* – this title has been translated in different ways – deals with how to time the various alchemical operations in a sequence which is relatable to the hexagrams of the *I Ching*, what materials and procedures are necessary for the manufacture of elixirs guaranteeing long life and immortality, and the theories connecting *yang* and *yin* and the five elements to the alchemical process, and is thus a remarkably comprehensive overview of and guide to the science. Unfortunately, its literary style is so convoluted – to the point of obscurity

– that translation is extremely difficult, although attempts have been made and many commentaries on the text provided. Wei Po-Yang, however, is by no means alone in employing such a style, at once highly poetic, allusive and rhetorical, for his communications on alchemy. It is, as we shall see later, characteristic of writers in the West, too, and these latter cases at least may have contributed to the notion that alchemy is not a serious science, since science should not be couched in a high-flown literary strain. (One is tempted, of course, to ask why not.)[15]

The great alchemists of the third and fourth centuries AD were Ge Hong and Ko Hung. Ge Hong's works are an interesting mixture of magic, astrology, pharmacology and alchemy interleaved with a high degree of scepticism in relation to popular beliefs, and at the same time a dismissal of Confucianism on the grounds that its ideas were not sufficiently exalted, and that its rationalism was restricted to a mere manifestation of common sense beyond which the intellects of its practitioners were afraid to venture. So on the one hand Ge Hong is sarcastic about what he regards as superstitious adherence to the cults of divinities and spirits and their attendant rites, while on the other he seeks to preserve and defend as almost holy the integrity of his Taoist and alchemical approach to the study of Nature. 'The ordinary, unbelieving people cannot be permitted to laugh at elixirs and blaspheme them,' he wrote, before advocating specific sacrifices and rituals he regarded as necessary to the success of alchemical endeavours. Are such apparent contradictions evidence of a kind of hypocrisy? They need not be. Ge Hong criticizes 'the common folk' for not understanding the nature of minerals, metals and herbs, an ignorance which made them turn to superstitious practices for preference. But he does not deny the existence and the importance of divinities and spirits: hence the necessity of god- and spirit-directed ritual in what would otherwise be little more than a series of technical experiments in the laboratory.

Ko Hung (AD 253–334), a near contemporary of Ge Hong, differed from him in certain ways. Ge Hong, for example, thought it essential for the alchemist to withdraw from human society and practise his or her science in the silence of a mountain retreat. Ko Hung disagreed. 'To turn one's back on wife and children and make one's abode in the mountains and marshes, uncaringly to reject basic human usage … is hardly to be encouraged. If by some good fortune they can become immortal and still go on living at home, why should they seek to mount specially to the heavens?' Born into the aristocracy, Ko Hung was both a scholar and a man of action – he is said to have got himself transferred at one point to Vietnam, an inferior posting, because he would then have ready access to the cinnabar he needed for his alchemical experiments – before he decided to retreat into the mountains of southern China to pursue alchemical studies. (Was it personal experience of such solitude which made him change his mind about its desirability as a physical condition for the work?) Impulses to study alchemy may have come from his family, since his uncle, his father-in-law and his wife were all practising alchemists. But it was a passionate interest in medicine, particularly in exotic herbs and unusual minerals, which drew him into the science and to concentrate on those aspects of it which were meant to produce elixirs of longevity and immortality. Diet, breathing exercises, gymnastics and sexual techniques all formed essential parts of his method, as did the use of magic to empower talismans for personal protection. So too did making gold for, as he wrote, 'if you wish to seek divinity and immortality, you need only acquire the quintessence, which consists in treasuring your sperm, circulating your breath, and taking one crucial medicine' – that medicine being either potable gold or reverted cinnabar (cinnabar subjected to a series of transformative treatments which bring it back to the state of being cinnabar again, but with all impurities removed).

Of all Chinese alchemists, Ko Hung is perhaps the most interesting because of the nature and extent of his surviving works. He compiled alchemical recipes, recorded legends, made lists of earlier alchemical books and writers, and expressed in remarkably clear language both his philosophical cogitations on alchemy and his lifetime experience of manipulating ingredients provided by Nature:

> The alchemist must previously fast for a hundred days and purify himself by perfume ... Only two or three persons should be present at a transmutation. It must be done on a famous great mountain, for even a small mountain is inadequate. It is impossible to perform a transformation in a palace. The adept must moreover learn the method directly from those skilled in the art. Books are inadequate. What is written in books is only enough for beginners. The rest is kept secret and is given only in oral teaching. Worship of the proper gods is necessary. The art can moreover be learned only by those who are specially blessed. People are born under suitable or unsuitable stars. Above all, belief is necessary. Disbelief brings failure.

He also provided an explanation other than seeking immortality for the alchemists' drive to manufacture gold. 'Seekers of the Tao usually go in groups of five or ten, counting the teacher and his disciples. Poor as they are, how can they be expected to get the necessary gold and silver? Furthermore, they cannot cover the great distances to gather the gold and silver which occur in nature. The only thing left for them to do is to make the metals themselves.' It is a reasonable enough sentiment, but it does not appear to have done Ko Hung himself much good, for he died, we are told, in poverty.[16]

Other writers on alchemy in succeeding centuries made individual contributions to a body of work whose principal themes and preoccupations had now largely been set. Tao Hung-ching (AD 456–536), for example, added extensively to what was then the standard Chinese pharmacopoeia, and rearranged the drugs listed there into six categories, retaining the traditional classifications only as subdivisions within his own rearrangement. Astrology was important to him, as it was to other alchemists – he built a planetarium, and a globe round which a mechanical sky was made to revolve – and, as we have seen already in the case of Cheng Wei, if the stars were against you, success would never be yours. Hence the ability of Cheng Wei's wife to achieve what he could not. Her stars were favourably aspected. So, too, we may presume were those of Keng hsien-seng, the daughter of Keng Chhien, who lived during the ninth century AD. A praiseworthy poet and magician, she also distilled perfumes and was an adept in the 'art of the yellow and the white' (i.e. alchemy), performing a number of successful alchemical experiments at the Imperial Court. To test her still further, however, the Emperor observed that everything she had managed so far had been done by the use of fire. Could she, he asked, accomplish a transmutation without it?

> She answered, 'Let me try. It might be'. So the Emperor took some mercury and enveloped it in several layers of beaten bark-cloth, closing it with the [Imperial] seal; this she placed forthwith in her bosom. After a long time there suddenly came a sound like the tearing of a piece of silk. The Teacher [Keng hsien-seng] smiled and said: 'Your Majesty did not believe in my methods, but now you will see for yourself. Ought you not to trust me ever hereafter?' Then she handed the packet back to the Emperor who saw that the seal was unbroken and upon opening it found that the mercury had all turned to silver.[17]

This talk of mercury reminds us how important it was not only in Chinese but also in Western alchemy. For, as George Agricola explained in his book on metals (*De re metallica*) in 1530, when mercury and sulphur are combined, the sulphur behaves like male semen and mercury like female, and thus is born the ore. Taoist alchemists were obsessed by the notion that mercury and sulphur be combined, separated and recombined in a series of transformations and for these the numbers five and nine were particularly significant. There were, for example, five cardinal colours (red, yellow, white, blue, black), represented by five important minerals (cinnabar, realgar, alum, azurite, magnetite), and five elements – by which the Chinese meant five powerful forces flowing perpetually in cyclical motion throughout all created things – and these were linked to the five planets (sun and moon not included). Each planet in turn was linked to a significant mineral, and thus we find in *Huai Nan Tzu* (c.125 BC) reference to a five-mineral elixir made from the essences of the five planets.

The significance of nine stems from the magic square of three, which seems to have been invented in China, and can be seen in the nine storeys or layers of the heavens, nine provinces of China, nine cauldrons associated with them, and nine continents. Hence we find alchemical treatises describing a 'ninefold radiance elixir' which could be made by transforming the five minerals – cinnabar, realgar, alum, malachite, and magnetite – or a 'nine-cycle potable gold great cyclically transformed elixir', or a 'ninefold cyclically transformed numinous elixir'.[18]

Element	Planet	Essence
water	Mercury	magnetite
fire	Mars	cinnabar
wood	Jupiter	malachite
metal	Venus	arsenolite
earth	Saturn	realgar

Numbers are thus part of the magical or perhaps mystical ground of the alchemical process, a somewhat obscurantist aspect which one can see in the names given to many of the component materials which were used. So, orpiment (a golden-yellow mineral, important because it was believed to transform copper into gold), could be known as 'blood of the divine woman', 'mid-month moon at the mystic platform' or 'blood of the yellow dragon', forays into the realms of metaphor of which alchemical poems, as one might expect, take full advantage: 'Behold, the mother, when she has sons, becomes a furnace and a pot. At the time when the soul of the sun and the essence of the moon are in a state of mutual influence, when one portion sinks and the other portion floats, the pearl will fly naturally. This black pearl will fly straightway to the peak of K'un Lun.'

Here the black pearl is probably mercury sublimating to a distant part of the alchemist's furnace. But, as Nathan Sivin has pointed out, the degree of mystification in this recondite language has been exaggerated. It is not too difficult, on many an occasion, to work out to what the flowery phrases are referring, and quite often, indeed, Chinese alchemists write more or less openly of what is being used and what is going on in their laboratories.[19]

One very important aspect of their alchemical work – one we have noted before and will note again in connection with both Indian and European alchemy – is the presence of sexual imagery throughout its processes. Those complementary forces of the universe, *yang* (male) and *yin* (female), represent the fuel in the smelting furnace of heaven and earth, wrote Chia I in c.170 BC, and fire for this furnace was produced by the two rubbing together like fire-sticks, a sexual simile which persisted thereafter in an immense variety of expressions: 'entwining of the tortoise and the serpent', 'union of the red and the white', 'the crow and the hare in the same cave', 'conjugal felicity', 'reunion of the herd-boy and the weaving girl'. A treatise written by Wei Po-Yang in c.AD 142 makes this explicit. 'The interaction of the five elements makes them in turn fathers and mothers. The mother possesses the nourishing fluids and the father functions as the fertiliser.' Not, as we have also seen, that the association of sex with alchemy was entirely a figure of speech. Analogy between the laboratory processes and actual intercourse between the alchemist and his wife or female assistant was of great significance: the woman's body was the crucible or reaction-vessel, the man's the furnace, and the conjunction of these two mirrored and indeed affected what was going on in the laboratory's apparatus. Alchemical experiments and procedures were thus a hierogamic exchange of attributes in which the inferior trait of each gives birth (so to speak) to something which is neither and yet both at the same time, a refinement and a union of their essences.[20]

Alchemy, as it developed in China, then, took several different forms. It made, or purported to make, gold artificially, although by 'gold' the alchemists did not necessarily mean the lustrous metal *Au*, and in the process of their experiments they discovered chemical and metallurgical methods of giving substances the appearance of gold, sufficient either to warrant the use of the term 'gold' to describe them, or to deceive those who wanted to be deceived. Eating or drinking from golden vessels was believed to prolong life, and so Chinese alchemy also extended its researches into looking for a variety of edible or potable substances composed from minerals and metals which had had their inner spirits released and recombined during a lengthy process of refinement and purification, whose hoped-for success was both prefaced and attended by religious and magical procedures, often in the solitariness of a remote laboratory. The elixirs thus produced frequently proved fatal – not necessarily an undesirable outcome, since a form of immortality as well as physical longevity was the declared aim of ingesting them. Chang Pang-Chi, a twelfth-century scholar, tells the following monitory anecdote:

> When Chang An-Tao was living at Nantu he also kept a furnace laboratory for transmuting elixirs, but it was only after several dozen years of maintaining the fire that any were achieved. He himself, however, did not dare to eat any of them. At that time Chang Sheng Min, the prefect of Nantu, was very thin and debilitated, so when he heard about this he importuned An-Tao to be allowed to take some. But the latter said: 'I do not want to be miserly, but this elixir has been heated in the fire for a very long time, so it is either very efficacious or extremely poisonous. It must not be taken rashly.' But as Sheng Min kept on begging for it, he finally gave him a piece the size of a millet-grain, warning him once more to treasure it and not to take it lightly. He swallowed it as soon as he got it, however, and before a few days were out, he went down with an effusion of blood, all his viscera becoming rotten, and death shortly ensuing.[21]

Naturally such details made many people increasingly nervous, and so the search for personal longevity or immortality turned inwards as the alchemist sought to rejuvenate his or her body and its spiritual parts so that, by a combination of diet, meditation, sexual techniques, gymnastics and a variety of elixirs he or she might eventually etherialize the body and so become a true Immortal. Following the individual examples of Wei PoYang and Ko Hung during the second and fourth centuries AD, efforts to develop or uncover the secrets of making elixirs continued with official encouragement. Indeed, between AD 398 and 404 the Emperor of the Northern Wei dynasty created a Professor of Alchemy and became the active patron of large-scale experiments in his capital, and it is possible, such was the interest in the subject, to produce a kind of 'family tree' of alchemists between the fourth and tenth centuries, showing how the traditions were handed down from teacher to pupil over succeeding generations.

This golden age was followed by another less consistent in its alchemical pursuits, overlapping with it at the start, and lasting until the fourteenth century. Joseph Needham observes some of the changes which occurred, 'a general trend in alchemical writings from originality to compilation, from clarity in style to obscurity, and from proto-chemical techniques (*wei tan*) to psycho-physiological (*nei tan*)'. Thus, under the powerful influence of Taoist thought and practice in particular, Chinese alchemy came to lay particular emphasis on the quest for spiritual perfection as well as physical longevity of immortality, an emphasis which to a remarkable degree eclipsed – although it did not abolish – the search for means of transmuting one metal into another more noble and more precious, and encouraged the practitioner 'to obtain the art of *yin* and *yang* [so as] to avert all harmful dangers and to tread the path of life eternal'. Political upheavals and civil strife, of course, played their parts in lessening interest in the pursuit of elixirs; but even so imperial encouragement did not die out altogether, and we find evidence of it from time to time, such as the alchemical laboratory maintained for 70 years in the Imperial Academy at the end of the tenth and beginning of the eleventh century. 'It was supplied daily with five loads of charcoal, and down to [AD 1068] the fire was continually kept going. But then [Liu Yen-Chung] received an Imperial order which cut down the size of the civil service establishment, so that the upkeep expenses of the laboratory were cancelled. The elixir which had been produced looked dark like iron.'[22]

After the fourteenth century, however, imperial favour and interest waned. A few Ming emperors were enthusiastic, but the intellectual climate had changed and an increasing number of stories intended to pillory alchemists as charlatans and their clients as gullible fools started to become popular. Direct contact with Western modes of thought, first of all perhaps through Jesuit missionaries from the late sixteenth century onwards, not only stimulated Chinese enquiry to divert itself into more material and less exalted channels of investigation and experiment, but also initiated a two-way intellectual traffic whereby Chinese inventions were increasingly revealed to the West and received approbation for their material foundations and goals in return. Even so, however, the alchemical tradition did not die out altogether, and there are small pieces of evidence that the making of elixirs and the manufacture of gold were still going on quietly during the hostile years of the twentieth century.[23]

2

India: The Way of Tantra and Mercury

If China is to be regarded as the birthplace of alchemy, what about India? By the time the peak of Chinese interest in the science was beginning to wane a little, others were uncertain where to locate its origin. 'The Egyptians especially', noted Ibn abi Ya'qūb al-Nadīm, a noted Iraqi bibliographer of the tenth century AD, 'have many alchemical writers and scholars, and [some say] that that was the country where the science was born . . . But others say that the discussions on the Art originated among the first Persians, [while] according to others the Greeks were the first who dealt with it. And others say yet again that alchemy originated either in India or in China.'

That there was relatively frequent contact between India and China was well known and recorded. In c.AD 649, for example, an Indian alchemist was welcomed at the Chinese Imperial Court, while Tuan Chheng-Shih in his *Miscellany of the Yu-Yang Mountain Cave* (*Yu-Yang Tsa Tsu*), written in AD 863, observed that the Chinese ambassador to the Court of Patna brought back with him to the Imperial Court an Indian scholar who claimed to be 200 years old and who told the Emperor about a remarkable water from his own country, which arose in the mountains, appeared in the guise of seven different colours, and could dissolve all kinds of things – herbs, wood, gold, even human flesh – and was both hot and cold by turns. The Emperor was fascinated and commissioned the Indian to make elixirs of longevity, with what success we do not know.[1]

Translations of Indian alchemical works into Chinese were also frequently undertaken, one of the earliest being a *Commentary on the Great Sūtra of the Perfection of Wisdom* (*Mahāprajñapāramitopadeśa Śastra*), dated to AD 406 and attributed to Nāgārjuna. Unfortunately, there were several writers by that name, all living at different times, so it is difficult to know which Nāgārjuna should be credited with this particular work; but since the one living in the second century AD is usually associated with it, and since he is associated with the beginnings of Tantrism, a religious philosophy involving both magical and sexual techniques as a means of bringing the human mind and soul into contact with the Divine, and one which, as Prafulla Chandra Ray observed, largely gave Indian alchemy its colour, flavour and nourishment, the proposition that he is properly said to be the author of this commentary has much to recommend it.

Therein he is supposed to have noted, 'By means of drugs and incantations one can change bronze into gold. By skilful use of chemical substances, silver may be transformed into gold and gold into silver. By spiritual strength a man can change even clay or stone into gold.'

Stories belonging to Tamil Tantrism talk of 18 magician-alchemists, two of whom at least were historical figures. The better known, Bogar, is the subject of two traditions. One has him come to India from China in the third century AD and live in Madras before returning home with a number of Tamil students; the other makes him a Tamil who went to China. In either case, he provides an indication that maritime exchanges between India and China were taking place at that time, and Chinese texts of the seventh century mention more than one Indian alchemist. What is more, nearly all the mercury Indian alchemists would later use came from China, so there can be no doubt that both nations fed each other's knowledge of the science and contributed to its practice in various ways. But in spite of Ray's claim that alchemy in India can be dated to Vedic times (second millennium BC), the heyday of Indian alchemy came very much later and, in the words of David White, 'seemingly out of nowhere, the alchemical science burst upon the Indian scene in the tenth century [AD] with a laboratory full of specialized equipment, and mineral and botanical raw materials in its theoretical inventory, which magical alchemy had in no way anticipated'.[2] It appears, therefore, as though India will have to yield precedence to China as the birthplace of alchemy, although she certainly developed features which, however similar they may have been to Chinese ideas, were nonetheless rooted in her own individual religious, philosophical, magical and pharmaceutical history.

We have already seen that Nāgārjuna recorded the possibility that one metal can be changed into another, up or down the scale of nobility, by the use of chemical substances. He also noted the use of magic and spiritual 'power', to which we shall return in a moment. Other texts deal with the gold-making process, too. A different Nāgārjuna, who lived in the middle of the seventh century AD, is credited by a collection of alchemical stories, *The Eighty-Four Siddhas*, with changing an iron mountain into copper, telling us that he would have changed it again into gold had he not been warned by a Boddhisattva of the dire consequences of doing so. This same Nāgārjuna was also said to have sprinkled a few drops of some extraordinary liquid over a number of stones, whereupon they all turned to gold. But aurifaction was not the only process followed by Indian alchemists. The eleventh-century *Flood of Mercury* (*Rasārnava*), for example, notes that 'a mercurial pill capable of transmuting one hundred times its mass of base metals into gold, when held in the mouth for a month, yields a life-span of 4,320,000 years'; and similarly, the more or less contemporary *Manifold Powers of the Ocean of Mercury* (*Rasārnavakalpa*) describes not only how base metals may be turned into gold and silver by the use of various other substances, but also how one may concoct elixirs which cure diseases, rejuvenate the human body and confer a number of extraordinary powers such as the ability to levitate, or fly through the air, or achieve physical immortality.[3]

The *rasa* in these titles is mercury, the substance par excellence of all al-chemical operations – so much so, indeed, that the regular Sanskrit word for alchemy is *rasayana*, 'the way of mercury'. Chinese alchemists noted that mercury kills the 'poison' in gold, silver, copper and tin, a purifying process which then allows the 'real' essence of the metal to emerge – death followed by resurrection – and this is repeated by their Indian counterparts. But not only is the motif of death and resurrection central to the interpretation of many alchemical laboratory techniques, it also underlies many of the associations practitioners discovered or made between the substances with which they were working and other apparently unrelated objects. Thus, for example, the thirteenth-century *Amassing of Rasas and Gemstones* (*Rasaratnasamucchaya*) tells us how the god Śiva is to be worshipped in the form of a penis (*lingam*) made from an amalgam of gold and mercury. Why? Because mercury is identified with Śiva's semen and so is gold, and hence quite logically flow a number of inferences. Since Śiva represents the destructive principle of the Hindu Triad, but destroys only to renew and instil fresh life, so mercury 'kills' only to transmute a substance into a better version of itself. Death and rebirth may thus be imitated in the apparatus of the laboratory, and human fluids be regarded as directly sexual (semen) or indirectly (menstrual blood) can be made to play their art in magical imitation of the divine transmuting elements.[4]

As in China, then, Indian alchemists had two broad aims in view, each of which easily merged into the other and spread to embrace a variety of other disciplines. As Peter Marshall puts it, 'the alchemists who were seeking to transform base metal into gold were interested in refining and purifying nature. Those who were seeking to prolong life and to attain immortality were trying to transform their base nature into a more spiritual form, their gross body into a subtle body.' This brings us to the basic division in alchemical interests between aurifaction and the making of elixirs. Manufacturing gold never died out. David White records an experiment which took place in Benares (Varanasi) in 1984:

Krishna Pal Shastri, a *vaidya* from Jamnagar in Gujarat, performed the experiment in the laboratory of Benares Hindu University chemistry professor Phaldevasahaya Varma, in the presence of nine or ten Ayurvedic scholars and practitioners and the great industrialist Birla. Shastri hollowed out a soap nut, which he filled with mercury, two or three grams of borax, and a grain of a secret powder. He sealed the nut with a paste of lime and molasses and put it inside a crucible, which he placed on a charcoal fire. He fanned the fire until the nut inside the crucible began to burn. When the smoke cleared, he split the nut open with an iron wedge. Inside was a metal that looked like silver. Half of this metal was taken by Professor Varma and the other half by Mr Birla. Varma tested it at BHU and Birla at one of his firm's laboratories in Calcutta. In both cases, the metal tested out as pure silver, with only the spectroscopy showing a slight variation from that of natural silver. Shastri had informed those who were present that he could also produce gold by the same procedure, by merely substituting ammonium chloride for borax. Later on, at Birla's instigation, he produced gold this way. He continued to make gold in this way, at the rate of three grams per week, to cover his laboratory and personal expenses.[5]

Reducing various substances to their basic form in order to reconstitute them into elixirs which would produce remarkable effects on the human body, however, rapidly became the more important alchemical activity, and the one more deserving of people's concentrated attention. But such elixirs were very dangerous. The seventh-century AD playwright Bānabhatta tells the story of a Dravidian ascetic who was blind in one eye because of an invisibility salve which had been given to him by a quack, and also suffering from a premature fever caused by his ingesting a badly prepared mercurial elixir he had taken to dispel intestinal worms. So it is not surprising that, in a situation similar to one we have already come across in China, we find that from about the thirteenth century onwards there was a move in northern India away from the goal of achieving physical immortality to the purely therapeutic use of elixirs and mercurial preparations, probably because so many people, like Bānabhatta's ascetic, had suffered actual harm from them, or had died from mercury poisoning.

What transformed Indian alchemy more than anything else, however, was the advent of Tantrism which started to flourish from the fourth century AD. Hindu Tantrism offers its adherents a practical way to attain supernatural powers (*siddhi*) and close association with a particular deity, while liberating oneself from the bonds and constraints of normal physical existence. Tantrists conceive divinity as having both male and female aspects, and union with such a deity is described in sexual terms. Matter, in whatever form, is a gross condensation of the subtle energy which characterizes divinity and with which creation is suffused in a number of different ways. Sound (in the form of mantras), control of the body (through *hatha* yoga), and worship of the divinity (typically through offering of the five substances, alcohol, meat, fish, grain and sexual intercourse), constitute the various ways in which personal transformation and integration can be attained. The Tantric universe, then, is both bipolar and sexualized, and any change takes place as the result of the commingling of male and female principles, a coition which can be mirrored in the alchemist's workplace. As David White explains, 'In the alchemical laboratory, [homologies between minerals and divine fluids] come to be practically applied through techniques that involve the commingling of human, divine, and mineral blood and semen. Here, the point of convergence between these interpenetrating systems is the person of the alchemist's female laboratory assistant.'[6]

This sexual aspect of both the metaphors, the theories and the practices of alchemy can be seen informing the importance of *hatha* yoga to control of the body. One etymology of the word *hatha* divides it into *ha* = 'sun' and *tha* = 'moon', thereby suggesting not so much a balance as a conjunction of male and female. With both male and female elements and energies combined and controlled by and within the body of the practitioner, then, analogies were created which might extend their influences into the laboratory, and thus the attempt to perfect Nature through manipulation of her processes upon certain of her constituent parts (such as metals or minerals) might in turn be more successfully effected. These personal controls would also give rise to or release magical powers: invisibility, invulnerability, ability to fly, to make oneself heavier or lighter at will. (The ability to manufacture gold, was, of course, another.) Purifying one's body until it changed its gross nature and turned into something at once less material and more spiritual did not just provide an analogy for the work of the alchemist in his or her laboratory; it projected asceticism upon the physical substances with which he or she was operating and thereby transferred in a kind of spiritual *and* physical reciprocity transmuting energies both to and from the primordial substance (*prakrti*) of which both alchemists and their working substances were made.

But magic can be seen not only in the powers thus potentially obtained, but also in such aspects of the work as numbers, the importance of which we have noted in connection with Chinese alchemy; and indeed, just as five was significant for Chinese alchemists, so it was for their Indian counterparts who recognized pentads of gemstones, salts, poisons, animal oils, urines, biles and excrements, as well as other, less tangible things such as the five faces of Śiva, the five tastes and the five dispositions. Even mercury itself was supposed to have divided itself into five when it first made its appearance in the world, locating itself in five wells – north, south, east, west and centre – in five different colours. So not only did Indian alchemy have a distinctively magical aspect, but prior to the tenth century this aspect was probably dominant until other concerns, such as concentration upon the search for life-prolonging elixirs, began to take over.[7]

Now, it is worth asking, as we did in our discussion of Chinese alchemy, whence this information about Indian alchemy can be drawn. Prafulla Ray and David White provide lists of authors and their actual or supposed works, some of which have survived, others appearing simply as references in both alchemical and medical literature. Their dates range from the tenth to the fourteenth century, and many contain a reference to mercury in their titles: *Heart of Mercury, Flood of Mercury, Effulgence of Mercury and Wellspring of Nectar, Auspicious Ornament of Mercury* (*Rashardaya Tantra, Rasarnava, Rasaprakāśa Sudhākara, Rasendra Mangala*), for example. Their contents tend to be explanations of the divine origins of mercury and sulphur; aphorisms; descriptions of the kind of ritual to be employed; descriptions of the laboratory and its apparatus; directions for the principal alchemical operations; discussions about how to prepare and combine one's ingredients, and how these are to be applied to the alchemist's body to render him or her immortal; and (in later works) descriptions of therapeutic elixirs and aphrodisiacs. Legend and legendary or actual history also provide information, as in the following story which has one or two echoes of the Chinese tale about Cheng Wei and his wife, and provides the reader with a moral, as well as a reminder that female contribution to the Great Work, no matter how made, is essential to its success:

> The Brahmin Vyali . . . was an ardent alchemist who tried to find the elixir of life. He spent his entire fortune in unsuccessful experiments with all sorts of expensive chemicals, and finally became so disgusted that he threw his formula book into the Ganges and left the place of his fruitless work as a beggar. But it happened that when he came to another city further down the Ganges, a courtesan, who was taking a bath in the river, picked up the book and brought it to him. This revived his old passion, and he took up his work again, while the courtesan supplied him with the means of livelihood. But his experiments were as unsuccessful as before, until one day the courtesan, while preparing his food, by chance dropped the juice of some spice into the alchemist's mixture – and lo! – what the learned Brahmin had not been able to achieve in fourteen years of hard work, had been accomplished by the hands of an ignorant low-caste woman.

Alchemical laboratories in India, like their counterparts in China, were not mere collections of apparatus in a convenient place. The laboratory itself was known as 'the temple of mercury', and was laid out in strict accordance with rules which took into account associations made between apparatus and materials and relevant divinities. Herbs and other plant matter were stored on the eastern wall because the east belongs to Indra, King of the gods. In the south-east, the distilling instruments; in the south, oxidizing chemicals; in the south-west, the alchemist's mortar, pestle and instruments for grinding and pulverizing; in the west, his liquefying apparatus; in the north-west, bellows; in the north, colouring agents (because alchemists tinge substances a golden colour or cover their surfaces with gold or gold-coloured material); and in the centre, upon a square stone slab is erected the lingam made from mercury and gold or sulphur, set in a yoni, which serves as his or her daily object of worship, along with the fire-pit needed to effect the various purifications and transformations. The alchemist, however, as we have seen more than once, will not carry out the operations alone; for at least one female assistant is necessary, a menstruating woman with whom he will have sexual congress, since both male and female fluids are essential to the work.[8]

We see, then, that there are several similarities between Chinese and Indian alchemical goals and practices. Both were interested in manufacturing gold and both claimed to do so. They made it partly for its own sake – it provided the money or at least the means whereby further experimentation could be afforded and tried – and partly because gold represented immortality, which in turn stood for invincibility and transcendence of human limitations, a goal to which Tantric alchemy, such as that we have been discussing, especially tended. Indian alchemy also produced mercurial and mineral-based preparations intended on the one hand to cure the body of its ills, and on the other to transform the practitioner into a perfected immortal. Chinese and Indian alchemy supposed the existence and active cooperation (or hindrance) of a multitude of divinities who had to be worshipped, placated and drawn to assist the alchemist in whatever trials he or she was undertaking; and for this purpose, a sexual interpretation of the interaction between cosmic forces and powers was intrinsic to any operation in the alchemical laboratory. This aspect of alchemy, and the practice of *hatha* yoga in particular, were perhaps peculiar to India, or at least received a special emphasis there, and thus the alchemy which spread from India to other countries – Tibet is a case in point – tended to concentrate on Hindu erotico-mystical techniques rather more than on the production of transmutation into gold and elixirs of immortality which appear to have been the staple of Chinese practice.[9]

Tantrism, the principal medium whereby esoteric theories and teachings were enabled to flow, carried alchemical notions between India and China through the trade-routes which not only linked both, but spread still further afield into Central Asia and Persia and thence far west into Europe. Nearly all the Tibetan alchemical texts with which we are familiar were translations of Sanskrit or Chinese originals, or were composed in the Tantric tradition and display characteristics associated with non-Buddhist influence and the cult and worship of Śiva. These Tantric traditions emphasized both spiritual and physical purification, sometimes of an extreme nature, in an effort at once to prolong life so that the search for ways of escaping the bonds of matter might be given a better chance to reach its goal, and for this purpose mercury-based elixirs were frequently employed. As Michael Walter explains, 'The goal of medical practices in Tantrism – like those of its alchemical, astrological, and hatha-yogic techniques – is to provide the yogi's body with a state of development favourable to attaining an ultimate religious goal ... He will achieve either an ethereal, transcendent body, a *ja'lus*, or an undecaying, physically perfect body which enjoys unending earthly existence.'[10]

Medicine, pharmacology and alchemy, then, are intertwined, their goals often similar or at least expressible in each other's terminology and metaphors.[11] Several texts deal with extracting the essences of the materials to be used, a form of distillation after distillation we have come across before in Chinese practice, after which the essence is transformed into an elixir, and it is noteworthy that this extraction of essences might well be preceded or attended by magico-ritual practices. Thus, a fourteenth-century Tibetan text requires an altar in a deserted place. On top of the altar is a mandala and on top of that are placed items to be consumed – a 'life-pill' and 'life-beer'. After an invocation, there appears Padmasambhava, a magician with power over life. In this context, 'magician' refers to one of a group of spirits or of deified human beings with great magical powers. The human practitioner must activate the life forces of various similar spirits and these will then be made to flow into the ritual objects on the altar. (It is a process familiar to Western magicians who consecrate their magical weapons so as to imbue them with power and thus transform them into implements mediating power between preternatural and natural modes of existence.) From east, south, west and north there appear further magicians who extract the essences of water, earth, fire and wind, while from the south-east, south-west, north-west, and north-east come four more who conjure up the life force of the practitioner. Thus are the materials transformed into an elixir of immortality and the practitioner him- or herself into a being purified and freed from death.

Clearly here we are talking about a ritual whose principal procedures take place internally and whose workings are described in alchemical terminology and metaphors. But physical alchemy of the kind we have met in China and India was certainly practised, and again we can see a description of it expressed in terms of a magical ceremony. Here the instructions are more specific. The ritual is to begin on the eighth day of a waxing moon. Some time in the morning, the practitioner must paint a mandala and cover it with excrement and urine. (This requirement is interesting because it reminds us that Chinese alchemists also used similar human excretions for their elixirs; and it is a commonplace of European alchemy to require the same. 'Our stone is . . . cast out into the dunghill and trodden under men's feet. It is counted a most vile and contemptible thing,' said the anonymous *Philosophia Maturata* in words which were taken literally by a number of alchemists, thereby allowing satirists to have fun at their expense. 'Panurge', wrote François Rabelais, 'fairly threw up his food when he saw an archasardpenim fermenting a great tub of human urine in horse-dung, with plenty of Christian shit. Pooh, the filthy wretch! He told us, however, that he watered kings and great princes with this holy distillation and thereby lengthened their life by a good six or nine feet.')

Five human skulls taken from a cemetery are then placed at the four corners of the mandala and the centre, each accompanied by a lamp fuelled by human fat. Five hundred more lamps should be lit before the ritual can start, and then the practitioner moves to the four cardinal points in turn, starting with the south. In the centre of the mandala is a Brahmin's skull, and into this are poured five ingredients whose nature is not altogether clear, except that all five are fragrant and possess *rasa*, that is, a vital fluid. These five are mixed with eight metals including camphor, pearl and salt; to these are added five others, principally fruits, and then five kinds of flesh mixed with materials made from the five sense organs. All kinds of other stuff is mixed in with these, always in multiples of five – again, we have come across the importance of this number before – some of which are aromatic, such as nutmeg and sandalwood, some of which are 'metals' – gold, silver, copper, iron and turquoise – ground to a powder and mingled with the rest. All this, we are told, is enough to bring the practitioner supernatural powers.[12]

The mention of vital fluid (*rasa*) may be particularly significant, since *rasa* is also one of the terms used for mercury, and we know that mercurial medicine was exported from India to Tibet and China, and that Tibet was obliged to import its mercury from China – further examples of the two- and three-way traffic in substances as well as ideas. Legend also illustrates exchanges between India and Burma. An alchemical tradition among the *zawgyis* – a word derived from 'yogi' but referring in Burmese to a kind of alchemist-monk – relates that an alchemist died during the course of his experiments and that his body was taken to a local monastery, roasted, and eaten. Those who ingested the flesh then became possessed of extraordinary powers, able to lift whole buildings and place them upside down. Slightly more sober claims (and ones we have met before) say that a man becomes a *zawgyi* as a result of introducing modified metal compounds into his body, first one based on mercury, secondly one based on iron. Thereafter he can fly through the air, attains physical immortality and becomes invulnerable, all of which powers, and many others, depend on his swallowing 'the stone of living metal', as it is called, a 'stone' which can also turn base metals into gold or silver. As a character says in an early nineteenth-century Burmese play, 'I have obtained the stone of live metal, and I have also become a *zawgyi*. My stone can turn lead into silver, brass into gold. I have eaten that compound of alchemy, which makes me above nature, above this earthliness. I cannot be hit by bullets and bombs, and swords and spears wound me not at all.' Two points are worth mentioning. First, a *zawgyi* is a man, not a woman – most unusual since females, as we have seen, play a crucial role in alchemical operations elsewhere; and secondly, the *zawgyi* attains his powers purely as a result of alchemy, not because he has combined the ingestion with magic or asceticism. Nevertheless, even if his personal aim was to get an immortal and eternally youthful body, the fact that he possessed the secret of manufacturing gold and silver from less noble metals made him a figure of interest to a succession of Burmese kings who encouraged their priests, already masters of magic, to experiment with and practise alchemy with a view to supplementing the royal treasuries.

Further east still, alchemy also spread into Japan, almost entirely from China, but this was the alchemy of elixirs rather than aurification. Japan had plenty gold of her own and was therefore not hard pressed to obtain more by manufacturing it. Human greed, of course, might have posed a counter-argument to this, but it

seems that from the eighth to the twelfth century the Imperial Court and nobility
were far more interested in elixirs of longevity and immortality and that it was
these which caught the attention of people who were in a position to encourage
and pay for the science which would produce them. Indeed, the Emperor himself
was prepared to ingest powdered quartz and potable gold – this last a mixture of
magnetite, sulphur and young men's urine, all heated together.[13]

Like China, then, India produced and exported more than one version of
alchemy. The gold-making so much associated with it in the West, however,
while practised, did not constitute anything like the principal focus of interest
among Indian alchemists, who were far more concerned with wedding *hatha*
yoga, asceticism, breath control and religious ritual to the manipulation of subtle
energies or 'fluids' derived from such basic elements as human excretions and
mercury, a substance identified in one of the most notable of Indian alchemical
systems with the semen of the god Śiva. Ingestion of the resulting elixir, or
attainment of the physical and spiritual changes attendant upon this kind of
alchemical practice, meant that the operator acquired a variety of magical
powers as well as physical longevity – or even, in the most successful cases,
transformation of the body itself into something beyond and aloof from the
limitations of physical matter. As in China, Indian alchemy was closely associated
with medical tradition, and the focus on gold-making shifted – largely during the
tenth to the thirteenth century – to that of producing elixirs to help the individual
practitioner identify him- or herself with Śiva and so become an immortal, and
supernaturally powerful; and, as in China too, we see the search for a means
of transmuting an inferior metal into a higher gradually take second place to
spiritual, self-transformational goals.

3

Roman Egypt: The White and the Yellow
Arising from Blackness

The tenth-century Byzantine lexicon attached to the name 'Suidas' defines *khēmeia* as 'the fabrication of silver and gold'. Popular etymologies of the word which has given us 'alchemy' have ranged from a supposed founding father Cham or Ham, one of the sons of Noah, a great magician who hid the written repository of his knowledge to await discovery by a later generation; a putative name for Egypt, indicating the blackness of its soil, a word also related to the pupil of the eye; an Egyptian word for 'completion'; a Greek word for 'melting' or 'pouring'; and a Semitic root connected with fermentation. All these have their problems, some more than others, and in view of the prior claims China and India seem to have as countries in which alchemy made its earliest appearances, and because Chinese rather than any Indian language offers one or two credible etymologies for the word, we may, as we did before, adhere to the proposal that the *chem-* of 'alchemy' comes from a Chinese word referring to transmutation of metals. Trade along the ancient Silk Road brought interchanges of all kinds between the West, Persia and China, and thus the possibility of transferring a Chinese word to the technical vocabulary of Roman Egypt. From the beginning, therefore, Western interest in the science focused on the aurifactional side of alchemy rather than its creation of elixirs of longevity or immortality. Indeed, as Needham points out, 'the "drug of immortality" was primarily a metaphor in the Greek context and primarily a real material thing for the Chinese.' But what it meant to the Graeco-Roman Egyptians turns out to have been something peculiar to this particular time and place.[1]

We are speaking of Greeks and Roman Egypt because it was during the post-Alexandrian period when Egypt became a province first in Alexander the Great's empire and then in that of Rome that, as John Read put it, Greek philosophy was applied to specific chemical techniques of Egypt and of other ancient cultures. But what parts of Greek philosophy in particular, and which range of chemical techniques? Plato noted that God had compounded the observable universe out of all the fire, water, air and earth which was available, and that these elements did not remain one, stable, immutable thing but changed in appearance when certain forces were directed upon them. Hence, water becomes stone and earth through condensation, but vapour and air through evaporation. Air, when heated, becomes fire: but when fire is condensed, it becomes air again. Air, when collected together and condensed, turns into cloud and mist which in turn produce water. Then water condenses into earth and stones, and so the natural cycle of mutability continues. Aristotle agreed, observing not only that the four elements can transform themselves into each other, but that these elements have properties in common.

$$\text{Fire} = \text{hot and dry,}$$
$$\text{Air} = \text{hot and moist,}$$
$$\text{Water} = \text{moist and cold,}$$
$$\text{Earth} = \text{cold and dry.}$$

Two of these (hot and cold) are active and two (dry and moist) passive. Hence various combinations of the four will produce different results and will be further influenced by the kind of force brought to bear on them – heating, cooling, evaporation, condensation, distillation and so forth. 'We maintain,' he said, 'that there are two exhalations, one vaporous, the other smoky ... The vaporous exhalation is the cause of all things mined – things which are either fusible or malleable, such as iron, copper, gold. All these originate from the imprisonment of the vaporous exhalation in the earth, and especially in stones,' But the basis of all the different levels or grades of existence in Nature was a kind of potentiality, the *prima materia* sought by all subsequent alchemists, the form without substance which rendered everything capable of assuming any number of different forms, and discovery of which would enable the alchemist to manipulate it into the form of gold or silver, or indeed anything else.[2]

These theories were not new. Many had been proposed by Greek philosophers long before Plato or Aristotle, but the writings of these two, as well as others attributed to them, provided the means whereby such ideas were developed and handed down from the Classical period to later centuries, and thus gave authority – more or less incontrovertible for a considerable time – to these basic alchemical assumptions. Everything grows; everything strives for perfection; this growth and striving happens according to a series of natural cycles over long periods of time; therefore by imitating Nature and hastening her processes, the alchemist can act as midwife and transforming demiurge, and speed inferior metals to their destined perfection as gold. Thus transmutation, as Cyril Stanley Smith said:

Was a thoroughly valid aim, a natural outgrowth of Aristotle's combinable qualities, and its truth was demonstrated by every child growing from the food he ate, by every smelter who turned green earth into red copper, or black galena into base lead and virgin-hued silver, by every founder who converted copper into gleaming yellow brass, by every potter who glazed his ware, by every goldsmith who produced niello, by every maker of stained glass windows, and by every smith who controlled the metamorphosis of iron during its smelting, conversion to steel, and hardening. Such changes of properties, seen physically, *are* transmutations.

Now, as we have seen, the gold which alchemists produced was not necessarily the metal *Au*, and the gold which alchemists aimed to produce was not necessarily intended to deceive other people into thinking it was the real thing. Real gold in Egypt was much prized as a symbol of immortality and deification, but only the rich could afford it. Cheaper versions – like our costume jewellery – imitated the real thing but might, depending on the skill with which the imitation had been effected, more or less easily be distinguished from it. Brass was known in Hellenistic and Roman times, and so were amalgams. If gold is dissolved in boiling mercury, for example, the amalgam so produced can be smeared over the surface of an object and thus plate it. The mercury is then volatized and removed by heat, leaving behind a smooth gilded surface. The set of alloys known as 'Corinthian bronze', much prized in the ancient world, consisted of copper alloyed with gold and silver and then gilded in a process called 'depletion' (i.e. converting the base metals near the surface of the gold alloy to chlorides or oxides, using chemicals or heat), to impart a particularly notable sheen.

A similar gilding process was known to the alchemists and metallurgists of Roman Egypt:

> *To give objects of copper the appearance of gold.* So that neither contact with nor rubbing against the touchstone will find them out, but so that they can help to make a fine-looking ring, here is what you do. Grind lead and gold to a dust as fine as flour, 2 parts lead to 1 part gold. Mix them together, blend them with gum, and smear the surface of the ring with this mixture. Then apply heat. Repeat this several times until the object has taken on the [gold] colour. It is difficult to discover [what has been done], because rubbing [the ring against a touchstone] produces the mark of a gold object. The heat burns away the lead but not the gold.

This is one of the 99 chemical recipes contained in a papyrus of the third or fourth century AD, called the *Leiden Papyrus X* from its present resting place. It probably came originally from Thebes in Upper Egypt. Based on much earlier sources, the papyrus illustrates the various techniques familiar to late Egyptian alchemist-metallurgists. The one quoted above, for example, tells one how to create a film on the surface of an object. It was also possible to strip away an inferior or unwanted surface to reveal a richer or more desirable surface underneath, and to augment, or appear to augment, the original metal. Thus, says another recipe from the same papyrus, one should take equal parts of 'Thracian' or 'Gaulish' *cadmia* [impure zinc oxide], partly oxidised iron or copper pyrites, haematite and gold: put the gold into a furnace and then, at the appropriate moment, add the other ingredients. After the mass has been removed and allowed to cool, it will be found that the gold has doubled in quantity (although actually, of course, the result would be an alloy of gold and zinc with copper and lead additions, depending on whether the *cadmia* contained one or other of their oxides). There are, in fact, several kinds of *cadmia* produced in such furnaces, and this recipe specifies that one is to use the sort known as *placitis* which resembles a crust. Hence Berthelot's translation, rather charming to English-language ears, 'make the mixture with the *cadmia* en croûtes'. Of similar date is a papyrus now kept in Stockholm, *Papyrus Holmiensis*, which contains recipes for manufacturing precious stones. To make a pearl, for example, one mixes ground mica with wax, egg-white and mercury. This produces a paste which is softened in gum, remixed, moulded into shape, and then allowed to harden. 'If managed properly,' says the writer, 'it will excel the natural.'[3]

It is generally assumed that much of this kind of alchemical endeavour was intended to deceive. Earl Radcliffe Caley's translation of the Leiden Papyrus's recipe to give objects the appearance of gold, for example, introduces 'the fraud' after 'it is difficult to discover', where I have chosen the less judgemental 'what has been done'. No one can deny, of course – and I should not want to do so – that such amalgams and augmentations could easily have been intended by certain persons on certain occasions to impose a deceit upon potential buyers or patrons. But not, surely, all the time, and sometimes at least with no more intention to deceive than anyone producing what is clearly costume jewellery would automatically try to pretend his goods were genuine Cartier. In this connection, then, it may be interesting to note that when the Emperor Diocletian ordered the burning of books on alchemy in Egypt, he did so, not because he condemned them as fraudulent. Far from it. His fear was that the Egyptians might use the science to accumulate wealth which would enable them to rebel 'wildly and murderously' against their Roman masters and occupiers.[4]

A review of the alchemical tradition in Hellenistic and Roman Egypt reveals how firm was its emphasis on the technical and aurifactional aspects of the science, and that neither occult theory nor obscurity of language plays any major role in it during the first two or three centuries. One of the earliest alchemical treatises from Egypt which has come down to us dates from about the first century AD and is attributed to Demokritos – either as a gesture of respect to the fifth-century BC Demokritos of Abdera, one of the founders of atomic theory, who was said to have studied mathematics and physics in Egypt – or in the hope that the treatise would actually be taken as one of his and thus gain both respectability and wider currency on the back of his name. Known as *Physika kai Mystika* (*Things to do with Nature and Things which are Mysterious*), the book is divided into four parts describing how to make gold, silver, precious stones and crimson dye, and the form of their recipes is similar to those of the Leiden and Stockholm papyri:

Take *claudian* [lead and copper mixed with zinc], make a stone of it, and treat it in the usual way until it becomes yellow ... You can turn it yellow with sulphur derived from degraded alum, yellow orpiment, realgar, or gypsum, or whatever you contrive. If you apply this to silver, you make gold; if you apply it to gold, you make 'gold-shell', because once the powers naturally inherent in one of them have overcome those naturally inherent in the other, they get the upper hand and hold sway.

The Greek verb here translated 'apply to' may also mean 'throw on to', and may remind us of the alchemical technique known as *projection* whereby a small amount of powder (the philosopher's stone), was added to a substance and thus converted it into gold or silver. Perhaps the original philosopher's stone actually was a single hard object rather than powder and thence derived its name.

Suddenly, however, we find an address to fellow-alchemists interrupting the flow of recipes:

O natural powers, fabricators of natural powers! O immense natural powers which overcome [other] natural powers by means of changes! O natural powers which enjoy natural powers beyond the natural power [which is in them]! These are indeed things which possess great natural power. There are no other natural powers among colouring agents greater than these. There are none equal, none which have put themselves in an inferior position. All these work while they are being resolved into their separate elements. So, fellow-prophets, I know you did not disbelieve, but that you were astonished because you know the capability of the basic material. [You also know] that those new to the science will be very much deceived, and that [on one particular occasion] they did not believe in what was being written [or 'drawn'] because they were in ignorance of the basic material, and did not know that whenever doctors' children want to prepare a wholesome medicine, they try to do so in a headstrong, impulsive manner ... But those who want to prepare the remedy of the spirit, and ransom-money for every distress, will not understand they will be hindered from doing so [if they adopt] a manner which is headstrong, absurd, and impulsive. They suppose we are telling a story which belongs to legend and yet is not mysterious, and makes no close examination of the things they see.[5]

There are one or two points worth noting briefly about this passage. It falls into three stages: (a) exclamations which celebrate the *physis*, the inherent natural power which exists in everything and which, as the author has just demonstrated, can be harnessed and manipulated in such a way as to render certain natural powers stronger than others; (b) an address to his fellow-alchemists, following what appears to have been a public demonstration of the kind of alteration or 'transmutation' he has been describing; and (c) a regret that the young, or at least beginners in both medicine and alchemy, are too eager to achieve the desired result, and do not take time to observe and learn from the various stages of the work they are doing. Calling natural powers 'fabricators' of natural powers is an interesting way of describing how one set of such powers can work on, mould and change another. The Greek *dēmiourgoi* is used of skilled workmen, examples being surgeons, carpenters, makers of bridal-cakes and medical practitioners. They are essentially artisans who work for the people – *dēmos* and *ergon* are the roots of the word – and, as we see from the examples, they either call forth the pleasing and useful forms inherent in their basic material, or they restore what has been damaged to its perfect form. (Xenophon and Plato used *dēmiourgos* as an epithet of the divine Creator, but they recognized only one, so clearly this aspect of the word does not apply here.) The alchemist, therefore, is working with powers which are, in a sense, very much like himself – concerned with practicalities and intent on drawing out from his raw material a form or shape which will be superior to the material from which it has been drawn.

But can we see a reference to some kind of elixir in 'those who want to prepare the remedy of the spirit'? The key words are 'remedy' (*iama*) and 'spirit' (*psykhē*). *Iama* simply refers to a method of healing and does not imply any particular one, although it is interesting to note that its cognate verb *iaomai*, while meaning 'I cure' in general, is also frequently used of what surgeons do, and this ties it in with *dēmiourgos*. *Psykhē*, of course, is notoriously difficult to pin down (like the Latin *anima*). It begins as 'breath as the sign of life', then turns into 'life' itself, 'ghost', an abstract notion of 'spirit' or 'soul', 'a sensual desire', and finally, 'reason' or 'understanding'. Clearly there is no hint here of any substance which will prolong physical life or confer immortality. It is noteworthy, too, that the Greek speaks of *the* remedy, not *a* remedy – the author, it seems, has something specific in mind – and perhaps a clue to our understanding of the whole phrase is contained in its companion, 'ransom-money for every distress'. This last is remarkably vivid. It paints toil, hardship, distress as though they were an enemy force laying siege to the individual, a force which can be bought off. *Lytron* means 'a price which is paid', 'ransom', 'recompense', and is obviously associated with money. Since 'remedy' and 'ransom' are so closely connected here, it seems reasonable to suggest that the remedy is intended to cure or satisfy one's sensual appetite: and one sure way of doing that is to provide it with money. The notion of money has been suggested by earlier reference to 'doctors' children', of course, but in spite of the initial temptation to see an elixir in the *iama*, it is unlikely that the author had in mind anything more than the production of gold and silver by alchemical means.

His mention of the impatient young, or novices in the practice of alchemy, reminds us that the science, no matter where it was to be found, consisted of tradition as well as experiment, and that results, advice, teaching and admonition were handed down orally to pupils and assistants. The omission of these 'secrets' from alchemical writings is one which is deliberately lauded by the writers themselves and one can see further hints of this oral tradition in alchemists' habit of referring to 'our' mercury, 'our' sulphur' and so forth – clear indications that the substances they are describing or whose use they are advocating are not the same as the mercury or sulphur known to the general public. There is also the slight puzzle in Pseudo-Demokritos's reference to the youngsters or novices not believing what was written down, because they did not know what was the basic material being used in the demonstration. 'What was written down' (*graphē*) can also mean 'what was drawn', or even 'what was painted'; and 'they did not believe' is expressed in a tense which implies that this happened on a single occasion in the past. So too are the verb-forms relating to the writer's fellow-alchemists. 'You did not disbelieve'; 'you were astonished'. These imply that Pseudo-Demokritos was thinking of a particular occasion when he or someone else conducted an alchemical experiment or demonstration for their benefit, and it may have been during this same occasion – he says to his fellow-alchemists, 'you know' this happened – that the youngster-novices were shown a drawing or a painting or a piece of writing they found difficult to credit. We are thus provided with one or two brief insights into the actual experience underlying this interruption of a collection of practical recipes.

Pseudo-Demokritos refers to his fellow-alchemists as 'fellow-prophets', meaning 'fellow-interpreters of things which the gods usually keep hidden', and this title reminds us of one of the most famous alchemists from Roman Egypt, Maria the Jewess. Our knowledge of her is derived very largely from the surviving writings of the fourth-century AD alchemist Zosimos who came from Panopolis in Upper Egypt, and if we believe what he says of her – and there is no good reason we should not – she appears to have been one of the most innovative and influential of the early practitioners. It is well known that the water-bath which is even now called after her, the bain-marie, is supposed to have been one of her inventions. But she also constructed various kinds of oven and different types of apparatus for cooking and distilling, preferring to have them made from glass rather than clay or metal, and described how such apparatus was to be put together and how it worked. Here is her version of a still known as a *tribikos* ('rubbed three times'):

Make three tubes of ductile copper a little thicker than that of a pastry cook's frying pan. Their length should be about a cubit and a half. Make three such tubes, and also make a wide tube of a hand's breadth width and an opening proportioned to that of the still-head. The three tubes should have their openings adapted like a nail to the neck of a light receiver so that they have the thumb-tube and the two finger-tubes joined laterally on either hand. Towards the bottom of the still-head are three holes adjusted to the tubes, and when these are fitted they are soldered into place, the one above receiving the vapour in a different fashion. Then, setting the still-head upon an earthenware pan containing the sulphur, and luting the joints with flour paste, place at the ends of the tubes glass flasks, large and strong, so that they may not break with the heat coming from the water in the middle.[6]

This is followed in the text by a drawing of the apparatus. Is some such diagram the *graphē* which Pseudo-Demokritos's youngster-novices found difficult to understand, or perhaps impossible to believe would actually work? Within these pieces of apparatus the various stages of the work took place, their progress verified by the changes of colour the alchemist could see. Thus, as Raphael Patai describes it, 'if the copper [*that is, alchemists' copper, not necessarily the same as Cu*] is properly nourished with solids and liquids, it undergoes four phases of colour transformation: it becomes in turn black, white, yellow, and red'. Now, these colours and the sequence in which they appeared were important and remained crucial to gauging the stages of the alchemical process, and one can immediately understand Maria's preference for glass over clay or metal as the material for her laboratory apparatus. The colours needed to be seen easily. Black signified the complete putrefaction or 'death' of the material, white its partial fixation, and red (sometimes called 'violet') its complete fixation and therefore perfection. From this, it is easy to see what another female Egyptian alchemist, 'Kleopatra', meant when she likened the alchemical process to the resurrection of the dead. 'The waters, when they come, awake the bodies and the spirits which are imprisoned and weak. For they again undergo oppression and are enclosed in Hades, and yet in a little while they grow and rise up and put on divers glorious colours like the flowers in Springtime.'[7]

But Maria, it appears, was not only an inventor. She understood the theories of matter underlying the work and passed them on to others, recorded for us by very much later writers as sayings or *aperçus*. For example: 'Join the male and the female and you will find what is sought' – a reminder of the essential requirement that polarities must be balanced for success. She also spoke of the 'death' of copper and silver, and of the necessity to render physical substances incorporeal and vice versa, which means that one must make metals volatile through sublimation, and then restore them to a new form of their original state. This, according to another of her sayings, releases the spirit of the metal and enables the alchemist to transform the nature of the substance when he turns it back into corporeal form. One of her sayings which was taken up and reproduced in varying forms by later alchemists is recorded by an early seventh-century alchemist Khristianos ('the Christian'): 'One becomes two, two becomes three, and by means of the third and fourth achieves unity. Thus two are but one' – an enigmatic pronouncement over which Carl Jung exercised much ingenuity, but which seems to mean simply that the alchemist combines a number of substances which begin the process as distinct entities, but end it as one transmuted substance.

Khristianos says that Maria announced this in a very particular way: she shrieked it. His verb, *kraugazei*, is used of dogs and ravens as well as human beings, in the latter case being related to a noun meaning 'scream' or 'shriek'. Raphael Patai, indeed, refers to it as an *ecstatic* shriek, which is perfectly possible, except that the Greek may equally well refer simply to a loud voice and hence to 'shouting' or 'proclaiming'. So Maria may not have been in some kind of trance when she voiced her proposition, but rather spoke or exclaimed it in excitement at the realization of an important idea, rather as Archimedes is said (alas with no basis in fact) to have shouted 'Eureka!' at a crucial moment of discovery. It is also possible that we have here a reference to her naturally loud speaking voice, or to her voice raised as she delivered a public lecture, or to her having to shout to make herself heard above a clamour of objections, or to a voice made hoarse because her throat and lungs had been adversely affected by the materials with which she was accustomed to work in her laboratory. Nevertheless, it is still worthwhile for us to consider the 'ecstasy'. Tradition gave Maria more than one additional appellation. Not only was she 'the Jewess', she was also 'the Prophetess', and prophets proclaim those revelations or messages which God has given them, as in Jer. 3.12, 'Go and proclaim (*qara*) these words'. The Hebrew verb means 'to raise one's voice'; the Greek Septuagint translates it as *anagnōthi*, 'read aloud'; and the Latin Vulgate as *clama*, 'shout'. So loud speaking of one form or another is definitely implied. References to Maria as a prophetess may be a later development from her identification with Miriam, the sister of Aaron, herself a prophetess, as Exod. 15.20 tells us, although these late traditions call her the 'sister of Moses', perhaps a more potent identification, since Moses became one of the great magicians of antiquity in mediaeval and early modern legend. Certainly Maria is credited with saying that alchemical secrets were revealed to her by God, which would make the notion of her as a prophetess both apt and logical. But these identifications come very late indeed – perhaps as late as the sixteenth century – and so pursuit of this tradition is scarcely going to be profitable. If Khristianos is right about her voice – and even this cannot be relied on – he is more likely to have preserved an echo of the way she spoke, or the way she spoke on one occasion, than to have hinted at some kind of trance or ecstatic utterance.[8]

Still, it is worth noting that there seems to have been a tradition connecting alchemy with divine realms and supernatural beings of one kind or another. An anonymous first-century AD transcript relates the following incident. The goddess Isis, speaking to her divine son Horus, tells him that at one astrologically significant moment she was seen by an angel from the first sphere, who wanted to have sex with her. He nearly succeeded in doing so, but Isis wanted to discover how to prepare gold and silver, and did not yield to his advances. The angel informed her that he did not know the secrets, but that next day a greater angel would come and answer her question. Sure enough, the following noon, the greater angel – called Amnaël, a name which appears nowhere else in Jewish or Egyptian angelology – descended and immediately wished to have sex with her. But once again Isis put him off until he was obliged to reveal the sign or mark

he carried on his head, and reveal to her the secrets she wanted to know. These
consisted of variations upon the themes 'like engenders like' and 'the naturally
inherent power [in one thing] enjoys the naturally inherent power [in another],
and the naturally inherent power [in one thing] overcomes the naturally inherent
power [in another]', followed by specific alchemical recipes. 'Take mercury. Fix it
either with a small lump of earth, or the substance of magnesia, or sulphur, and
hold on to it. This is the "amalgam".'

It seems clear we are meant to associate the two angels with the moon and
the sun, and therefore with silver and gold, and that Isis represents 'Nature' or
'the inherent natural power in things', whose act of sexual intercourse with the
astral force of the sun will enable her not only to effect the transmutation of
metals into their highest form, but will also permit her to pass on her secrets
to those who are legitimately 'born' from her. The implication of the tract
is that alchemists will have to seek out the secrets of their science in Nature,
and that their work will entail astrological knowledge of the appropriate moment, and a willing interaction with angelic powers. Now, there are obvious
connections between all this and the apocryphal second-century BC Book of
Enoch:

> And it came to pass when the children of men had multiplied that in those days were
> born unto them beautiful and comely daughters. And the angels, the children of the
> heaven, saw and lusted after them . . . And all the others together with them took unto
> themselves wives . . . And they began to go in unto them and to defile themselves with
> them, and they taught them charms and enchantments . . . And Azazel taught men to
> make swords and knives . . . and made known to them the metals of the earth and the art
> of working them . . . and all kinds of costly stones, *and all colouring tinctures.*[9]

Angels, sex, secrets: so far the parallels are suggestive, for they seem to mirror
certain linguistic usages which act as bridges between physical substances or
actions performed either in reality or through symbol to the outer, material
world, and to substances or actions pertaining to the realm of the spirit. The word
'dyeing', for example, is the same in Greek as that for 'baptizing', and 'sulphur
water' can also be understood as 'divine water', since etymology makes *theion*
mean both 'sulphur' and 'divine'. The terminology of corruption, death and
resurrection applies, as we have seen, to stages of the alchemical process, and the
uniting of two substances and production of a third is referred to in terms of
marriage or sexual intercourse, followed by birth. We can see these clearly in the
Dialogue of Philosophers and Kleopatra, a text dated between the first and third
century AD, in which Kleopatra (not the famous queen, but a female alchemist)
explains 'how something which is very high comes down to something which
is very low, and how something which is very low rises up to something which
is very high'. *High* and *low* in Greek may also refer to this world and the world

of the dead respectively, and Kleopatra's exposition of the process of regeneration illustrates this as she speaks of the dead lying in chains and darkness, who are woken by 'the drug of life', their 'bodies' and 'spirits' roused by penetrating waters. The 'body' is now filled with light, clothed in 'animating spirits' and 'made divine' (literally, 'fumigated with sulphur'), and vested in a shining colour which comes from the fire. The science, then, has reached its fulfilment in the yoking together of the bride and the groom, a conjunction which has made them a single entity. Régine Charron has outlined the chemical processes here being described in allegorical language. A lead-copper alloy is 'killed' by burning or boiling. This separates the volatile substance (its 'soul') from its 'body', and the remaining black mass lies inert on the bottom of the vessel. Sulphur water is poured on it. This turns the metal white, the process being a 'marriage' between the 'body' of the material and its 'soul', a marriage which results in a further change of colour from white to yellow as the 'spirit of gold' hidden in the sulphur water reacts upon them.

Like Maria, Kleopatra claimed that her knowledge came from God, the word she uses for 'God' being *dēmiourgos*, a term we have met before, and here used as a technical appellation for the god who created the world of matter as opposed to the God who is supreme and absolute and removed from material creation. Such a concept, as well as the way motifs of dead spirits, awakening and resurrection are here expressed, suggests that Kleopatra may have belonged to, or been influenced by, one of the systems of religious speculation and philosophy known collectively (although not very helpfully) as 'Gnosticism'; and the close similarity between Kleopatra's theories and practices and those attributed to Maria may also imply that she was familiar not only with the teachings of Gnostic groups in Egypt but also with some of the Jews of Alexandria.[10] Now, we have to bear in mind the ferment of various kinds of intellectual activity which was bubbling under the surface of the early Christian period, especially perhaps in Egypt. Notions, later dubbed heretical, of what constituted reality, and whether the Physical was inferior to or co-equal with the Spiritual, provided a rich ground for those who wished to investigate the precise relationship between the two; and while some people concentrated on trying to work out whether Jesus was wholly God or wholly human or some kind of mixture of both, or whether there had actually been two Christs, one divine and one human, others turned their fascination with Matter into the form of alchemical experiments, endeavouring to see whether their various separations and conjunctions of different substances could illustrate and explain by analogy what might happen in the spiritual world. Indeed, such operations might be made to work in reality, creating from inferior matter another more pure and more subtle, the kind of etherealized substance from which the human soul itself was created – a way of thinking entirely alchemical, since alchemy supposed that a substance such as metal consisted of a lifeless physical base (its 'body'), and an invigorating principle (its 'soul'). Thus, as Garth Fowden explains:

> The physical base was the same for all metals, but the 'soul' was present in varying degrees of purity – hence the different characteristics of each metal, and the belief that it was possible to transmute base metals into gold by manipulating the 'soul'. But the same distinction between the body and soul of metals stimulated in some alchemists another, more analogical line of thought, which used alchemical imagery in order to describe the purification of the human soul and its ascent to its divine source, so that a physical process became a generative symbol of a spiritual experience. The alchemists themselves were 'philosophers', and the aim of their 'philosophy' or 'divine art' was 'the dissolution of the body and the separation of the soul from the body'.[11]

There was, then, in Roman Egypt a vigorous strain within alchemy, which allied it to religious and philosophical theory, but in a way quite different from that found in Far Eastern and Indian practice. It can be seen again in the surviving works of or attributed to Zosimos of Panopolis (fourth century AD). This uncertainty of authorship is a constant problem for anyone discussing the early Christian centuries, but rather than invent periphrases for Zosimos, I shall refer to him by name, with the caveat that the reader should always bear in mind that the 'Zosimos' of any particular work could actually be another author whose name we do not know. Zosimos's principal treatise, *Apparatus and Furnaces*, was part of a great volume in 28 books entitled *Alchemical Matters*, dedicated to a fellow alchemist Theosebeia, called his 'sister', although this may refer to their alchemical rather than any sibling relationship; and like Maria the Jewess and Kleopatra, he was both a practical exponent of the science and a Gnostic interpreter of it. Thus, Zosimos invented alchemical equipment, in his case a cold-still which was intended to provide a greater evaporating surface suitable for distillation at low temperatures – significantly, in view of the constant interplay of the sexes which is found running through alchemical terminology and practice, his still was called a *mastarion* because it resembled a woman's breast – and he provides many drawings of alchemical apparatus, including those said to have been invented by Maria the Jewess. He also describes various experiments, such as one during which arsenic sulphide first releases sulphur and then deposits the arsenious oxide which, after heating with other, reducing substances, produces what Zosimos calls 'the second mercury', a substance which can then be used to convert copper into 'silver' (that is, copper arsenide); and he is even credited with a formula, called 'the formula of the Crab', which purports to contain the secret of transmutation itself.[12]

But alongside these evidences of technical interest appears a great deal more which bears witness to a spiritual eclecticism entirely natural to the era in which he was living. The gallimaufry of religious beliefs and speculations known as 'Gnosticism', but forming no single system or school, Platonism, Judaism, Hermeticism and magic mingled with alchemy to produce a rich fusion of disparate notions which suggested that the true or inner aim of the alchemist was to purify his or her soul in preparation for contemplation of the divine. Like Maria and other alchemists, Zosimos seems to have had an acute sense of being in touch with God, in his case through dreams or visions. His most famous vision, commented upon at length by Carl Jung in a less than helpful discussion, are recorded in his *Concerning Virtue*:

> I fell asleep and saw a person who offers sacrifices, standing in front of me on the upper side of an altar which was shaped like a broad flat bowl. This particular altar had fifteen rungs leading up to it, and it was there that the priest was standing. I heard [his] voice speaking to me from above. 'I have completed my descent of these fifteen rungs which radiate darkness, and my ascent of the rungs which blaze with light. It is the one who offers sacrifices who is making me into something new by throwing away the coarse thickness of the body, and while I am being turned into a priest by force I am initiated as a spirit.'[13]

The dream or vision continues at length, in five episodes, each interrupted by a period of wakefulness during which Zosimos meditates on what he has seen and tries to work out its meanings. Extreme violence is the *leitmotif* – dismemberment, burning, self-mutilation, boiling – the different stages of the alchemical process in the laboratory being described quite clearly under allegorical forms. Was Zosimos recollecting his experience of some kind of trance-like state during which he envisaged an alchemical experiment in images reminiscent of those of Hieronymus Bosch? We have already come across this suggestion of trance in connection with Maria the Jewess, but it is all too easy to fall into the trap of pushing these early writers down a mystical route which may not, in fact, have existed. In Maria's case, the speculation depended upon a verb (*kraugazei*) and an appellation, 'the Prophetess', both of which come from very much later traditions and may or may not reflect genuine aspects of her behaviour. In the case of Zosimos we have to bear in mind a long-established oneirological genre in literature. Plato, Aristotle and Cicero discussed the function of dreams and dreaming; so did Macrobius, Philo, Iamblichus and Epictetus. In the second century AD, Artemidoros provided a handbook and guide to the interpretation of dreams, while in a work written at the beginning of the fifth century AD, Synesios of Cyrene tried to account for why people dream by saying that during sleep the dreamer's *pneuma* (his psyche or soul) travels to all parts of the universe and collects impressions of things, which are then conveyed to the imagination (the faculty which stores and preserves images), from where they are relayed to the understanding (*nous*). The more virtuous the dreamer, the truer (in the sense of more accurately prophetic) his or her dreams will be. There also existed not only theoretical speculation on dreaming, but also the practice of incubation during which divine figures visited the dreamer and cured ailments or suggested solutions to problems. So, just as it is possible to interpret aspects of Maria's behaviour and reputation in more than one way, so it is too with those of Zosimos, and those interpretations inclining to the mystical side of explanation need to be tempered with other, more mundane possibilities.

Still, one does not deny that Maria and Zosimos and their several alchemical contemporaries lived during a period of immense religious ferment during which streams of speculation were bound to cross, mingle and generate further streams. So the allegorical possibilities of alchemy, numerous and varied throughout the different stages of the laboratory processes, could always be drawn into any discussion of the science and its technical stages – the word *pneuma* we noted above, for example, could also refer to colour, which was envisaged as a kind of activity and could be transferred from one substance to another during an alchemical procedure – and in a spiritual and philosophical world dominated by Gnostic and Manichaean ideas about the nature of matter and divinity, the relationship between them, and the possibility of separating oneself from the former and attaining (in whatever measure) the latter, could easily be taken for granted. One can begin to see, then (as Joseph Needham expresses it) 'something of the mystical significance which would have attached to the vapours and volatile substances, whether aqueous or oily, arsenical or sulphurous, in the minds of the Graeco-Egyptian and Persian proto-chemists, "spirit" rising from the "hell" of the distilling flask to be caught in the heaven of a receiver'. Hence Zosimos urged Theosebeia not to follow Aristotle by concentrating her energies upon the world of matter, but to direct herself to the non-material sphere and communicate to other, worthy individuals what she saw therein, and so direct their souls towards a Nature which is incorporeal and incorruptible.[14]

This strain of voice continued in later centuries, the writers, like Zosimos, mixing practical description and mystical commentary in their various works which, however, were more often derivative than original. Of these, Stephanos of Alexandria (seventh century), a scholar at the Court of Emperor Herakleios in Constantinople, produced an alchemical tract which expounded alchemical theory up to that point, presenting it as an intellectual and spiritual process rather than a coherent chemical and metallurgical science, infusing the still-fashionable Platonic and Gnostic notions of his day with Christian imagery and symbolism. With Stephanos, alchemy seems not only to have moved from Egypt to the Byzantine capital, but also to have shifted its principal focus from the laboratory to the study where it provided a rich bran-tub whence poets could draw romantic phrases and sentences to describe human regeneration and transformation. 'Body', 'soul', 'spirit', 'darkness' and 'unification', technical terms for aspects of the substance to be worked on and the initial processes of the alchemical experiment, take on religious connotations of death and resurrection. Thus the eighth-century poet Arkhelaos:

> When the spirit of darkness and of foul odour is rejected, so that no stench and no shadow of darkness appear, then the body is clothed with light and the soul and spirit rejoice because darkness has fled from the body. And the soul, calling to the body that has been filled with light, says: 'Awaken from Hades! Arise from the tomb and rouse thyself from darkness, for thou hast clothed thyself with spirituality and divinity, since the voice of the resurrection has sounded and the medicine of life has entered into thee.' For the spirit is again made glad in the body, as is also the soul, and runs with joyous haste to embrace it and does embrace it. Darkness no longer has dominion over the body, since it is a subject of light and they will not suffer separation again for eternity. And the soul rejoices in her home, because after the body had been hidden in darkness, she found it filled with light. And she united with it, since it had become divine towards her, and it is now her home. For it had put on the light of divinity and darkness had departed from it. And the body and the soul and the spirit were all united in love and had become one, in which unity the mystery had been concealed. In their being united together the mystery has been accomplished, its dwelling place sealed up and a monument erected full of light and divinity.

Joseph Needham, however, makes a notable point when he says, 'There is something ominous about alchemical poems. They presage and preside over the decaying end of a tradition, when the hard factual side has been pushed as far as it will go within the prevailing intellectual cadre, and there is no real way further forward.'[15] But, as the sixth-century alchemist Olympiodoros said, the ancients were in the habit of veiling the truth and hiding, by means of certain allegories and philosophical cunning, things which were in every way abundantly clear to people. In the case of Romano-Egyptian alchemy, this increasingly meant seeing laboratory processes more as a ritual than as chemical procedures – Zosimos, for example, seems to have regarded practical work not so much as attempts to manufacture gold itself as to produce ways of gilding metal alloys, which were symbolic of transformation in the human psyche – and so the colour-changes observable in the laboratory, from black through white and yellow to red-violet, became indicators of the practitioner's psychic journey from death to resurrection; from personal destruction and revival through marriage and sexual union to rebirth and transcendence; from ignorance through graded initiatory stages to wisdom; from time to timelessness; from being human to becoming in some sense divine, or at least achieving a more-than-quite-human apprehension of what was going on in the mind of God. Such progress had to be fought for. The laboratory was a severe and often dangerous testing-ground, and failure was in constant attendance. But there was also the comfort and expectation of a personal revelation, a dream or vision which would impart occult truths in the same kind of way an adept might instruct a favoured pupil. For it was a common understanding among alchemists that not all their secrets were written down, and that oral instruction was not only desirable but necessary in order to prevent the unworthy from gaining knowledge they might either abuse or misunderstand completely.

Yet in spite of these lofty ambitions and hopes for the science, by the time of these later alchemical writers all was not well. As C.A. Browne has pointed out, ancient clarity had been seduced by the wiles of rhetoric, and genuine expression of emotion to the 'empty jingling of an inflated style', of which Stephanos of Alexandria provides an all too typical example:

> O wisdom of teaching such a preparation, displaying the work. O moon clad in white and vehemently shining abroad whiteness. Let us learn what is the lunar radiance that we may not miss what is doubtful. For the same is the whitening snow, the brilliant eye of whiteness, the bridal procession-robe of the management of the process, the stainless chiton, the mind-constructed beauty of fair form, the whitest composition of the perfection, the coagulated milk of fulfilment, the moon-froth of the sea of dawn, the magnesia of Lydia, the Italian stibnite, the pyrites of Achaea, that of Albania, the many-named matter of the good work, that which lulls the All to sleep, that which bears the One which is the All, that which fulfils the wondrous work . . . For it is white as seen, but yellow as apprehended, the bridegroom to the allotted moon, the golden drop [falling] from it, the glorious emanation from it, the unchangeable embrace, the indelible orbit, the god-given work, the marvellous making of gold.[16]

As a practical science, then, alchemy clearly stood in need of being brought back to earth, and in the following centuries alchemists from a different tradition in the Middle East, albeit inheritors of the Alexandrian schools of natural philosophy, were to achieve this purpose.

4

The Islamic World: Balance and Magic Numbers

The extensive corpus of alchemical writings attributed to Jābir ibn Hayyān, an alchemist of the eighth century AD, cites many if not most of the names of those Romano-Egyptian alchemists we have been discussing, as well as a number of divine or legendary figures such as Isis and Hermes Trismegistos. It is therefore clear that not only were Islamic alchemists acquainted in greater or lesser measure with that earlier tradition which Islam encountered as it swept through Egypt during the previous century, but that they were happy to acknowledge the work already done and the theories already formulated by their pagan and Christian predecessors. The inclusion of Hermes Trismegistos among the ancestral adepts of alchemy is interesting, since the collection of treatises known as the *Corpus Hermeticum* contained a short exposition of one version of the Egyptian creation myth, one which can easily be interpreted as an allegory of the alchemical wedding of the sun and moon: 'As all things were by the contemplation of one, so all things arose from this one thing by a single act of adaptation. The father thereof is the Sun, the mother the Moon. The wind carried it in the womb, the Earth is the nurse thereof ... If it be cast on to the Earth, it will separate the element of Earth from that of Fire, the subtle from the gross.'

This text, known as the *Emerald Tablet* (*Tabula Smaragdina*), passed into both Arabic and Latin European magical tradition, and sentences from it were quoted in almost every Arabic alchemical work. It was considered important partly in its own right and partly because of the name 'Hermes' attached to it. 'Hermes' was the Greek name given to the Egyptian god Thoth, patron of writing, learning and occult knowledge. The Greeks called him 'three times great' (*Trismegistos*) in imitation of Egyptian linguistic usage which simply repeated an adjective instead of using a separate word as a superlative. Arabic tradition, however, divided him into three persons. One was identified with Enoch who built the pyramids and inscribed his contemporaries' scientific achievements on their walls to preserve this knowledge against the destruction of the Flood. A second lived after the Flood and made his way from Babylon, where he revived the sciences, to Egypt; and a third lived in Egypt, taught this revived knowledge, and also wrote it down. One of these, probably the last, was actually the inventor of alchemy and was buried in the Great Pyramid, one among several immense buildings which acted as alchemical laboratories and libraries. Thus the tenth-century scholar Ibn abī Ya'qūb al-Nadīm al-Warrāq al-Baghdādī. But this multiplicity of Hermeses is surpassed by the number of references to him – that is to say, references to his philosophical and ethical dicta – in extant Arabic texts dealing not only with alchemy but also astrology and magic, and it is clearly by means of his authoritative name that much of the Gnostic content of Romano-Egyptian alchemical theory was passed on to Islamic practitioners and, via their works or works attributed to them, to the European Middle Ages.[1]

Arabic alchemical texts also reproduce a Hellenistic symbol, the *ouroboros*, which appears in slightly different forms, but is based on the figure of a snake biting or swallowing its own tail. As a symbol it is much older than any of our extant alchemical writings – it is to be found, for example, in the Pyramid Texts of ancient Egypt, and Paola Carusi has suggested that the double *ouroboros* which makes its appearance in tenth-century Muslim alchemy may have originated in accounts of solar eclipses – but it has peculiar value for alchemists inasmuch as it can be seen to represent the constant cyclical nature of the work, rebirth and regeneration, and the action of corrosive vapours devouring the base metal of an alchemical experiment. Gnostic philosophers and magicians also used the *ouroboros* as a symbol of eternity or of the serpent of Genesis or of primeval darkness. A poem attributed to the eighth- or ninth-century alchemist Theophrastos describes it as a white snake with a spotted skin, which springs from the union of 'male' and 'female' after an incubation period of 20 days in horse dung, a clear indication of yet another identity for it, that of mercury, the substance which both transforms and is itself to be transformed by the alchemist. Other 'Greek' borrowings can be seen, too, in the notion that the 'body' of a metal is penetrated during the laboratory process by a 'spirit' (that is, a vapour), which changes its properties, expressed in the Arabic texts by *ajsād* (something new or renewed) which refers to the bodies of metals, and *arwāh* (spirit) which refers to their volatile parts or to the vapours which enter and transform the 'body'. Arabic also seems to have borrowed a number of technical terms from Greek: *al-iksīr* = *xērion* = elixir; *al-uthāl* – *aithalion* = a vapour-chamber; *al-anbīk* = *ambix* = alembic, a form of still.[2]

During the course of the early Islamic period, the centres of alchemical learning shifted. Constantinople had preserved a knowledge of the science but, as we have seen, tended to reduce it to a source of philosophical imagery. More important, the practical as well as the speculative side of alchemy removed from Egypt to Syria, which provided just that cultural and religious melting-pot especially favourable to the reception and development of the occult sciences, in which all kinds of texts – those of astronomy, philosophy, natural science, medicine – were translated and presented to interested parties as genuine works by Plato, Pythagoras and Aristotle, not to mention Hermes whom the native Harranians held in such esteem that he was sometimes called their 'prince'.

Harran – nowadays a small town alongside the River Belikh, 24 miles south-south-east of Urfa – was an important meeting place for travellers from Egypt and Persia, and traders with India and perhaps China, too. It had been since the beginning. Its name means 'journey' or 'caravan' or 'crossroad'. The town was famous for its metal working, and for its worship of planetary divinities with whom specific metals were associated, herbs, colours, days and numbers. Hence, perhaps, some of the emphasis placed by certain scholars on the importance of astrology for successful alchemical working. 'If you, [an astrologer], are asked about a work of alchemy,' wrote Sahl ibn Bishr (first half of the ninth century), 'whether it is true or false, then look at the lord of the ascendant and the moon, and if they are free from the malefics, then it is a true being. And if they are malefics, then it is false.'[3]

Muslim alchemy, however, imbued as it may be with the theories and terminology of Roman Egypt, traditionally begins in earnest with Khālid ibn Yazīd, an Umayyad prince, about whom little is known for certain beyond assertions in later literature that he was interested in alchemy, and that he composed a number of alchemical treatises. But there is so much doubt about his connection with alchemy that it is best to pass him over and come at once to the work which really does define Muslim alchemy – that of Jābir ibn Hayyān and the extensive corpus of writings which bear his name. 'Jābir' was not necessarily the same person as the alchemist 'Geber', although this is not always realized and the two men are confused as one, 'Geber' being both the Latinized form of his name attached to at least three genuine 'Jābirian' treatises translated from Arabic during the Middle Ages, but also the pseudonym of a Latin alchemist of the late thirteenth century. There is also no certainty that 'Jābir' himself was an historical person. All one can safely do is to say that books and treatises under his name, dating to the late ninth and tenth century, initiate the great period of Muslim alchemy during which certain specific ideas make their influence felt in the science.

One of these ideas is *balance*. According to 'Jābir', metals arise as the result of the wedding of mercury and sulphur in different proportions and under particular celestial influences. All metals have internal and external characteristics peculiar to themselves, and the alchemist's task is to ascertain exactly what these characteristics are and in what proportion they appear in any given metal, so that he or she can bring about chemical change by mixing these primary characteristics. By 'characteristics' the texts mean the Aristotelian principles of hot, cold, moist and dry, and a metal can exhibit two externally and contain two internally. (Thus, for example, gold is hot and moist externally, but cold and dry internally.) Metals look and feel as they do because their individual characteristics are held in a certain balance. Alter that balance, and the composition of the metal will inevitably change, the agents for such alteration being elixirs, substances made specifically to alter or correct the proportion or 'balance' of characteristics in any given metal.

Knowledge of the various balances was therefore a prerequisite to embarking upon the work, but could be gained by means of complex numerological computations. These, however, were not mere exercises in arithmetic, and certainly had nothing to do with computing the weights or measurements of metals or their constituent parts under laboratory conditions. As Seyyed Nasr says, 'Jābir, who employs numbers exclusively as the basis of the balance, also uses the qualitative number of the Pythagoreans, since the Jābirian balance is essentially an instrument for measuring the tendency of the World Soul towards each substance.' Nevertheless, what may seem to be a certain arbitrariness in 'Jābir's' numbers is more apparent than real. In fact, there were certain numbers to which he attached particular significance – 1, 3, 5, 8 and 28 – and the sum of 1, 3, 5 and 8 was the most significant number of all. Everything, he said, was governed by 17, a number he almost certainly derived from a magic square.

$$4 \quad 9 \quad 2$$
$$3 \quad 5 \quad 7$$
$$8 \quad 1 \quad 6$$

As we can see, 1, 3, 5, 8 = 17 and 4, 9, 2, 7, 6 = 28 and, as Holmyard points out, not only did 'Jābir' write a book on magic squares, this particular square had important associations for the Sufi sect to which he is said to have belonged. Now, 28 was the significant number when it came to working out the constitution of metals. Each of the four elementary natures had four 'degrees' – heat, cold, dryness, humidity – and seven subdivisions, and so each elementary nature had 28 'positions' on the table of 'qualities'. There are 28 letters in the Arabic alphabet, and so the Arabic name of a substance could be made to yield the composition and the ratio of its constituent qualities to one another. Moreover, since each substance has an internal and an external composition, its internal and external qualities will be found to be in opposition to one another, in the ratio of either 1:3 or 5:8. Hence the overriding importance of the numbers contained in this magic square.[4]

It is a system closely akin to magic, of course, but then magic was never far away from the Jābirian corpus. The various authors who produced these works had interests extending far beyond the relatively simple transmutation of metals and production of elixirs. One was 'the science of theurgy and apotropaics', specifically magical and directed, among other things, to the creation of amulets and talismans ('*Ihn al-Tilasmat*); another involved the generation of ores, plants, minerals, animals, and even human beings, the latter under the form of a foetus or homunculus, an endeavour picked up and developed by Latin alchemy; while several volumes related the chemical proportions of substances to the constitution of the universe via cosmology and astrology. Still, it would be unfair to leave the impression that 'Jābir' was simply a theorist after the Byzantine mode. If we are to believe one of the stories about his 'life', he appears to have spent time at the Court of the Caliph in Baghdad and had a secret, or at least a private laboratory at Kufa, which was rediscovered 200 years after his 'death'. No matter, really, whether this is told of a real or a legendary person; it was obviously important to the tradition that 'Jābir' be associated with practical as well as theoretical alchemy, and we see this again in the *Book of Properties* which bears his name, for therein we find entirely clear and practical recipes for the preparation of various substances, such as this one for white lead:

> Take a pound of litharge, powder it well and heat it gently with four pounds of wine vinegar until the latter is reduced to half its original volume. Then take a pound of soda and heat it with four pounds of fresh water until the volume of the latter is halved. Filter the two solutions until they are quite clear and then gradually add the solution of soda to that of the litharge. A white substance is formed which settles to the bottom. Pour off the supernatant water and leave the residue to dry. It will become a salt as white as snow.

But the practicalities of the Jābirian corpus, a very large body of writings with no fewer than 500 separate titles, its extensive concern with chemical processes and techniques, its development of several key procedures such as crystallization, distillation, calcination, sublimation and evaporation, and its preparation of a number of acids – nitric, hydrochloric, citric and tartaric – along with its description of how to prepare steel, how to dye cloth and leather, how to make varnishes to render cloth waterproof and how to prepare hair-dyes, reveal that 'Jābir' was not particularly interested in what is supposed to be the principal characteristic of an alchemist, namely, the transmutation of inferior metals into gold. On the contrary, macrobiotics and chemotherapy prevail, and help to show that by and large Muslim alchemy had a much greater connection with medicine than its Romano-Egyptian and Byzantine predecessors.[5] So to 'Jābir' and his corpus can be assigned a number of striking theories and pioneering endeavours: the notion that all metals consist of sulphur and mercury in various proportions; that there is an ontological equivalence between the name of a thing and the thing itself, and that numbers can be made to reveal this relationship; that living creatures can be brought into being by artificial generation in the laboratory; and that experimental investigation will yield knowledge of the different ways chemicals interact with one another – for which new or improved types of laboratory equipment may well be necessary. It is to 'Jābir', for example, that alchemy owes the *alembic*, strictly speaking the head of a still used for distillation, but commonly applied to the whole of the still itself. Never mind, therefore, that 'Jābirian' alchemy included magical numerology as an essential component of its method. Nothing could have been further removed from the highly Christianized, analogically driven system it inherited from Egypt and Constantinople. The coming-down-to-earth which was necessary for progress to be made in the science had overtly and unmistakably happened.

The connection between Muslim alchemy and medicine can be seen in the work of Abū Bakr Muhammad ibn Zakariya al-Razī (AD 865–925), known in the West as Razes or Rhazes, a Persian who, like many others, was drawn to the remarkable academic and medical facilities in Baghdad. Here he studied under a famous Jewish convert to Islam and later produced 'a hundred' books on medicine, as well as other treatises on such subjects as natural philosophy, mathematics, astronomy, logic, theology and alchemy. Recollections of him by a contemporary from his native town describe him as having a large square head and a generous nature which led him to look after the poor and sick. His eyes, we are told, were always watering on account of his excessive consumption of beans, although the likelihood is that they were watering from fatigue and strain as a result of his constant reading and copying books. A sceptic when it came to many of the therapeutic theories and procedures based on the works of the second-century AD Greek physician Galen – which still held common sway and continued to do so in the West for many more centuries to come – al-Razī expressed his doubts in writing (while gracefully acknowledging Galen's stature in medical history), and produced a kind of home manual for the general public, to which people could turn if they could not find or afford a doctor. He himself used a wide variety of mineral drugs in his therapies, and here, of course, is where his medicine and his alchemy overlapped.

Of all the volumes attributed to his pen – and we always have to treat numbers with a degree of caution – two, *The Book of Secrets* (*Kitāb al-asrār*) and *The Book of the Secret of Secrets* (*Kitāb sirr al-asrār*) contain the bulk of his final thoughts on alchemy. In them, he divides what he has to say into three categories: (a) drugs derived from plants, animals and minerals, and their application in therapy; (b) apparatus; and (c) the basic techniques and procedures used in alchemy. It becomes clear to anyone who reads these texts that al-Razī knew exactly what he was talking about, and that his knowledge had almost certainly been gained from practice in the laboratory rather than reading in his study. Indeed, he tells us himself that once, during a visit to Baghdad, he used an elixir to gild two metals to such effect that they had the appearance of actual gold, and in *Kitāb sirr al-asrār* he describes the techniques for doing this, along with others which will successfully reverse the process.

Like 'Jābir', al-Razī was keen to classify substances although, as we might expect, his classifications sprang from practical rather than from philosophical roots. Thus, in addition to listing the materials and apparatus which should be found in a well-equipped laboratory and store-room, he devised a system which classified substances used in alchemy under four headings – mineral, vegetable, animal, derivative – and then further subdivided the minerals into six categories: spirits (including mercury and sulphur), bodies (seven metals corresponding to the seven planets), stones, vitriols, boraces and salts. It is evidence of an orderliness of mind which can be seen again in his medical encyclopaedia, *Kitāb al-Hāwī fi 'l-tib*, in effect an edited version of his medical notebooks, in which his notes are organized anatomically from head to toe, with the materia medica arranged in alphabetical order. If this published version came from his students rather than from al-Razī himself, as seems likely, it shows that the urge to classify was well entrenched among those he had taught, either by nature or by training.

Unlike 'Jābir', however, al-Razī did not accept the theory of balance. But he was happy to accept the proposition that metals could be transmuted on a growing scale of worth, and that stones could be improved in similar fashion by treating them with elixirs of appropriate strength, and he described his method of transmutation in a certain amount of detail. It involved four stages. First, the substance had to be cleansed of its impurities by subjecting it to such processes as distillation, calcinations, sublimation, and so forth. Secondly, it had to be reduced to a condition in which it was readily fusible. Thirdly, the results of this process were to be dissolved in solutions which were alkaline and ammoniacal rather than acidic, and then recombined. Fourthly, this recombination was to be coagulated or solidified, and if the process had worked successfully that coagulated or solidified substance would be the elixir – not actually called 'the philosopher's stone' by al-Rāzī – which had the power to transmute baser metals into metals more noble, such as gold or silver.[6]

Not every Muslim alchemist accepted the validity of transmutation, however, and indeed opponents and defenders of the theory conducted a scholarly debate among themselves until the beginning of the fifteenth century. Al-Rāzī himself was obliged to refute Ya'kub ibn Ishāk al-Kindī (AD 800–67), who wrote that humankind is unable to achieve those things which are peculiarly the preserve of Nature; Abū 'Alīal-Husain ibn Sīnā (AD 980–1037), known in the West as Avicenna, flatly denied that either transmutation or manufacture of gold were at all possible; and Abū Hayyān al-Tawhīdī, his contemporary, likewise denied that alchemists could do more than produce imitations of precious metals. The Iraqi traveller and geographer al-Masūdī (died AD 956), summed up their negative attitude. 'As far as I am concerned, I seek refuge in God from becoming obsessed by researches which weaken the brain, damage the sight and darken the complexion with clouds of vapours rising from sublimations, emanations from vitriol, and other chemical substances.' But criticism continued. In the fourteenth century, both Ibn Kayyim al-Djawziyya (died 1349) and Ibn Khaldūn (1322–1406) agreed that the claims of alchemy were largely false, the former saying it could produce only appearance, the latter that alchemy was, in effect, a branch of magic. Ibn Khaldūn, indeed, went even further and suggested that, although alchemists might have acquired genuine chemical knowledge during the course of their experiments, they were charlatans almost to a man, and he gave examples of Berber alchemists in the Maghrib who would cover silver with a gold veneer or blanch copper with mercury to make it look like silver. 'Those who claim to have made gold with the help of alchemy,' he observed sarcastically, 'are like those who might claim success in the artificial creation of Man from semen' – a swipe at those Jābirians who practised what they called 'the science of generation' in an effort artificially to create various forms of life, especially an homunculus.

But none of these objections passed without equal challenge. Maslama ibn Ahmad al-Majrītī (died c.1007), for example, was one of a group of Muslim scholars and alchemists from Spain – 'al-Majrītī' indicates he came from Madrid – whose work shows a close familiarity with the alchemical processes of the laboratory. He believed in the power of elixirs to transmute metals, while his contemporary al-Fārābī (died AD 950) argued that transmutation must be possible because, as Aristotle had pointed out, metals constitute a single species and can therefore change from one to another of their own accord. The same kind of argument was used by another contemporary, al-Hamdānī (died AD 945), who noted that metallurgists are able to subject iron and steel to processes which improve their quality, and so alchemists should be able to imitate the way Nature matures metals into gold simply by speeding up her protracted form of working. In 1034 al-Katī wrote a book whose alchemy was very much in the Romano-Egyptian tradition and asserted that the science was perfectly capable of making gold; and in the early twelfth century, Mu'ayyid al-Dīn al-Tughrā'ī (1061–1121) defended it against sceptics in a number of treatises on the subject, particularly one written in 1112 as a response to Ibn Sīnā, in which he maintained that although each mineral did indeed belong to a separate species and therefore had its own specific difference, as Ibn Sīnā had said, nevertheless the alchemist could alter this condition and so prepare it for intervention by God, who would then suspend the arrangement of His own creation and effect the change at which the alchemist was aiming. Taken by and large, then, scholarly Islamic opinion on the validity of alchemy tended to be split evenly between the yeas and nays, with al-Djāhiz (AD 776–868/9), a theologian and polemicist from Basra, carefully sitting on the fence, suggesting that perhaps, once in 5,000 years, when the qualities of the metals were just right and the alignment of the planets was just so, it might not be impossible to make gold after all.[7]

Ibn Sīnā, like 'Jābir' and al-Rāzī, is one of the dominant names in Muslim alchemy. Born in Persia, he received quite a good education but soon outstripped his tutors and resorted to teaching himself, concentrating on medicine which, he remarked later, 'is not a difficult subject'. His two most important works were *The Book of Healing*, which dealt with a large number of different topics, and *The Canon of Medicine* whose influence on generations of medical students was incalculable; but there is controversy over whether he himself practised or wrote about alchemy. As Donald Hill says, 'Properly speaking ... Ibn Sīnā cannot be considered as an alchemist at all, since in his *Kitāb al-Shifā'*, and elsewhere, he denied the main belief of alchemists, namely, the possibility of transmutation. Moreover, modern research has shown that most of the alchemical works that bear his name were not from his pen.' One such, *The Book about the Soul* (*Liber de anima*), deals with the history and aims of alchemy, and details the procedures of preparing an elixir; a second, *The Soul in the Art of Alchemy* (*De anima in arte alchemiae*), defends the reality of transmutation, and exists only in a Latin translation. It could *au fond* be genuine, but has been altered and revised considerably by the Latin translator; and a third, *A Letter about the Elixir* (*Risālat al-Iksīr*), is to all intents and purposes a laboratory handbook describing various ways of colouring substances and preparing the elixir. We need not be surprised, therefore, to find that Ibn Sīnā's opinions on alchemy (if they are indeed his) accept some aspects of it while repudiating others:

> I do not deny that such a degree of accuracy in imitation may be reached as to deceive even the shrewdest, but the possibility of transmutation has never been clear to me. Indeed, I regard it as impossible, since there is no way of splitting up one metallic combination into another. Those properties that are perceived by the senses are probably not the differences which distinguish one metallic species from another, but rather accidents or consequences, the essential specific differences being unknown. And if a thing is unknown, how is it possible for anyone to endeavour to produce it or to destroy it?[8]

By the middle of the eleventh century, however, the great days of Muslim alchemy were on the wane. But from Baghdad in particular, and from Muslim Spain where Islamic and Jewish alchemists flourished – especially, perhaps, in Córdoba during the second half of the tenth century AD, issued large numbers of translated works, a legacy from the late antique to the mediaeval world; and of these one of the best known is the first Arabic work on alchemy to appear in Latin, *The Company of Philosophers* (*Turba Philosophorum*), dating to c.AD 900. Originally written by an anonymous author from Akhmīm, a town in which scientific traditions rubbed shoulders with Greek, Coptic and Arabic, the *Turba* was probably composed in Arabic but is likely to have been based on older Greek sources. It is cast in the well-tried form of a set of an extended 'conversation' pieces – actually more a succession of speeches than genuinely interactive discourse – involving famous figures who have gathered together at the invitation, or in the house, of a noted individual, in this case, Pythagoras. Nine early Greek natural philosophers take part in this static drama, each summarizing his particular teachings (although, as Plessner points out, these are not always quite in accord with what we know from elsewhere these pre-Socratic philosophers actually taught), and then 63 other speeches from a variety of people set out dicta directly related to the practicalities of alchemical procedure. Thus 'Cerus' in the preparation of an elixir:

> I direct you to take quicksilver in which is the male potency or strength. Cook it with its body until it becomes a fluxible water. Cook the masculine together with the vapour until each becomes coagulated and turns into a stone. Then take the water, which you have previously divided into two parts, one of which is for liquefying and cooking the body, and the second, its companion, for cleansing that which is already burnt. The two are made one. Soak the stone seven times and cleanse it until it disintegrates, its body is purged from all defilement, and it becomes earth. (Be aware, too, that in a period of forty-two days, the whole [thing] is changed into earth.) Liquefy it, therefore, by cooking until it becomes like true water, that is, quicksilver. Then wash with water of nitre until it becomes like a liquefied coin. Then cook it until it congeals and becomes like tin, at which stage it is a very great arcanum (that is, the stone which comes out of two things). Exercise control over this by cooking and pounding until it becomes a most excellent crocus. (Be aware that we have called water desiccated with its companion 'crocus'.) Cook it, therefore, and soak with the residual water you have put by until you attain your goal.

It was perhaps partly because of this semi-overt language – and we shall see that alchemical writers could be extraordinarily obscure in an effort either to hide their secrets from the uninitiated, or to appear more learned and advanced in the science than they actually were – that the *Turba*, in one version or another, became a popular text in mediaeval Europe. For it is a most interesting attempt to express Romano-Egyptian alchemy in Arabic and to adapt it to the most recent forms taken by Muslim science; and throughout its multiple dicta we can discern those twin principles which were to inform European alchemy, Aristotle's concept of the four elements and the nature of minerals, and 'Jābir's' theory that all metals are composed of sulphur and mercury. Everything else – the development of apparatus, the classification of substances, the debate about the validity or non-validity of transmutation, the increasing sophistication of laboratory methods – rested upon these two pillars. Taken as a whole, it was a formidable tradition of practicalities suffused by disputed theory, which Muslim alchemists built up and handed on to their Western counterparts, and with the flood of translations emanating from Spain from the twelfth century onwards, European alchemists were not slow to take advantage of this intellectual windfall.[9]

5

Mediaeval Europe: Translations, Debates and Symbols

The first mention of alchemy in a Western source (c.1050) reported a fraudulent transmutation into gold by a Byzantine Jew called 'Paul'. It is an anecdote which draws attention to three points worth noting: first, that the alchemical tradition mediated by Constantinople from Roman Egypt was still available; secondly, that fraud was an ever-present worry to everyone who patronized alchemists and put money into their ventures; and thirdly, that Jewish contribution to the science was both notable and important. We have already remarked on the existence of translations and adaptations of Greek texts by Arabic scholars, supplemented by original theories and practical descriptions and recommendations by Muslim alchemists, all of which started to make their way into Europe early in the twelfth century. As De Pascalis observes, 'For the men of the 12th century, thirsty for new cultural experiences, the Spanish peninsula became a sort of "promised land" where mathematics, astronomy, medicine, and alchemy could be studied ... [and] the work of translating Arabic manuscripts was often encouraged and protected by the ecclesiastical authorities, such as the Archbishop of Toledo or the Bishop of Tarragona.' Alchemy thus came into Europe as a new and intriguing branch of knowledge apparently under the patronage and guidance of the Church, and it came, by and large, from Spain.

Alfred of Sarashel, for example, was an Englishman who lived there towards the end of the twelfth century and translated part of Ibn Sīnā's work on alchemy into Latin. Robert of Chester was another. He concentrated on astrological treatises but also translated *A Book about the Structure of Alchemy* (*Liber de compositione alchimiae*) in 1144, feeling obliged, since alchemy was a science relatively new to Europe, to explain that *alchemy* referred to the transmutation of substances into 'better' substances in accordance with the operations of Nature. Toledo in particular attracted scholars from all over Western Europe to render an immense variety of Arabic texts into Latin for the benefit of their less learned colleagues and pupils, an enterprise which took place under the patronage of King Alfonso X of Castile and with the encouragement of Raimundo, the city's Archbishop who, together with Domingo Gundisalvo, Archdeacon of Cuéllar, supported a number of Hispanic Jews in this work of translation and dissemination.

One of the best known of this Toledan school of translators was Gerard of Cremona (1114–87). Born, as his name suggests, in Italy, Gerard came to Toledo in 1167 and there learned the art of translating from Arabic into Latin. His greatest achievement therein was to provide the West with a Latin version of the Arabic translation of Ptolemy's *Almagest*, a major astronomical work; but he is also credited with translating one of al-Rāzī's books on alums and salts, and perhaps also one of the Jābirian corpus dealing with the balance of metals. 'Translation', however, can be misunderstood in this context. What often (but not invariably) happened was that the European scholar did not have good enough Arabic to be able to work directly from his text, so someone, often a Jewish convert, would render the Arabic into Castilian or Catalan, and from this the scholar would produce his Latin version. In Gerard's case, this assistant seems to have been a Mozarab called 'Galippus', although it has also been suggested that his knowledge of Arabic improved to the point where he could translate without the help of an intermediary.[1]

Mediating the Romano-Egyptian-Muslim alchemical tradition, then, was part of a great wave of translation which streamed out of Spain and, to a somewhat lesser extent, Italy during the twelfth and thirteenth centuries. This tradition, however, emphasized the practical aspects of the science over the theoretical, and hence mediaeval European alchemy tended to take its tone more from the Jābirian corpus than from the earlier 'Hellenistic' model. Still, we must not exaggerate the distance between them. 'Practical' and 'theoretical' did not become two distinct features of European alchemy, as can be seen from Robert of Chester's translation of the *Liber de compositione alchimiae*.

Attributed to 'Morienus', a supposed Christian hermit and teacher of Khālid ibn Yazīd ibn Mu'āwiya who, legend said, was a practising alchemist and author of alchemical poems, the treatise in Robert's version opens with the story of the three Hermeses, the last of whom, Hermes Trismegistos, discovered and first published this book after the Flood. Rediscovered by Adfar of Alexandria, the *Liber* gave up its secrets to him and allowed Adfar to achieve a certain fame which then reached the ears of 'Morienus', who was living in Rome at the time. Leaving everything at once, 'Morienus' travelled to Alexandria, learned 'the secrets of all divinity' from Adfar and after Adfar's death retired to become a hermit in Jerusalem. A garbled history of Khālid follows, with an account of how 'Morienus' came to meet him and ask him to provide him with a laboratory in which he could transmute substances into gold. This Khālid granted, but once 'Morienus' had successfully completed the work, he ran away and it took many years before Khālid's scouts managed to locate him and bring him back to their master. The next section of the treatise is devoted to a set-piece 'conversation' between the two men, in which Khālid asks questions about alchemy and 'Morienus' answers, first in general terms and then in specific detail about the conduct of alchemical operations. Von Lippmann, as Thorndike points out, had no time for this account, referring to its 'vacuity, lack of clarity, and silly twaddle'; but it does illustrate the way in which appeal to antiquity, apparently corroborated by a mass of circumstantial evidence, gave confidence in and support to the technicalities of a 'new' science with its own particular jargon (which 'Morienus' takes care to explain to Khālid, and thus to his European readers).[2]

How, then, did alchemy fare in mediaeval Europe? Frankly, its status and claims were uncertain. There was a widespread view that technology in its various forms provided at basis an imitation of Nature and her capabilities, and so alchemy's assertion that it could, in effect, not only imitate Nature but actually do her work for her in accelerated time was bound to produce controversy. Universities, for example, steadfastly refused to include alchemy in their curricula, even though alchemical texts often display what Chiara Crisciani has called 'a confident mastery of both medical and Aristotelian naturalistic doctrines' and 'purposeful adaptations of these doctrines to the specific needs of alchemical knowledge'. This refusal of the institutions of learning is somewhat surprising, since Aristotle, the doyen of Mediaeval studies, was credited with writing on alchemy, partly, at least, because one section of Ibn Sīnā's *Kitāb al-Shifa* was translated and tacked on to the end of the fourth book of Aristotle's *Meteorologica* under the title *The Freezing and Cohesion of Stones* (*De congelatione et conglutinatione lapidum*), thus, as far as many scholars were concerned, passing into the Aristotelian canon. In it Ibn Sīnā attacked the doctrine of transmutation, and so inevitably provided a focal point for those such as Albertus Magnus, himself a great Aristotelian, who wished to defend it.

Albertus (1193/1206–1280), a German Dominican, was one of the most influential European scholars of the thirteenth century and produced studies within an extraordinary range of disciplines – theology, astronomy, geography, botany, zoology, mineralogy and medicine. Needless to say, he had further works fathered upon him, principally those dealing with occult sciences such as magic and alchemy; but in one of his genuine books, *Minerals* (*De Mineralibus*), he made the interesting observation that of all the arts, alchemy was the one which most closely imitated Nature and that its processes acted on mercury and sulphur analogously to the way medicines act on corrupt matter, by purging away what was rotten and restoring to health the substance which was left. Nevertheless, while acknowledging that transmutation was possible in theory, Albertus did say he had tried burning alchemically produced gold and found that after it had been subjected to this test six or seven times, it was finally consumed altogether, which would not have happened had the gold been as genuine as Nature's. So he concluded that, whatever the theory, alchemists had not yet discovered a method whereby true gold could be manufactured and made to withstand a trial by fire. But he did suggest that skilled alchemists, working under favourable astrological conditions, might be able to produce a form of metal which was an improvement on an earlier stage of its existence and open to beneficial influence from the stars

– a connection between alchemy and astrology we have noted before in both Chinese and Romano-Egyptian texts.

Now, as William Newman points out, the tone of Albertus's argumentation is perfectly even and he does not seem to be taking part in any general heated debate on the subject. This, however, changed in c.1266 when Roger Bacon produced his *Opus Tertium* in which he argued for the study of alchemy as a way of reforming the natural sciences as they were understood and taught in his day, since he clearly regarded it as greater than any other similar branch of learning, and lamented the fact (as he saw it) that people in general seemed to be ignorant of its importance:

> There is another branch of learning which is about the generation of things from the elements, and about all inanimate objects: for example, the elements, simple and composite humours; ordinary stones, gems, and marbles; gold and the rest of the metals; sulphurs, salts, inks; lapis lazuli, cinnabar, and the rest of the colours; oils and burning tars; and other things without number about which we have nothing in the books of Aristotle. Natural philosophers know nothing about them, and neither does the whole orb of writers in Latin. Now, because the generality of students is ignorant of this branch of learning, it follows that they do not know anything about the things in Nature, which follow [from it] – namely, the generation of living things such as [plants, animals, and human beings . . . [*This also includes ignorance about the theory and practice of medicine*], and neither the terminology of these two aspects of medicine, nor its meaning, can be known except by means of this branch of learning; and this branch of learning is speculative alchemy which investigates every inanimate object and the entire generation of things from the elements.
>
> But there is an operative and practical alchemy which teaches [us] how to make noble metals, and colours, and many other things through technique, which is better and more productive than Nature can manage. This particular branch of learning is greater than all those I mentioned before, because it produces greater advantages. For not only can it provide for the state's expenditure, and numberless other things, but it teaches [us] how to discover things which can prolong human life (to that length of time it can be prolonged in accordance with Nature) . . . [But] almost everyone is ignorant of these two branches of the science of alchemy. For although many people throughout the world labour to make metals and colours and other things, very few genuinely know how to make colours profitably. Almost no one knows how to make metals, and even fewer how to achieve those things which have the power to prolong life. There are also few who know how to distil well, to sublimate, to calcinate, to dissolve, and carry out the operations of this kind of craft, through which all inanimate objects are validated and through which speculative alchemy, natural philosophy, and medicine are validated [too].

Those who teach natural philosophy and those who teach medicine – 'the mob of writers in Latin', whom Bacon contrasts with Arabs such as Ibn Sīnā with whose work he himself was acquainted and which he clearly admired – are hamstrung by their ignorance of alchemy in both its speculative and its practical aspects, and therefore their students turn out to be equally ignorant. So many other subjects stem from the kind of knowledge acquired from a study of alchemy that none can be apprehended properly unless alchemy be studied first. But while it is worth noting that in his *Wonderful Power of Art and Nature* (*De mirabili potestate artis et naturae*, Paris 1542) Bacon observed that 'the science [of alchemy] can increase the purity of gold a lot, and likewise deliver gold without deception' (p. 45) in his *Opus Tertium* from which the passage above is taken, he remarks that not only can the state treasury benefit from the practice of alchemy, so also can the individual by producing or acquiring an elixir to prolong natural life. These are themes to which he returns more than once, as in his *Opus Maius*:

> The experimental science (of the future) will know, from the 'Secret of Secrets' of Aristotle, how to produce gold not only of twenty-four degrees but of thirty or forty or however many desired. This was why Aristotle said to Alexander, 'I wish to show you the greatest of secrets', and it is indeed the greatest. For not only will it conduce to the well-being of the state, and provide everything desirable that can be bought for abundant supplies of gold, but what is infinitely more important, it will give the prolongation of human life. For that medicine which would remove all the impurities and corruptions of baser metal so that it should become silver and the purest gold, is considered by the wise to be able to remove the corruptions of the human body to such an extent that it will prolong life for many centuries.[3]

This life-prolonging elixir seems to have been one of the principal reasons for Bacon's interest in and hope for alchemy, and it is worth noting, as Bruce Moran has done, that in spite of those historians of science who would like to claim Bacon as an early chemist, it was actually alchemy, not chemistry, which engaged his attention. Humans could live longer naturally if they corrected the causes of physical corruption, and this correction can take place by creating a balance between the elemental parts of the body and temperament, its *complexio*. 'Even Adam in his state of innocence did not have complete equality of the elements, because he lacked the food of the tree of life,' he wrote, but 'at the resurrection, bodies of those to be damned as well as of those to be glorified will be immortal because of [this] equality'. Gradually, however, since the time of Adam and Eve, human life has become shorter and shorter, 'and people born after the Flood have not been able to live as long as they used to'. Nevertheless, there were many examples of what a strict régime could do, even in Bacon's time, and he mentions a woman in the diocese of Norwich in England, who did not eat for 20 years and yet retained her weight without being fat, as was ascertained by the Bishop after careful examination. This example, Bacon notes, 'was not a miracle but a work of Nature, because some pattern of the stars (*constellatio*) at that time had the power to return the elements in her body to a state closer to that of equality than they had been in before'. But regulating a person's diet and getting him or her to follow a healthy regimen was not the only means to help prolong someone's life. Assistance could also be found in ingestible gold, since gold already embodies incorruptibility and is thus a body in which the elements exist in equal balance; and to obtain gold in digestible form, one relies upon alchemy because 'alchemical gold, as Avicenna says in his book *Anima*, is better than the natural. Likewise, there is a great difference between the grades of alchemical gold, the best being that which comes from an equality of its constituent parts. [This one] prolongs life'.

Elixirs and potable gold were thus part of the armoury of fourteenth- and fifteenth-century physicians who frequently interpreted both the sick body and the intended cures in alchemical terms. In his *Book of Surgery* (1306), for example, Henri de Mondeville, surgeon to Philippe le Bel of France, saw the body as an alchemist's furnace or oven in which boiling, combustion and calcination were constantly taking place, and the surgeon's or physician's task was to preside over this process in such a way as to restore healthy balance to the temperature of the humours. Likewise, the late fourteenth-century Catalan Carmelite, Guillem Sedacer, suggested that since a metal was a 'body' [*corpus*], it could be sick and therefore cured – lead, for example, was gold suffering from leprosy – and elixirs could be employed to penetrate the 'body', solidify its inherent mercury, fix it, harden it, and change it into something both solar and lunar, that is to say, into a substance in which the male and female components were in perfect balance. Producing the philosopher's stone in such a form is thus the first step towards manufacturing a superior form of gold which, when ingested, will help to prolong human life. This conjunction of an alchemical elixir with medicine was also made by Albertus Magnus who referred to it in his *De Mineralibus*, treating 'medical antidote' and '[that] which alchemists call elixir' as synonymous; and he was by no means unusual in making such a linkage. For, as Chiara Crisciani has pointed out, 'alchemists made abundant use of [medical] doctrines taught at universities – the humoral theories, the doctrines of radical moisture, and the various kinds of doctrines concerning digestion, degree measurement, embryology, and mixtures', and she suggests that it would be useful to conduct further research into 'the analogies detectable in the epistemological structure of the two disciplines, often pointed out by alchemists, physicians, and natural philosophers alike; the discussions on the role of practice in medicine, and on the forms of transmission of operative skills, as compared with similar discussions in alchemy; [and] the medical competence that some alchemists displayed, as well as the interest in alchemic doctrines shown by several doctors'.[4]

Now, alchemical medicine in England seems to have been especially popular during the second half of the fifteenth century. The universities of Oxford and Cambridge both sheltered practising alchemists, and Peterhouse in Cambridge saw the rise to prominence of large numbers of physicians who had an active interest in the science, one of whom, physician to Edward IV, donated several alchemical treatises to the college before his death in 1477, while John Aldeward, Fellow of Exeter College in Oxford, presented to the university a collection of tracts on the philosopher's stone and the quintessence, 'the fifth essence', that most refined substance found in everything, which can be extracted with difficulty by alchemical procedures. George Ripley, a canon of Bridlington in Yorkshire, dedicated his *Compound of Alchymie* to the King, describing laboratory procedures, and ending his versified introductory epistle with praise of a medicinal elixir thus produced:

> This natural process by help of craft thus consummate
> Dissolveth the Elixir spiritual in our unctuous humidity;
> Then in the balneo of Mary together let them be circulate,
> Like new honey or oil till they perfectly thicked be,
> Then will that medicine heal all manner infirmity,
> And turn all metals to sun and moon most perfectly:
> Thus shall ye have both great Elixir and Aurum potabile,
> By the grace and will of God, to whom be laud eternally.

That such an elixir was not purely a theoretical construct can be seen from the following passage taken from *True Alchemical Practice* (*Practica vera alkimica*) by someone calling himself 'Ortulanus'. The treatise appeared in 1386:

Take rectified aqueous alcohol in whatever quantity you wish and put it, drop by drop, into what is left over from the perfected Stone – as much as can be dissolved therein. In this solution will emerge burning or flaming golden sparks, and there will appear as many colours as anyone can imagine. When the colours have stopped appearing and the water clears, it will be golden or a kind of bright red, transparent and unclouded. This is perfected aqueous alcohol and a sound medicine for the body, a more valuable medicine than those of Galen, Avicenna, Hippocrates, and any other doctor, having the power to pluck out, uproot, purge, and expel all infirmities from the human body. Even if the infirmity has lasted for a hundred years, it will be completely cured in one month; and if it has lasted for fifty years, it will be completely cured within a fortnight. If some infirmity has lasted for twenty years, it will be completely cured within twenty days; and if some infirmity has lasted in the human body for seven years, it will be cured within three days; and if some infirmity has lasted for one year, it will be cured in a single day. This is quite obviously the secret of secrets. Its power cannot be bought, and it is rightly called 'the blessed stone' because there has not been anything which Almighty God has given humankind, which is more precious.

Here is how the medicine should be taken. Take one draught of wine as strong as the patient's condition and appetite warrant, and put therein one drop of this aqueous alcohol – two, if the patient is very ill, but no more at one time. Warm it a little by the fire and the medicine will immediately begin to mix with the wine. Once the two are thoroughly mixed, give the draught to the patient, and he will begin to recover in the name of the Lord and will be well, by the grace of God. Do this every third or fourth day until the patient has recovered and is out of danger. The same medicine can be taken in any concoction the patient finds agreeable. In a case where the patient is weak and feverish and cannot drink wine, he may be given the medicine in any concoction by maintaining a conveniently appropriate dose in everything.

The alcohol to which Ortulanus was referring appears in an alchemical context a few years earlier in a treatise by the Catalan Franciscan, John of Rupescissa, *A Study of the Fifth Essence of Everything* (*De consideratione quintae essentiae omnium rerum*), dated 1351–2. Praising alcohol for its extraordinary therapeutic powers, he says it can actually be improved by heating gold and leaf and then extinguishing it in alcohol, thereby 'fixing the sun in our sky'. Alcohol – in the sense of the fifth or quintessence – could however be obtained from anything, not just from wine, as the title of the tract says, and John describes how to extract it from gold or antimony or mercury. Gold, he says, is to be reduced to an amalgam in the usual way, after which the amalgam should be turned into powder and saturated with vinegar or urine. The quintessence will then show itself as a layer floating upon the surface of the liquid. Antimony (i.e. antimony sulphide) should be saturated with 'acetum' (vinegar) and then distilled, which will eventually allow the quintessence of the antimony to appear in the form of blood-red drops. Mercury is to have its quintessence drawn out by dissolving or sublimating the mercury in *aquae fortis*.

The practical benefits of alchemy could thus be seen and argued without much difficulty. Nevertheless, there was still a problem. For alchemy suggested that not only could it produce curative elixirs or draughts to prolong human life, but that it was capable of altering the very composition of metals so as to speed their transmutation into gold, and this was a proposition defenders of alchemy had to prove against their opponents. How was their science different *in kind* from that of craftsmen such as painters? Because if alchemists could produce their effects merely by gilding or plating a surface, in what way could their 'art' be said to differ from that of painters who also changed surfaces, but without affecting the basic nature of the substance whose surface they were altering?

This question was addressed by Paul of Taranto, a thirteenth-century Franciscan, in his *Theorica et Practica*, a treatise written specifically to deal with the difference between *ars* and *natura*, that is, between the application of a technical skill or technique, and the operation of Nature as the power which determines the physical properties and conditions of all created things. One can divide 'art', he said, into two categories. The first uses the primary qualities familiar from Aristotle – hot, cold, wet, dry – as instruments to achieve its goals. The second employs secondary qualities such as colours and tastes for the same purpose. Agriculture and medicine are examples of the first category: painting and sculpture of the second. The first can actually alter substance itself, whereas the second can merely introduce superficial changes which do not affect the substance of the material which is being worked on. So, because 'arts' such as medicine (and, of course, alchemy) are able to induce change at such a basic level, they can therefore alter species. Now, as far as alchemy is concerned, laboratory experiments have enabled us to discover the essential principles of different metals, and it is also clear from these experiments that metals contain mercury and sulphur in various proportions, depending on the metal involved. So, since alchemists can recognize these principles and the varying proportions of their qualities of hot, cold, wet and dry, they can manipulate their material so as to produce fundamental alteration, as opposed to sculptors and painters who make merely surface changes and do not understand, at the same basic level, the materials with which they work.

Petrus Bonus Lombardus, a fourteenth-century physician in Ferrara, however, adopted something of a midway position between accepting and rejecting the possibility of transmutation in the 1330 treatise *The Precious New Pearl* (*Pretiosa Margarita Novella*). His remarks are worth quoting in full because they illuminate very clearly contemporary metallurgical theory:

It should be noted that in the generation of metals, there are two kinds of moisture. One is viscous, external, does not come to a complete union with the earthy parts of the matter, and is inflammable and sulphurous; the other is a viscous, internal humidity, exactly alike throughout with the earthy parts, not inflammable, but incombustible because in all its smallest earthy parts it has been so strongly balanced and mixed together that the smallest part of one has become the same as the smallest part of the other, and they have turned into mercury by their own digestive process. Therefore the moist part does not abandon the dry part in the fire, nor vice versa. Either it withdraws from the fire with its substance intact, or it stays there intact: and it does this because the moist part does not adhere to what it touches. The earthy parts bind and temper it in equal measure. The dry part is not restricted to its own boundary, either, because the watery parts loosen and temper it in equal measure; and so the moist and the dry are balanced within [the matter].

So the first matter of all metals is moist, viscous, incombustible, subtle, assimilated to the subtle earthy part, strongly mixed in balanced fashion throughout its smallest parts in the mineral caverns of the earth. Their nearest matter is mercury which is generated out of their strong admixture. But it does not produce its essential self with the matter. Therefore discerning and most wise Nature has joined to it an appropriate agent, namely sulphur, so that she may change the form in the metal by a process of digestion and 'cooking'. For sulphur is a certain fatness of earth, generated, thickened, and hardened in its minerals by a controlled decoction. Sulphur is related to mercury as male is to female, and appropriate agent to appropriate matter. One type of sulphur can be melted naturally, another cannot; and according to whether Nature has been willing to make it fusible, it joins fusible sulphur to them so that it may extract a like liquefaction from capacity of matter. This is why metals liquefy in fire and coagulate when then they are removed from the fire, although mercury is always naturally in a liquid state. But when Nature has not wanted things to be fusible, she has added infusible but coagulated sulphur to them – for example, marchasite, magnesia, and antimony. The sulphur in marchasite is not fixed, and combustible, whereas in antimony it is fixed and incombustible . . .

Just as the elements are scarcely removed from the basic matter out of which they arise, and so are generated one after the other in turn, in a manner like that of a circle: so metals are generated, but in a somewhat different fashion . . . Metals are a different case because they are all imperfect in themselves, the sole exception being gold . . . So they are all organised [to tend] towards gold as to their final goal and do not revert after they have become gold. The sign of this natural transformation into gold is their being mingled in a single mineral followed by their successive stages of change. For if they were perfect and complete so that they had one nature and one completion which was defined and concluded – that is, they had already reached their final state – then undoubtedly they could not be converted into anything else unless they were first reduced to something which was not a metal . . .

So Nature adopts two ways of generating gold: one, first and foremost, through herself by generating gold in her own minerals and according to her own principles; the other – not first and foremost – through herself by first generating imperfect minerals, and then finally converting them gold. Alchemy therefore follows Nature in generating gold according to her second method, generating gold out of imperfect metals, just as Nature does. It is not possible for alchemy to follow Nature's first method.[5]

But alchemists continued to protest that they could indeed imitate or even surpass Nature in this regard, and that the transformative substance which enabled them to speed up the processes of Nature to an extraordinary extent was their stone. They differed, however, in their views on what exactly constituted the stone. Bacon concluded from his reading of Ibn Sīnā's treatise on the soul that the basis of the stone, its *prima materia*, was a purified form of human blood:

The alchemist looks for a way to separate [its] humours from each other and to free each from the impurities [associated with the others].When, by means of operations which are hard to carry out, they have been brought back to their unadulterated singleness of nature, they are then combined in a secret and quite individual proportion. To these are added mercury, once its outward form has been altered or destroyed and then sublimated several times. Likewise, the 'calx' or powder of the baser metal from which the nobler will be produced. Likewise [in the case] of the nobler. After this, let them be amalgamated with each other until they produce a single 'body'. [This] is then thrown on to the liquefied baser metal and it becomes more noble.

The author of *The Book of Light* (*Liber Lucis*), often said to be John of Rupescissa, on the other hand, maintained that:

The material of the Stone is one and the same thing, small in value. Whenever it is found in the viscous water which is called 'mercury', and since [people] say it is found in places of no account, many of the irrational sort who do not comprehend what philosophers mean have looked for this Stone in [piles of] dung. But please understand, my son, that the material is prepared by removing the earthiness which mercury has, and applying the 'sulphur' of the philosophers to it. This is not sulphur as it is regularly understood. Our 'sulphur' is invisible. I shall give it its proper name, 'Roman vitriol', which certain philosophers call 'magnesia'.

About 100 years later, the Englishman John Lydgate described the philosopher's stone as 'sometimes citrine in colour, like the golden-haired sun beaming down as is his nature, who makes hearts very happy with more treasure than the King of India has [in the form of] precious stones made each in its own fitting way: the citrine colour for the bright sun, white for the moon which shines all night'.[6] By the time one reaches the early seventeenth century, the philosopher's stone has gathered to itself a remarkable variety of names and attributions. Martin Ruland the Elder, physician at the Court of the Holy Roman Emperor, compiled a *Lexicon of Alchemy* (1612) in which he listed 50, including 'poison, spirit, medicine, sky, cloud dew, saltpetre, spouse, virgin, bath, pomegranate juice, lead, natural sulphur, moon-spit, jewel of Scotland, white smoke, chaos, and Venus'.

Positive arguments in favour of the science, however, were countered by others just as assertive. St Thomas Aquinas (1225/7–1274), to whom various alchemical treatises were attributed, including a mishmash of biblical and alchemical texts, entitled *Dawn Rising* (*Aurora Consurgens*), rejected this notion that alchemists could create and have a fundamental effect upon metals, even with the help of evil spirits, because such creations and effects were reserved to God Himself; and Egidio Colonna (c.1243–1316), Archbishop of Bourges, followed this by asking two questions, one theoretical, the other practical. Can humans make real gold by 'art' and, if they can do so, is it permissible for them to sell such gold? Gold, he argues from Ibn Sīnā, is a product of Nature and so it cannot be made by artificial means. Therefore one cannot sell alchemical gold as real gold because it does not have all the medical properties of real gold.

It is a fascinating argument which, once again, links medicine and alchemy, although it does so quite contrary to the linkage made by Bacon and Ortulanus. But whereas Albertus Magnus and Bacon concentrate on arguments rooted in natural philosophy, Egidio and St Thomas base their opposition on theological claims, a dichotomy which seems to be straightforward until one remembers that ever since the time of Maria the Jewess alchemists had been eager to assert that their science was special, a gift of God, a claim more or less constant throughout Islamic sources and therefore (since these were largely the sources of European alchemy, obtained via translation), a claim transmitted to mediaeval workers in the field. Yet, as Vladimír Karpenko points out, 'the claims of alchemists concerning the transmutation of metals, not to mention the elixir of life, must have sounded like a direct attempt to attain divine power. Therefore it was advantageous to accentuate alchemy as *donum Dei* in order not to attract the unwanted attention of the Church.' It is a judgement with perhaps a trace of cynicism in it, one which does not make sufficient allowance for the sincerity with which some alchemists, at least, genuinely felt they were engaging directly with the mind of God. God, after all, was the great Technician, humankind had been created in His likeness and, as Genesis 1.26 says, humankind had been given dominion over all other created things. Therefore, by seeking to change and even surpass Nature, humankind was doing no more than behaving in accordance with its special status as a technician following in the footsteps of the divine pattern.

Such an argument, of course, represents a possible theological quagmire, and so alchemists tended to say that they were both imitating and assisting Nature and, in as far as their science allowed them to go further and change or even create Nature, it was done by permission and through the influence of God, which was why the successful exercise of their 'art' could be described as a gift of God. Curiously enough, however, when papal condemnation came in the bull *Spondent Pariter*, promulgated in 1317 by Pope John XXII, it was not the possible theological ramifications of the science to which the Holy Father directed his ire:

> Alchemists solemnly promise riches to the poor, and do not produce them. Likewise, thinking themselves so full of knowledge, they fall into a pit which they have dug; for there can be no doubt that people who profess this art of alchemy are deluding each other when they express astonishment at those aware of their ignorance and who have drawn attention to their self-delusion. When the real thing they have been looking for does not turn up, these people fix a day, exhaust their resources, and paint a false picture so that – unable by the very nature of things to produce real gold or silver – they talk up a transmutation and produce it that way.

So it is the crime of manufacturing and distributing false coins which has angered the Pope. This is scarcely surprising. The papacy was lodged in Avignon at the time, and it was notorious that France at this time was suffering a surfeit of counterfeit money. But the problem was not confined to France, for the monetary environment of this period (and indeed later) was very poor indeed, partly because of frequent deficiencies in the supply of bullion. Cash was no longer the preserve of trade in towns but had spread to the countryside, and increasing commutation of payment of dues in labour to payment in coin meant that demand for silver and gold seemed to be never-ending. The technology of minting coins was fairly crude, too. Coins varied in weight and quality even when they were new, so deterioration through wear and such underhand methods as clipping and culling led to shortage of good coins on the one hand,

and proliferation of poor or false coins on the other. No wonder, then, that the English Benedictine, Matthew Paris, could write in his *Chronica Maiora* for the year 1248:

> At this period English money was so intolerably debased by money-clippers and forgers that neither the native English nor foreigners could regard it with an unruffled eye or equanimity because the coins were clipped almost to the inner circle, and the inscription round the border was either entirely destroyed or very badly defaced. So public criers proclaimed, in the name of the King, in every town, fair, and market, that no one was to accept a penny which was not of legal weight and circumference, and that no defective coin was to be accepted under any circumstances in buying, selling, or exchange. Anyone who disobeyed this decree would be punished. A fair amount of trouble was taken to discover these false-coiners so that if they were convicted of the crime by a court of law, they might be suitably punished.

Suitable punishment might well mean the death penalty, as in France where convicted coiners were hanged and left to rot on the gallows – not that that prevented Philippe le Bel from altering the weight of French coins in 1295, in effect debasing them – or in Italy, as we learn from Dante who refers to a notorious case in Canto 29 of his *Inferno*, that of one Capocchio, 'a good ape of Nature who altered metal by means of alchemy', who was burned alive in Siena in 1293. So Pope John XXII's particular concern for the probity of coinage and his animus against alchemists who might be seen to be tampering with economies which were already unstable is only to be expected.

Now, Capocchio may have been condemned as a false-coiner rather than as an alchemist, but either way, he was likely to have found himself the victim of a public attitude which, in spite of official condemnation, did not really quite know what to make of the science. Alchemists were mocked, and yet people still made use of their services. Consider the unfriendly portrait of an alchemist offered by Chaucer in the Canon's yeoman's prologue in his *Canterbury Tales* (late 1380s): 'My master has knowledge of such a subtle kind – but you can't blame his cunning on me: I just help him a little while he's working – that he could turn all this ground on which we've been riding, and from here to Canterbury, completely upside down and pave it with silver and gold.'

When the yeoman finished saying this, the landlord said:

> God bless you! I find it quite extraordinary that if your master has such lofty knowledge which ought to make people respect him, he pays so little attention to his personal dignity. His overcoat is not worth a farthing – and I am actually obliged to dress as he does. It is dirty and torn all over. Why is your master so slovenly when he has the power to buy better cloth, if he can do as you say? Answer me that, please! [*No, replies, the yeoman, I shall keep it a secret.*] 'My opinion of him is that he is both ignorant and foolish. When

a man has an over-great intelligence, he frequently misuses it. So does my master, and I am very sorry for it. God put it right! I can't tell you any more'.

'It's of no consequence, good yeoman', said our landlord. 'But, since you know about your master's skill, please tell me how he lives, since he is so cunning and so subtle. If you are willing to tell me, where do you live?'

'In the suburbs of a town', he said, 'lurking in corners and blind alleys where this kind of robber, these thieves by nature, live in secret and in fright, like people who dare not show themselves in public. This is how we live, if I'm to tell you the truth'.

'Now', said the landlord, 'let me go on talking to you. Why is your face so discoloured?'

'God damn it, Peter, I am so used to blowing the fire that I believe it has changed my complexion. I don't usually look in a mirror. I work hard and learn how to multiply [*turn base metal into gold*]. We are always making mistakes and staring into the fire; but in spite of all that, we fail to achieve what we want and never bring our work to a successful conclusion. We give many people illusions, and borrow gold – perhaps a pound or two, or ten, or twelve, or much greater amounts – and make them imagine that, at the very least, we could make twenty pounds out of one. It's always a lie, but we always really hope we can do it, and we blunder about, trying to achieve it. But that kind of knowledge has eluded us so far, and we are not successful, although we had sworn the contrary; it rushed past, it slid away so fast. It will make us beggars in the end . . . Yet they [*alchemists*] never weary of the art, for to them it is apparently something bitter-sweet. Even if they had only a sheet to wrap themselves in at night, and a cloak to wear during the day, they would sell them and spend the money on this craft. They can't stop until they have nothing left. Wherever they go, people always recognise what they are by the smell of brimstone. They stink for all the world like a goat. The smell is so much like that of a ram in heat that even if someone is a mile away, he is contaminated by the smell. People can therefore recognise them by their stink and their threadbare clothes. If anyone asks them very quietly why they are so poorly dressed, they will whisper in his ear and say that if it was found out they were alchemists, people would kill them for it. This is how these people deceive simpletons'.

Perhaps the most interesting assertion made in this self-condemnation, apart from the verification that being an alchemist could turn out to be a fatal trade, is that although the alchemist and his assistant lie to people in an effort to get money out of them to pay for their experiments, 'we always really hope we can do it, and we blunder about, trying to achieve it'. Not altogether deliberate fraud as far as the alchemy itself is concerned, then, but a genuine obsession which, like addiction, is prepared to deceive and cheat to attain or encompass ends it considers desirable and beneficial. Yet frauds there undoubtedly were, as Sebastian Brant averred in his *Narrenschiff* (1494). 'I shall not forget the great swindle which is alchemy: the making of gold and silver already concealed in the stick [*which stirs the pot*]. It uses tricks and diddles people dreadfully. It demonstrates a "proof", and then produces a serpent.' A mid fourteenth-century Jewish astronomer,

Themo, who taught at both Erfurt and the Sorbonne, thought that the goals of alchemy were possible but difficult, and that it was also dangerous to the individual because of the prevalence of counterfeit coinage 'by which a whole region can be deceived'. Alchemists also lost a great deal of money in pursuit of their aims, and even if they were successful, envy of their achievement would destroy them sooner or later. The best thing a person could do, therefore, was to abandon alchemy altogether, or not take it up in the first place.

Sometimes, however, one cannot quite tell whether alchemists should belong to the Chaucer or Brant camp. In 1350 Edward III had John de Walden thrown into the Tower after providing him with 5,000 gold crowns and 20 pounds of silver 'to work thereon by the art of alchemy for the benefit of the King', presumably, to judge by his imprisonment, without any success. Similarly, a commission issued by the English King Henry VI on 18 August 1452 to John Hewet, John Edmund and John Assheby, appointed them 'to arrest all persons in the city or suburbs of London or the county of Middlesex or elsewhere, who, pretending themselves expert in the science of multiplying gold and silver, have approached simple persons and received from them on such false pretences sums of money and jewels of gold and silver, making no restitution thereof'. Were these alchemists straight swindlers, or obsessives willing to lie to get their hands on funds to subsidise experiments they hoped one day would work?

Hope, indeed, sprang eternal not only in the bosoms of alchemists but in those of the authorities as well. There was a widespread hope that if alchemists' claims were good, the state treasury would benefit thereby, as Roger Bacon had premised, and so, for example, we find a stream of licences being granted by royal authority: by John I of Aragon on 5 April 1396 to a Jewish alchemist, Caracosa Samuel, and in England between 1444 and 1476, 'to transmute imperfect metals from their proper sort into perfect gold and silver', 'to search the doctrines and writings of the wise ancients and to practise transmutation of metals', 'to practise the art of alchemy with all kinds of metals and minerals for the space of two years in the King's manor of Woodstock', 'to practise the faculty and science of [natural] philosophy and the turning of mercury into gold and silver'. Nor was it kings alone who were hopeful of making themselves rich this way. On 3 April 1337, a commission was issued to John de Pulteneye, Mayor of London, enabling him and two fellow magistrates to deal with a case of kidnapping an alchemist:

On complaint by Thomas de Eboraco that, whereas he by the science of alchemy had forged silver plates and had them proved by goldsmiths and others of the city of London, one Thomas Corp of London, a 'spicer', and others plotting to disturb him maliciously took him by night at the said city and brought him to the house of the said Thomas Corp there, and made him bring with him an elixir and some other instruments wherewith he made such silver; and to compel him to teach them the art, [they] imprisoned him there until through fear of death he forged silver by his art in their sight, and made two bonds to the said Thomas in £100 each; and [they] carried away the elixir and instruments with other goods; and that they afterwards, by pretext of the bonds, although he was never bailiff of the said Thomas Corp or receiver of any of his moneys, before the mayor and sheriffs of the city they called him to account before auditors appointed for this sum in bonds and arrears, and procured him to be adjudged to Newgate gaol until he satisfied him of these, whereby he has been long and still remains in the said gaol.[7]

How did Thomas Corp make his silver and others their gold? Arnaldus of Bruxella (second half of the fifteenth century) gave practical advice:

To change copper into very good gold: take hens and keep them cooped up so that they are unable to eat anything except pulse, i.e. lentils. Then take a small, trough-like vessel with a big lip to it, and put in fifteen of their eggs until they have formed little eddies. Then take them and put them in a separate, secluded place and let them stand until they are all reduced to a single [mass]. Then take [the mixture], put it in an oven, and let it reduce to ashes with heat sufficient for this purpose. From this powder you will make very good gold, if you know how to conduct the operation with true understanding . . . To make silver from iron: another method on which great scholars are in agreement, having given some consideration to this craft, but have preserved only this [way of proceeding]. Take two toads which are carrying poison with them – you may actually have ten of them, or as many as you can find – take freshly gathered asphodels and a large quantity of white hellebore, and pound them really well. Then take a little vinegar and mix all these together in a rough pot; put the resulting mixture with iron, and if you add a little sublimated white sulphur, I guarantee you will be happy with it and that it will be happy with you.

The mention of toads is not as bizarre as it may seem at first. Ruland's *Lexicon* gives 'poison' as one of the names of the mercurial stone, for which Pietro d'Abano provided the explanation, 'this stone works in leprous metals and therefore is sometimes called *poison*', and George Ripley's famous vision is entirely about a toad whose venom is an essential ingredient in the production of an alchemical elixir:

A toad full red I saw did drink the juice of grapes so fast,
Till overcharged with the broth, his bowels all to brast;
And after that from the poisoned bulk he cast his venom fell,
For grief and pain whereof his members all began to swell,
With drops of poisoned sweat approaching thus his secret den,
His cave with blasts of fumous air he all bewhited then;
And from the which in space a golden humour did ensue,
Whose falling drops from high did stain the soil with ruddy hue:
And when this corpse the force of vital breath began to lack,
This dying toad became forthwith like coal for colour black:
Thus drowned in his proper veins of poisoned flood,
For term of eighty days and four he rotting stood:

> By trial then this venom to expel I did desire,
> For which I did commit his carcase to a gentle fire:
> Which done, a wonder to the sight, but more to be rehearsed,
> The toad with colours rare through every side was pierced,
> And white appeared when all the sundry hues were passed,
> Which after being tincted red, for ever more did last.
> Then of the venom handled thus a medicine I did make;
> Which venom kills and saveth such as venom chance to take.

Here the toad clearly symbolizes the *prima materia* obtained during the *nigredo* or blackening putrefaction stage. Toads were believed to have a jewel in their head, and this can therefore represent the stone hidden within the *prima materia*: hence the presence of a toad at the roots of the alchemical tree in Samuel Norton's *Mercurius Redivivus* (1630).

Pope John XXII's condemnation of alchemical activity, however, was answered by one John Dastin about whom we know very little save that he belonged to a religious order and felt strongly enough about the validity of the science to write to both the Pope and Cardinal Orsini in defence of it; but it is noteworthy that he concentrates on explaining how alchemical operations worked – by means of turning gold itself into some kind of leaven, he said, which will then change other metals into gold or silver – and how mercury can also be converted into an elixir over a period of about 100 days. Elsewhere, he emphasizes the power of alchemical elixirs. The text of a 'dream' attributed to him – 'not yet full sleeping, nor yet full waking/but between twain lying in a trance' – describes the alchemical wedding of a king and queen, and the birth of their alchemical child, in terms which were to become virtual clichés in a later period:

> The King thus entered in his bed royal,
> The Queen conceived under a sun bright;
> Under her feet a mount like crystal,
> Which had devoured her husband anon right,
> Dead of desire and in the maiden's sight;
> Lost all the colour of his fresh face,
> Thus was he dead, the maidens feeble of might
> Despaired, slept in the same place . . .
>
> The full moon half shadowed the sun,
> To put away the burning of his light;
> Black shadowed first the skies were to dunn,
> The raven's bill began who looketh right,
> Blacker than jet or bugle to fight;
> But little and little by ordinary appearance,
> The temperate fire which his cherishing might
> Turned all to white, but with no violence.

Time to the Queen approached of childing,
The child of Nature was ready to fly,
Passage was there to his out-going:
He spread his wings and found no liberty;
Of nine virgins he devoured three,
The other six most excellent and fair,
Fearful for dread in their greatest beauty,
Spread their feathers and flew forth in the air.

The child coloured first black, and after white,
Having no heat in very existence,
But by cherishing of the sun bright,
Of foreign fire there was no violence:
Save that men say which have experience,
He drank such plenty of the water of the well,
That his six sisters made no resistance,
But would have devoured. Dastin, can you tell?

Sometimes black, sometimes was he red,
Now like ashes, now citrine of colour:
Now of saffron hue, now sanguine was his head,
Now white as a lily he showed him in his bower,
The moon gave nourishment to him in his labour;
And with all their force did their business,
To clothe him fresher than any flower,
With a mantle of everlasting whiteness.

If this motley collection of images of sexual union, death, birth and the changing colours attendant upon a chemical process within the alchemist's apparatus can be interpreted with varying degrees of difficulty into the stages of a laboratory experiment, why is it that alchemists clothed their descriptions in metaphors instead of writing *en clair*? It is not as though they never wrote openly. John of Rupescissa, for example, had done so in describing how to extract the quintessence from antimony:

Reduce antimony to a powder to the point where you cannot feel it, and then put it in distilled vinegar of the best quality until the vinegar turns red. When you have done this, remove the coloured vinegar to another vessel and pour on top of it some fresh vinegar until it, too, has taken on colour over a moderate heat. Then take it off. Do this until the vinegar takes on no more colour; then put into a distillation vessel all the vinegar you have coloured in this way, and at first the vinegar will rise. Then you will see an absolutely extraordinary marvel, because through the beak of the alembic you will see as it were a thousand rivulets of the blessed mineral running down in reddish droplets, like blood. Keep this blessed liquid in a stout, closely sealed bottle because it is a treasure of which the whole world does not have an equal. See a miracle – such a great sweetness of antimony that it surpasses the sweetness of honey; and I say by the love of God that the human intellect could scarcely believe the power and strength of this water, or 'fifth essence' of antimony.

The standard explanation for the obfuscating rhetoric was that alchemy was too dangerous a science to be put into the hands of the ignorant or half-trained, and so constructing a kind of jargon would effectively confine its practice to those worthy and intelligent enough to use it for proper ends. A similar explanation applied to the esoteric side of alchemy. If the science was less a series of laboratory procedures and more a set of exercises in religious and philosophical advancement for the practitioner, the complex symbolism would conceal not so much genuine chemical information as evidences of spiritual trial and change, and thus provide some kind of guide, however generalized, to what such a practitioner might expect to undergo.

There is, however, another explanation which should be taken into account. It will not apply except in a minority of cases, but when it does, it is capable of throwing additional light on certain historical events. Jonathan Hughes has pointed out that every so often a number of alchemical works reflect or comment upon critical moments in the life of contemporary or near-contemporary figures. Sir George Ripley's alchemical poem 'Cantilena', the earliest copies of which date to the 1470s, describes in alchemical terms the sickness and recovery of King Henry VI. The King, says Ripley, has become enfeebled, old and sterile, in need of transformation and rebirth. So he undergoes an incestuous union with his mother (the moon) who becomes pregnant, eats peacock flesh during her confinement, drinks the blood of the green lion, and eventually gives birth to a child who begins by resembling the moon but then turns into the sun. 'The reborn King becomes a victor, a healer and the redeemer of all sins [and then undergoes], like the alchemist's metal, a psychic death and resurrection from which he emerges renewed, integrated, and balanced.' A similar impulse to interpret political events through alchemical imagery can be seen in Thomas Norton's *Ordinal of Alchemy* (c.1477) in which, for example, the white rose of the House of York is seen as an alchemical symbol of the fruition of peace after a breakdown of events during 1468–71.[8]

Whether this genre is confined to English alchemists of the late fifteenth century, or whether it is to be found elsewhere is a subject for further research, but the images and symbols they used were a common currency. In *The Rose Garden of the Philosophers* (*Rosarium Philosophorum*), an alchemical text which used to be attributed to the Catalan physician Arnald of Villanova (c.1240–1311), addressed, like part of Dastin's correspondence, to Cardinal Orsini, the sun = male = gold is united with the moon = female = silver in a bath of acid and turns into ('gives birth to') an hermaphroditic offspring. This 'sacred marriage' (*hieros gamos*) draws on very ancient notions of a union between two deities, or between a human and a divine being, to produce something or someone more distinctive and more powerful since, in the latter case at least, it represented the union between body and spirit. It entered European alchemy via the *Tabula Chemica*, a Latin version of *Letter of the Sun to the Crescent Moon* (*Risālat al-Shams ilā 'l-Hilāl*) together with *Book of the Silvery Water and the Starry Earth* (*Kitāb al-Mā' al-Waraqī wa 'l-Ard al-Najmīyah*) by Muhammad ibn Umail (c.AD 900–c.960), the first an alchemical allegorical poem which describes the courtship and wedding of the sun and moon, the latter a commentary upon it.

Seen in alchemical terms, this kind of union offered the possibility of integrating or reintegrating two modes of being which were usually conceived as opposites, and it was easy to see this further in Christian terms as the transubstantiation of the wafer into the body and blood of Christ during the Mass: the death, resurrection and transfiguration of Jesus: the *hieros gamos* between the Virgin Mary and the Holy Spirit to produce the divine Son. Fifteen of the 21 images published in the *Rosarium* are devoted to illustrating this sacred marriage: a king and queen fully dressed stand upon the sun and moon respectively, clasping hands in a prefiguring of their union; naked, they embrace one another in the act of sex; they lie in a tomb, now a single body with separate crowned heads; the hermaphroditic result is shown, fully clothed, its double but united nature depicted again by two crowned heads; the transformative union of body and spirit is shown in a picture which could have appeared in any church – the Holy Trinity holding a crown over the head of the Virgin who is kneeling in prayer and adoration; the risen Christ stands on the steps of the empty tomb, in the words of Karen-Claire Voss, 'the embodiment of the hierogamic union between human and divine'.

Ripley describes the union as incestuous. He was not alone in this. If we look again at the illustrations accompanying the *Rosarium*, the one showing the king and queen fully clothed and clasping hands has a dove flying down from a star with a plant in its beak. This downward motion emphasises the fact that the couple are conjoining their *left* hands, quite literally a sinister gesture, which reminds cognoscenti that these two people are, in fact, brother and sister – as were Apollo and Artemis, deities of the sun and moon – and that their subsequent intercourse will be incestuous, an interpretation underlined by a text accompanying the 1550 printing of the *Rosarium*, which adds to the illustration of the pair engaged in sexual intercourse, 'Therefore unite your son Gabricus, the one among all your sons dearer to you, with his sister Beya'. In a variation upon this theme, an illustration in Ripley's *Cantilena* shows the King crawling under his *mother's* skirt.

Many of these illustrations are vividly coloured, and this was not merely for the sake of aesthetic effect. As John Dastin said, 'The colours will teach you what you may do with fire, because they will show in how much time and when the first, second, and third fire is to be made. Consequently, if you have been an attentive practitioner, the colours will teach you what needs to be done.' Colours were important as a guide to the various stages of the alchemical process, and there were four of them: *nigredo* (blackness), the initial stage during which the body of the impure metal is broken down and dissolved into the *prima materia*; albedo (whiteness), when the purified body is washed clean by mercurial water or fire; *citrinitas* (yellowness), the third stage described as 'the messenger of the red', which seems to represent a point at which the stone is nearly but not quite perfect; and finally *rubedo* (redness), the colour of the stone itself. Naturally, these colours could also be associated with the four elements and with the four humours – black bile, phlegm, yellow bile and blood – so the predominant colour in any given picture will direct the onlooker's attention to a whole range of interconnections ranging from purely chemical to medical and help him or her to understand the complexities of change taking place in the laboratory apparatus. These complexities produce different colours, too. Immediately after *nigredo*, a rapidly altering sequence of colours shows itself in the glass vessel and is known as 'the peacock's tail'. It demonstrates that the integration of every colour into a single pure whiteness – 'eating the peacock's flesh', in Ripley's phrase – is being achieved successfully.

These illustrations were relatively new to alchemical literature. Antique manuscripts frequently contain drawings of apparatus, but the advent of allegorical and symbolic pictures can be dated to the fifteenth century in particular, when the illustrations became an integral part of the text and were highly organised supplements to it. They were there on the one hand to make clear, or at least make clearer, the inward and therefore non-visible processes of breakdown, purification and transformation as opposed to the visible apparatus and outward signs of inward change, and on the other to emphasise the status of alchemy as a *scientia*, a reputable branch of knowledge, rather than an *ars*, a mere craft or artisan's technique. Many of these pictorial representations were based on procreative acts, thereby helping the written text – if there was one: a number of alchemical works, such as the *Mutus Liber*, consist entirely of pictures – in the transmission of the theoretical principles of the science by encapsulating them in vivid, striking and therefore memorable images which would ensure the reader's attention and consequent instruction. By expressing themselves in Christian imagery and symbols, these principles suggested not only the basic respectability which alchemists sought, but also the similarity between the alchemists' creative operations and those of God Himself. As Constantine of Pisa expressed it, 'All strength and operation rest upon mercury, it being the mother and matter of all metals, just as "hyle" [*Aristotle's word for primordial matter*] is the first cause ... The material cause comes about through congealing as in the first *hyle*, the mother of all creatures, as established by the Supreme Artificer . . . And just as it is told of the Spirit of the Lord moving upon the waters as the first cause, so this Work consists of twelve waters.'[9]

One of the most celebrated books illustrated after this fashion is *The Splendour of the Sun* (*Splendor Solis*) by 'Solomon Trismosin', almost certainly the pseudonym of someone who has been ascribed to both the fifteenth and the sixteenth century. Its text is accompanied by 22 detailed pictures showing by means of allegory and symbolism both the outer stages of the work and the inner processes of spiritual transformation. The first four illustrate the *prima materia*; the next seven the seven stages of the work; the next seven – perhaps the best known because the most frequently reproduced – seven glass flasks in which the alchemical transformation is represented allegorically by means of (i) a boy working with bellows to stimulate a dragon into activity, (ii) three coloured birds (black, white, red), (iii) a cockerel with three heads, (iv) a triple-headed dragon, (v) a peacock displaying its tail, (vi) a queen (the white tincture or stone), and (vii) a king (the red tincture or stone). The whole sequence ends with four pictures which summarize the last four stages of the work, (i) a dark setting sun, (ii) children at play, (iii) women at work and (iv) the sun in glory.

But are these illustrations no more than allegorical representations of changes which take place in the laboratory? It is actually quite difficult to tell, although constant, unmistakably Christian images do suggest, as we have already proposed, that the alchemical process was easily and frequently interpreted in terms of personal death to the world and resurrection as a new, transfigured Christian person. But this is probably the only justifiable esoteric interpretation an historian may be permitted by the available evidence to discern. Non-historians, of course, are entirely free to find other significances in both the texts and the images – and Italo Ronca has issued a timely warning that historians of mediaeval alchemy need to exercise restraint in not importing modern esoteric ideas about alchemy into the texts they are reading, if only because 'the vast majority of mediaeval alchemical texts are utterly unreliable in the printed form given to them by unscrupulous editors in the sixteenth and seventeenth centuries'.

'Trismosin' is also the name attached to a treatise entitled *The Golden Fleece* (*Aureum Vellus*) which purports to give an account of the author's wanderings in search of the secrets of alchemy:

> From the year 1473 I betook myself to the road, and wandered here and there. Wherever I heard of an artist, I was diligent in going to him, and I spent one year and a half in these wanderings, and I came to know all kinds of arts of alchemy which I do not want to specify, but I saw the truth in several details, and spent 200 florins, and still did not think of giving up.
>
> I thought, and had the diligence, to raise expenses among my friends, and set out on a journey with a foreigner to Labach, and from there to Milan, and I came to a monastery

where I served as an amanuensis, and attended lectures for a whole year. Thereafter I wandered all about in Italy, and came to an Italian merchant and a Jew who knew German. They knew how to make English tin look like the best fine silver, they sold much of it. I offered myself to serve them if it pleased them: the Jew persuaded the merchant that he should take me on as a servant. I had to guard the fire when they made their art with the tin. I was diligent, and they liked it well, and therefore they kept nothing hidden from me. Thus I learned also the art which was carried out with poisonous things, and I was with them fourteen weeks.

Thereafter I travelled with the Jew to Venice [where] he sold forty pounds of silver to a Turkish merchant. While he negotiated with the merchant I took six lots of the silver and went to a goldsmith, who had two journeymen. He knew Latin, and I asked him to assay the silver. He referred me to St Mark's Place, to an assayer who was very portly and rich. He had three German assistant assayers. They quickly carried out the assay, with very sharp things, and thereafter they subjected it to the test, but it did not stand any of the tests, everything flew away in the fire. And they asked me harshly from where I had taken the silver. I indicated that I had had it assayed in order to see whether it would stand up as good silver. When I saw the fraud, I did not return to the Jew, and no longer paid attention to this art, and thought I would be caught in a misfortune with the Jew and the false silver.

There are several themes here which we have come across before: spending a lot of money on one's obsession with alchemy, but still being unable to tear oneself away from the pursuit of its promise to turn base metals into precious metals; and fraud based on some actual chemical ability, since the 'silver' produced from tin or by plating it was obviously sufficiently accomplished to allow the Italian and the Jew to sell it as the real thing to gullible customers. The use of 'poisonous' substances during their alchemical procedures, presumably a reference to such basic matter as 'toad' venom or the derivatives of antimony, hydrochloric acid, or any of the other venenous ingredients used or appearing in those same procedures is not altogether clear. What is puzzling is 'Trismosin's' assertion that the Italian and the Jew kept nothing from him, followed by his taking some of their 'silver' to be assayed and then being shocked by the discovery that it was fraudulent. But it is a reminder, perhaps, that we should not be misled by the apparent verisimilitude of the narrative. It could be true, it could be true in part, but the theme of a long journey in quest of an ideal goal, a search beset by trials and difficulties and disappointments, is all too recognizable a literary genre, and it is quite possible to read this life of 'Trismosin' as an allegory of the alchemical quest itself.

What is actually of more interest here is not so much the narrative as the presence of a Jew as one of the alchemists. Ever since Maria the Jewess had established herself as a major figure in the alchemical canon, Jews had appeared at intervals in the history of the science, and would continue to do so throughout the post-mediaeval period. One of the most famous names in the alchemical literature of the Middle Ages, Artephius, was supposed to have been a Jewish convert to Christianity, living in the twelfth century, but the evidence for this is somewhat shaky. In the thirteenth century, however, we have Jacob Aranicus who lived in France and taught alchemy to the Dominican encyclopaedist, Vincent de Beauvais; and we have already come across Caracosa Samuel who was granted royal permission to practise alchemy in Aragon in 1396. Fifty years previously, a Mallorcan Jew called Menahem (no other name is given) found himself in court, accused of being a counterfeiter of gold and silver coins, not to mention being a necromancer as well. We do not know the outcome of the case, but it is difficult to believe he was found guilty, because just over a year later, in July 1346, he was appointed physician to King Pedro IV of Majorca and apparently given leave to conduct 'certain experiments and business activities [*opera*]', which sound very much like alchemical experiments.

Johanan Alemanno (1435–c.1504) who, in spite of his name, was an Italian, and whose greatest claim to fame, perhaps, was introducing Giovanni Pico della Mirandola to the Kabbalah, wrote with especial interest about alchemy in his *Book of the Gate of Desire* (*Sefer Sha'ar hattesheq*). One passage links metals with the planets in a remarkable account of the palace which Japheth, son of Noah, built in the land of Zin – a useful reminder of the part astrology frequently played in alchemical theory and imagery. The second waxes hot in praise of gold which, he says, has several extraordinary properties, one of which illustrates most clearly the difference between real and alchemical gold:

> One, that if [somebody] eats [of it] as a charm, it makes him cunning like running water, or if it is cooked with food, behold, it will be in its power to restore to life the soul of the sick who is close to death. The second, that if he is used to his wine in which [the gold] is extinguished many times, then, behold, it purifies the intellect to sharpen [the mind of] the man who uses it. The third, that its sight gladdens souls with the special quality that is in it, and even more so in eating and drinking, if one drinks from a golden vessel. The fourth, that it greatly purifies and improves the digestion when it is found in the stomach, just as it makes it hard if it is swallowed whole in the shape of a skull. Behold, it improves the vision darkened by bad digestion, and not only the vision, but it also lights up the face darkened by leprosy or by ugly moisture. The fifth, that even if it is left for thousands of years in caves or in wet places underground, it will not be affected, nor will it be damaged, for it preserves its [original character] for ever, for it is not possible to forge it or to exchange it for another thing, even though the masters of alchemy do forge it and make beaten gold which resembles it to such an extent that one can as little distinguish between the two as between a mouse born out of dust and that which is born of its own kind. But as for verification, so that it should not be falsified, there is a feature preserved in it which cannot be forged by means of a charm, for the gold that is made by [alchemical] work raises blisters in burning, whereas real gold does not raise blisters.

The oddest Jewish writer on alchemy, however, is probably an anonymous Sephardi Jew living either in Spain or a suitable place of exile after 1492 – odd because his treatise is attributed to Maimonides, a scholar who disapproved most strongly of books supposedly by 'Hermes', and therefore who was almost certainly hostile to alchemy as well. Pseudo-Maimonides first directs his readers' attention to 'God the Helper', and then proceeds to give practical instructions on how to create a large pearl out of several small ones; how to make the stone out of gold, citron peel, jasmine violets, a sea-plant, arsenic and copper; how to prepare a medicinal elixir, 'a potion which I give to those who suffer epilepsy and the trembling disease, and to the paralytic, and to the melancholic, because of its effects on them'. This last is reminiscent of remarks by the mid fourteenth-century Ibn Aidamur al-Jildakī who wrote about the curative effects of alchemical gold and silver:

> The philosophers' gold, when applied three times to the eyes of a person suffering from continuous flow of tears, cures him; if an eyelash is plucked with a pair of tweezers made of this gold it will grow no more; if a plate of this gold is placed on the heart of someone suffering from palpitations he is sure to recover; and if this gold is dissolved and taken, it will cure all atrabilious diseases. Common gold exhibits none of these properties . . . The philosophers' silver cures hot fevers, and in solution in date-wine constitutes a remedy for atrabilious diseases, while common silver does none of these things . . . The elixir cures patients suffering from leprosy if it is applied to his sores and given him to drink as a potion. The sores burst and effuse a yellow water, after which new skin develops and no mark is left on the body.[10]

This strong link between alchemy and medicine is an integral part of the science itself. Chinese, Indian, Romano-Egyptian and Muslim alchemists all sought elixirs through their experiments, and Latin Europe of the Middle Ages, influenced as it was by the increasingly available translations of alchemical treatises largely Arabic in origin, followed suit in pursuing that same goal. Thus, a petition addressed to the English King, Henry VI, at the end of May 1456, noted that:

> Ancient wise and most reputable natural philosophers have taught and left behind, in their writings and books, under the form of diagrams and allegories, a record of how many estimable and noteworthy medicines can be prepared from wine, precious stones, oils, plants, living things, metals, and ordinary minerals, and especially a certain very valuable medicine which some of the natural philosophers have called 'the mother and empress of medicines'. Some people have given it the name 'inestimable glory'. On the other hand, some have called it 'quintessence', and others have designated it 'the philosophers' stone' and 'the elixir of life'.

The reference to 'diagrams and allegories' through which the natural philosophers passed on their knowledge reminds us that while alchemy continued to be perceived as a respectable *scientia* on the one hand – and its attachment to medicine would underline this aspect – there was also the gold-making side which threatened to bring it much closer to *ars*, the craftsmanship of the artisan, and therefore to lower its status in the eyes of the learned. In practice, however, this dichotomy was never as clear-cut as this. In spite of many alchemists' assertions that their texts must be expressed obscurely in order to keep their knowledge safe from the unlearned, the readership and audience for such texts were always widespread. But kings, noblemen and merchants, for example, were rarely in command of the kind of Latin required to be able to follow alchemical disquisitions with ease – and so vernacular texts were composed, from at least the fourteenth century onwards, in order to serve the wider interest. While the medical link undoubtedly stimulated the writing of some of them – a book on distillation translated into Italian by Michele Savonarola, or a pseudo-Lullian *Testamentum* in Catalan – the theme of transmutation of metals informed many others, and both the English texts we have met already and a Czech practical treatise indicate a deep interest in a craft which might produce gold and silver and so make one rich.

But to these two types can be added German versions – *Buch der heiligen Dreifaltigkeit* (1415/1419) and *Alchymey teuczsch* (1426) – both of which highlight religious themes, an interesting echo of an old Jewish tradition which saw Abraham as rich in silver and gold (Gen. 13.2) because he had learned alchemy from Hermes in Egypt; David as an expert alchemist who had used his art to raise the enormous sums of gold and silver expended on 'the house of the Lord' (1 Chron. 22.14); and likewise Solomon who had been taught by his father and was thus able to provide 'silver and gold to be in Jerusalem as stones' (2 Chron. 1.15). The *Buch der heiligen Dreifaltigkeit* seems to have been written by an anonymous Franciscan and contains a number of illustrations, two of which show Christ crucified in the form of a double-headed eagle. In the first, a triple-headed bird perches on the halo round his head. In the second, he appears twice: once on a shield as a doubled-headed eagle crucified, and once as himself accompanied by God the Father (labelled 'wisdom') and the Holy Spirit as a dove bearing the label 'earth'. Christ himself holds an orb labelled 'body' and places a crown on the head of a woman (the Virgin Mary) labelled 'soul', while at the corners of the picture are the winged symbols of the four evangelists.

Now, the early Latin alchemical texts were largely practical, in spite of their obligatory nods in the direction of the Creator. Albertus Magnus, for example, directed his attention to transmutation: is it possible or not? Bacon was interested mainly in the production of life-conserving medicines. In the thirteenth century, therefore, alchemy was considered to be essentially a superior brand of craftsmanship. Change came in the fourteenth century when alchemical writers began consciously to use biblical texts, especially those from Genesis relating to the creation of the world and the creation of Adam, as springboards for alchemical glosses and commentaries. Pseudo-Arnald of Villanova took this a stage further and compared the tribulations of alchemical mercury in the laboratory with the sufferings, death and ultimate resurrection of Christ, a mode of allegorical interpretation we have seen reflected already in some of the illustrations of the real Arnald's *Rosarium Philosophorum*.

Speculative alchemy thus became Christianized, a search for personal trans-mutation via the laboratory well illustrated by the famous image engraved by Hans Vredemann de Vries and inserted into Heinrich Khunrath's *Amphitheatrum sapientiae aeternae* (published 1609). It shows a large room with a tiled floor and high roof-beams. On the left-hand side is an oratory depicted as a kind of tent or tabernacle within which stands a table holding two open books on whose pages we can see circular diagrams and printed or written text. In front of this the alchemist (presumably Khunrath himself) kneels in prayer or supplication, his arms outstretched in cruciform fashion. On the right is his laboratory sheltered by a solid wooden canopy which is supported by pillars labelled 'reason' and 'experience'. Dominant in the foreground is a long table on which is displayed a variety of musical instruments representing sacred music, as the caption says. Cosmic harmony, it is suggested, rests in balance between religious contempla-tion or prayer and practical manipulation of Nature, and so also does the success of the work which the alchemist will be undertaking. Notably, we see him at his devotions. The laboratory is empty and waiting for his return. It is an emphasis that the late Middle Ages would have recognized and applauded.[11]

6

The Sixteenth and Seventeenth Centuries: Pretension, Fraud and Redeeming the World

With the early modern period we find alchemy rising to the height of what one might call popularity. The three main peaks of publication of alchemical books all occurred within this time: 1560–70, 1610–20, and 1650–85. The majority of these works were written in Latin (1703), closely followed by German (1667) which maintained quite a high level during the eighteenth century too, with a small peak round about 1780. French accounts for only a third of the German number (544), although once again there is also a small increase in publications after 1775; alchemical books in English are fewer than those in French (432), with a sudden notable increase in the 1650s; and relatively few were produced in Italian (223).

What can account for these separate peaks? The 1560s saw a disastrous change in the weather throughout Western Europe, and climate change became an extremely significant factor in fluctuating food prices. The winter of 1560–61, for example, was long and cold and there were hard frosts in the following spring. The summer of 1561 was dry and hot, but frequent hailstorms damaged the grain harvest. In 1562 the summer was attended by heavy rains. Again crops were badly affected and floods helped to spread disease among humans and cattle. The winter of that year was extreme. Alpine lakes froze and falls of snow were very heavy. Most of 1563 was equally disastrous – and so it went on. As Brian Fagan says, 'famine followed famine bringing epidemics in their train, bread riots and general disorder brought fear and distrust'. The 1560s also saw savage confessional wars between Catholics and Protestants in France, wars which not only devastated the countryside but also cost huge sums of money. Little wonder, therefore, if rulers and landowners, made nervous (and in some cases penurious) by this combination of circumstances, looked for ways to increase their threatened incomes, and others less fortunately placed in the social scale turned to anyone who might be able to provide them with gold and silver.

At the beginning of the seventeenth century, three publications – *Fama fraternitatis* (1614), *Confessio fraternitatis* (1615) and *Chymische Hochzeit* (1616) – saw a remarkable surge of interest in alchemy in learned circles throughout Europe. These books purported to be the manifestos of a secret organization, the Brotherhood of the Rosy Cross, which took alchemy as its language of mystical illumination and appeared to seek to use it as a means of influencing the basic structure of contemporary European knowledge. The medicine of Galen and the philosophy of Aristotle were to be ousted and replaced by new branches of learning based on wisdom derived directly from God and Nature; and the 'ungodly and accursed gold-making, which hath gotten so much the upper hand, whereby under colour of it, many runagates and roguish people do use great villanies, and cozen and abuse the credit which is given to them' was to give way to a true alchemy which would lead people into a more profound contemplation of God and the wonders of His creation. Transmutation was probably possible, and 'this so great gift of God we do in no manner set at naught or despise it. But because she bringeth not with her always the knowledge of Nature, but this bringeth forth not only medicine but also maketh manifest and open to us innumerable secrets and wonders, therefore it is requisite that we be earnest to attain to the understanding and knowledge of philosophy. And moreover, excellent wits ought not to be drawn to the tincture of metals before they be exercised well in the knowledge of Nature.' So far the *Fama* and the *Confessio*. The *Chymische Hochzeit* follows these thoughts by presenting the reader with an alchemical allegory along the same lines, using alchemy as the basis for a system of Christian mysticism which had nothing to do with a physical laboratory and everything with personal followed by social transformation along fairly distinctive lines.

The third peak of interest seems to have coincided with the activities of recently founded learned societies largely devoted to what we should call 'scientific investigation and experimentation'. First came the Academia Naturae Curiosorum, founded in 1652 in Schweinfurt by three physicians who were deeply interested in alchemy and its gold-making potential; secondly, the Royal Society of London for Improving Natural Knowledge, founded in 1660, which presided over what Charles Webster has called 'a last outburst of judicial astrology, the continuing flourishing of Paracelsian medicine, [and the] undiminished appeal of alchemy and medicine'; and thirdly, the Académie Royale des Sciences, founded in Paris in 1666, which included among its members Samuel Cottereau Duclos who had a reputation for being an 'amateur of spagyric medicine', and who disliked having to attend to his patients, preferring to work on both the speculative and the practical sides of alchemy, as he himself acknowledged on his deathbed.[1]

Between them, these three peaks of publication cover alchemy as gold-making, and alchemy as an allegory of a quest for personal transmutation and a deeper, more intimate knowledge of the mind of God. They therefore continue, in different forms and with different emphases, the preoccupations of earlier centuries, especially perhaps the two immediately preceding. One of these different emphases is, of course, the advent of Protestantism in all its varied manifestations; but in fact confessional divagations made no immediate break with past modes of apprehending the science. Luther himself, for example, professed admiration for both its theory and its practice:

> I very much like the science of alchemy which is, indeed, the philosophy of the ancients. I like it not only because, by melting metals, and decocting, preparing, extracting, and distilling herbs and roots, it produces profits: but also because of its allegorical and secret meaning. This is quite excellent and touches upon the resurrection of the dead at the Last Day. For, just as in a furnace the fire extracts and separates the various parts of a substance, and carries upward its spirit, life, sap and strength, leaving behind at the bottom the unclean matter, the dregs, like a dead, worthless corpse; so God, at the Day of Judgement, will separate everything with fire, the righteous from the unrighteous. The Christians, the righteous, will ascend to Heaven where they will enjoy everlasting life; but the wicked and the unrighteous, like dross and dirt, will remain in Hell and there they will be damned.

On the Catholic side, Pope Leo X's known tolerance of alchemy led to at least two books being dedicated to him. The first was an alchemical poem by Giovanni Aurelio Augurello, first published in 1515, which, as its title 'Chrysopoeia' suggests, purports to teach the techniques of gold-making to those capable of understanding the science, to explain the power inherent in alchemy, and to describe the miraculous effects of the stone. A story told of him by Charles Mackay in the nineteenth century (therefore probably not altogether reliable, but certainly *ben trovato*) informs us that Augurello dedicated his work to the Pope:

> in the hope that the Pontiff would reward him handsomely for the compliment. But the Pope was too good a judge of poetry to be pleased with the worse than mediocrity of his poem, and too good a philosopher to approve of the strange doctrines which it inculcated. He was, therefore, far from gratified at the dedication. It is said that when Augurello applied to him for a reward, the Pope, with great ceremony and much apparent kindness and cordiality, drew an empty purse from his pocket and presented it to the alchemist, saying that since he was able to make gold, the most appropriate present that could be made to him was a purse to put it in.

The second book appeared at the end of 1518, *Ars transmutationis metallicae*, by a Venetian priest, Giovanni Agostino Panteo, in which Panteo claimed he wanted to reveal only the truth about alchemy so that his readers could be forewarned of all the lies and nonsense which would otherwise cloud their perception of the science. The book was published by special permission of the Venetian authorities and the Pope himself, permission which was needed as the government of Venice had recently prohibited the practice of alchemy within its bounds. Indeed, Panteo seems to have become nervous in the years succeeding publication of the *Ars transmutationis*, and in 1518 he produced a bizarre treatise, *Voarchadumia as Opposed to Alchemy* (*Voarchadumia contra alchemiam*), in which he fulminated against alchemy while in fact repeating most of what he had written in the earlier book, employing the unconvincing device of merely naming alchemy as 'Voarchadumia' which he said was the true science of metals inherited from the biblical tubal Cain.

But the person whose name is inextricably associated with alchemy at the beginning of the sixteenth century is Philip Theophrastus Bombast von Hohenheim, most frequently known as 'Paracelsus'. He was born in Swabia in 1493 but began very early, at the age of nine in fact, a life of wandering all over Europe: Carinthia, Tyrol, several Italian universities, Vienna, Paris, Oxford and Köln saw him accumulate knowledge from anyone who would supply it, regardless of academic or social status. His principal reputation in his own time and afterwards was that of an unorthodox physician, and he was quite clear about what should be the supporting disciplines of his chosen science. 'The first pillar, philosophy, is the knowledge of earth and water; the second pillar, astronomy together with astrology, has a complete knowledge of the two elements air and fire; the third pillar, alchemy, is the knowledge of the experiment and preparation of the four elements just mentioned; and the fourth pillar, virtue, should remain with the physician until death, for this completes and preserves the other three pillars.'

The alchemical pillar of this system included expertise in gold-making as well as manufacture of elixirs. We are told, for example, that on one occasion Paracelsus had run out of money, so he gave his assistant a guilder to buy a pound of mercury. The mercury was then put into a crucible and heated over a fire, after which it was allowed to cool. The lid of the crucible was removed and the assistant saw inside the vessel a mass of solid gold, certified by a local goldsmith to be genuine, which was exchanged for a purseful of money. Clearly certain details are missing from this account, as heating mercury alone would not have effected the transmutation, so, if we wish to accept the story as a truthful version of what happened, we have to assume that Paracelsus added something to the crucible at some point during the proceedings, as was alchemists' usual practice. On another occasion, he met a farmer's wife whom he had cured of an illness many years before. She showed her gratitude once again and in return he smeared some kind of ointment on one of her kitchen forks and turned it into gold.

Paracelsus made it clear that such expertise was not to be gained without a great deal of hard, physical labour:

> [Alchemists] devote themselves diligently to their labours, sweating whole nights and days over fiery furnaces. These do not kill the time with empty talk, but find their delight in their laboratory. They are clad in leathern garments, and wear a girdle to wipe their hands on. They put their fingers to the coals, the lute, and the dung, not into gold rings.

Like blacksmiths and coal merchants, they are sooty and dirty . . . They perceive the work should glorify the workman, and not the workman the work . . . They rejoice to be occupied at the fire and to learn the steps of alchemical knowledge.

He also left details about his experiments in the science, in which he describes how gold can be increased in the laboratory vessel:

It is possible, by his industry and skill, for the alchemist to exalt gold so high that it grows in a crucible like a tree, with many wonderful boughs and leaves. This is a most pleasant and, indeed, an extraordinary sight. The process is as follows. Calcine gold with aqua regis until it turns into a kind of chalk. Put this into a gourd-shaped glass and pour some fresh aqua regis on it so that the gold is covered to a depth of four fingers. Draw it off again, with the third degree of fire, until nothing further rises. Distil water from it, pour this on again, and then distil the water once more. Do this as long as you see that the gold is rising and growing like a tree in the glass, with many branches and leaves. This is how a wonderful and delightful shrub is made from the gold. Alchemists call it their 'golden plant' and 'the philosophers' tree'.

His experience seems to have been gained, at least in part, from his spending time with Hans Kilian, librarian to the Duke of Bavaria, whom the Duke also retained as his personal alchemist. Together he and Paracelsus worked in a laboratory the Duke had provided in the basement of his castle at Neuburg, and whatever else they did there, Paracelsus appears to have used some of the time to write a book, *Archidoxa*, partly a collection of alchemical recipes and their medical applications, partly a manifesto for a new type of medicine in which the physician, rather than follow the Galenic system of readjusting the body's humours, was to direct and control the natural powers inherent in the quintessence of each individual substance. This manifesto is extraordinary, saturated with religious metaphors, a virtual proclamation that Nature is a vehicle through which God reveals to those who can read them the divine forces which bring about the process of healing. The *Archidoxa*, however, makes no mention of what was to become one of Paracelsus's most famous contribution to alchemical theory. Aristotle had said there were four elements, each a manifestation of the basic *prima materia* of creation. Muslim alchemists had suggested that, in addition to this, every metal consisted of two principles, mercury and sulphur, which subsumed Aristotle's elements. To these Paracelsus added salt, thereby not only creating a trinity of fundamental alchemical principles, but altering the way they should be understood. Mercury, sulphur and salt do not replace Aristotelian earth, air, fire and water but are so to speak spiritual propensities inherent in them.

'A peasant can tell you that you are holding a piece of wood,' he explained in his *A Work Which Surpasses Amazing* (*Opus Paramirum*), 'but you also know that you have a compound of sulphur, mercury, and salt. If you have a bone and can say whether it is mostly sulphur, mercury, or salt, you know why it is diseased or what is the matter with it. The peasant can see the externals, but the physician's task is to see the inner and secret matter.'

But what was the ground and ultimate origin of this 'secret matter'? Was it created especially by God or did it exist already, to be used by Him in the execution of His creative purposes? Paracelsus says, ambiguously, that it existed from the beginning, inherent in the word spoken by God to initiate the separate stages of creation: *Fiat*, 'let there be'. Such a mode of thinking has, of course, left the laboratory far behind. Philip Ball calls it 'chemical theology', and with this we are reminded that Paracelsus did not write merely upon alchemy and medicine, but upon theology, numerology and magic, too, the extraordinary and kaleidoscopic whole being shot through with Neoplatonist and Gnostic influences. In consequence, his alchemical philosophy gives the appearance of being a theory of evolution, but an evolution in which things evolve upwards not downwards, and this evolution upwards is expressed in alchemical metaphors and analogies which constantly speak of two things at one and the same time: the nature of humankind and the nature of God. As Alexandre Koyré expresses it, 'The Philosopher's Stone is the Christ of Nature, and Christ is the Philosopher's Stone of the spirit. Mercury, being the intermediary between the sun and moon . . . *is* Christ in the world of matter, in the same way that Christ, mediator between God and the world, is the spiritual mercury of the universe.'[2]

No surprise, then, that Paracelsus came under attack from several quarters, included among those impious individuals who, 'armed with alchemical or rather diabolical juggleries and monstrous sophisms, overthrow arts propagated in a continuous series from the first antiquity of the human race', and condemned for comparing the Holy Trinity with salt, sulphur and mercury, and fabricating Heaven from these same three substances. Heretical, contentious, iconoclastic, Paracelsus left a considerable mark on later medicine and iatrochemistry, although his influence on practical alchemy itself was not so great. As far as transmutational alchemy was concerned, the science continued very much as it had done before Paracelsus embarked on his career, as did its practitioners, endeavouring to avoid arrest, trying to make gold and wandering from place to place in pursuit of that combination of credulity, tolerance and need which would enable them to pursue their obsession in some degree of safety and comfort. We have a good example of the type in 'Denis Zacaire' (1510–56) who has left us what purports to be an account of his life, *Opuscule tres-eccellent de la vraye philosophie naturelle des metaulx*, published the year after he died. He says he was educated at home and then went on to study philosophy at Bordeaux where he met an alchemist and learned the science from him. His father then sent him to Toulouse to study law, giving him 200 écus to support him while he did so. Unfortunately, however, 'Zacaire' spent the entire sum on alchemical experiments:

Before the end of the year, my 200 écus had gone up in smoke and my master died of a continuous fever. It took him off during the summer because he had been blowing on the fire and drinking while he was hot, and he rarely left his room which was scarcely cooler than the Arsenal in Venice. His death distressed me, all the more so because my parents were willing to send me only the money I needed for my living expenses and not as much as I wanted to carry on my work.

To take care of these difficulties, I went home in 1535 to extract myself from tutelage, and rented out my whole property for three years at 400 écus. I needed these funds to carry out an operation details of which I had been given at Toulouse by an Italian who said he had seen it done. I kept him with me to see the process through. Then I carried out calcination of gold and silver with *aqua fortis*. But this came to nothing. I now had only half of all the gold and silver I had used, and my 400 écus were soon reduced to 230. I gave 20 to my Italian so that he could go and get an explanation from the author of the recipe, who (he said) was in Milan. I remained all winter in Toulouse, in the hope he would come back. But I would still be there had I waited any longer for I have never seen him again since.

The following summer brought the plague, which made me abandon the city. But I did not lose sight of my work. I went to Cahors where I stayed for six months. There I met an old man known to everyone as 'the Philosopher', a name which is easily acquired in the provinces by those who are less ignorant than the rest. I communicated to him the results of my procedures and asked for his opinion. He commented on only ten or twelve points which he found better than the others. The plague ceased and I returned to Toulouse where I resumed my work. I did so well that my 400 écus were now reduced to 170.

To continue my experiments on a firmer footing, I made the acquaintance, in 1537, of an abbot who lived in the neighbourhood of the city. He was smitten by the same passion and told me that one of his friends, who had been one of the Cardinal d'Armagnac's servants, had sent him from Rome a procedure which he believed reliable, but which would cost 200 écus. I gave him half, he supplied the rest, and together we started to work, sharing the expenses. As we had no spirits of wine, I bought some excellent vin de Gaillac, extracted the spirits and rectified them several times. We took four marks of these and added a mark of gold which we had calcinated for a month. Everything was artistically combined in one retort, then the materials were transferred to another which was placed on a stove to make a congelation. This work lasted a year. But so that we should not be idle, we amused ourselves by carrying out several other less important operations from which we derived as much profit as we did from the major work.

So the whole of 1537 passed without finding any change in our work, and we should have waited all our lives for the congelation of our spirits of wine, because the water which dissolves gold is not there. Still, we got all of it back, but with this difference, that the powder was a little finer than it had been when we first put it in. We made a projection with it on heated mercury, but this came to nothing. Judge how frustrated we were, especially the abbot who had already told all his monks that once our operation had been successful he had only to melt down a lovely lead fountain which was in their cloister to turn it into gold. Lack of success did not stop us from continuing. I leased my property again and drew 400 écus. The abbot added a similar sum, and I went back to Paris, the city which, more than any other in the world, produces practitioners of this science. I arrived with my 800 écus, fully resolved not to leave until I had either spent all my money or had discovered something worthwhile. I could not make this trip without incurring the indignation of my parents and the reproaches of my friends. They, imagining I was a great lawyer, wanted me to buy a councillor's post, and I deluded them into thinking I was taking this trip only to make such a purchase.

After fifteen days' travel I arrived in Paris on 9 January 1539. I stayed for a month, more or less unknown. But scarcely had I started to frequent those who were keen on alchemy (and even the makers of ovens) than I got to know more than a hundred alchemical operatives, who all had different ways of working: some used cementation, others dissolution, others essence of emery. There were those who laboured to extract the mercury from metals in order to fix it afterwards. So, to let each other know how our operations were progressing, we did not fail to meet every day in somebody's lodging – even on Sundays and Feasts of Notre Dame, which is the most visited church in Paris. Some of them said, 'If we had the means to start again, we should produce something worthwhile.' Others said, 'If our vessel could have withstood it, we should have been inside.' Others, 'If I had had a round copper vessel, tightly closed, I should have fixed the mercury with the silver.'

There was not one who did not have a reasonable excuse; but I was deaf to these conversations, knowing already from my own experience how far I had been the dupe of these kinds of promises.

A Greek introduced himself, and I worked uselessly with him on clouds made of cinnabar. I got to know, more or less at the same time, a foreign gentleman, newly arrived, who often used to sell the results of his experiments at the Orfèvres. I stayed a long time with him without his being willing to let me in on his secret. He did so, however; only it was merely a more ingenious piece of deceit than those of the others. I did not fail to let the abbot from Toulouse know everything. I even sent him a copy of this gentleman's procedure and, imagining I should eventually come to discover something useful, the abbot urged me to stay another year in Paris, since I had made such a good start. In spite of all my pains, I prospered no more in the three years I was there than I had before.

I had spent nearly all my money when the abbot told me to leave everything and come back and join him as soon as possible. I returned and found letters from the King of Navarre. This prince, who had an inquiring mind and was a great amateur of philosophy, had written to the abbot, asking him to get me to go and join the Court at Pau in Bearn where I was to teach him the secret I had learned from the foreign gentleman. The King said he would pay me 3,000 or 4,000 écus. These words, '4,000 écus', so tickled the abbot's ears that, thinking he already had the money in his purse, he gave me no rest until I had left him to join the prince's Court. I arrived at Pau in May 1542. I set to work and was successful according to the procedure I knew. When I had finished as the King wished, I got the payment I expected. Although the King had every intention of doing me some good, he was diverted from doing so by the gentlemen of his Court, even by those who had undertaken to have me come. So he sent me home with many thanks, saying I should look around and if there was anything at all I wanted – confiscations, anything like that – he would be happy to give it to me. This reply, which contented only empty hopes, gave me leave to return to the abbot in Toulouse.

Still, I had learned on my way that there was a monk who was very adept in natural philosophy, so I went to visit him. He could not help feeling sorry for me and told me, with a deal of enthusiasm and good nature, that his advice was not to amuse myself any longer with all these specific operations, all of which were false and full of sophistry, but to read the fine books of the ancient philosophers so that I could get to know the truth of the matter and find out exactly the order one must follow in the practice of this science.

I very much appreciated this wise advice, but before putting it into practice, I went to find my abbot in Toulouse to give him an account of the 800 écus we had put together, and at the same time give him his half of the reward I had received from the King of Navarre. If the abbot was not happy with everything I told him, he appeared even less so with the resolution I had taken not to continue any longer with our labours, because he thought I was a good practitioner. We each had only 90 écus left out of our 800. I left the abbot and went back home, intending to take myself off to Paris as soon as I could and to stay there for as long as it took me to read the philosophers. I arrived the day after All Saints in 1546. I spent a year in Paris, assiduously studying the great authors, namely, the *Turba Philosophorum*, the excellent Trevisano, the *Remontrance de Nature*, and several more of the best books. As I had none of the basic principles of the art, I did not know on what I should concentrate.

Finally I came out of my solitude, not to see my operative acquaintances, all of whom I had forsaken, but to frequent the company of true philosophers. Once again I fell into the greatest doubts because of the variety of their work and methods of procedure. Still, roused by a kind of inspiration, I threw myself into reading Raymund Lull and the *Rosarium* of Arnald of Villanova. My meditations and reading lasted another year, and at last I made up my mind. But I waited for the end of the lease on my property before carrying out my intention at home. So I arrived at the beginning of Lent 1549, determined to put into practice everything I had decided upon and, after making several preparations, I made provision for everything I needed and started to work on Easter Monday. Nevertheless, I did not do so without anxiety and without things getting in the way. Sometimes someone said to me, 'What are you doing? Haven't you spent enough of your income on all these follies?' Another assured me that if I continued to buy so much coal, people would suspect me of being a coiner, as indeed he had heard it whispered. Because I had a degree in law, people wanted me to purchase a legal position. But I was even more tormented by my parents who reproached me bitterly for my behaviour to the point of threatening to send the police to my house to break up all my furnaces.

I leave you to imagine the exhaustion and worry I suffered as a result of this kind of talk and complication. I found consolation only in my work and my operation, which I saw thriving day after day, and to which I paid the closest possible attention. The interruption of all business, caused by the plague, threw me into a deep solitude and gave me a chance to notice, with satisfaction, the progress and succession of the three colours which philosophers require before one arrives at the perfection of the work. I saw them, one after the other, and I made a test the following year on Easter Day 1550. Common mercury, which I put in a crucible on the fire, was changed into fine gold in less than an hour. You may judge how happy I was. But I was careful not to boast of it. I thanked God for the favour He had done me, and I prayed Him not to let me use it for anything other than His glory'.

The ramifications of this story are diverting and the verisimilitude is convincing, but in fact it is difficult to tell whether the account is genuine or not. Certainly there is no doubt that the author – 'Denis Zacaire' appears to have been a pseudonym – was well acquainted with the way alchemists explained themselves, but this means he was well enough acquainted to have been able to compose this supposedly autobiographical tale as a satire upon alchemists in general. Their prodigal extravagance, their constant search for a genuine master, their perpetual disappointments and frustrations, their gullibility – it is all there. But what makes one suspicious is that in many ways it is strongly reminiscent of the autobiographical account attributed to Bernardo il Trevisano (1406–90), which tells of similar journeys and unhappy failures. His journeys (if we are to believe a word of it) took place in Italy, Spain, Turkey, Greece, Egypt, the Barbary Coast, Persia, Sicily, France, Scotland, the Holy Land and Germany; and the substance of 13,000 écus he inherited, he spent in his lifelong quest for the stone, a quest which ended nowhere for, as he says, he was over 62 years old at the time of his writing and had still not succeeded in the task he had made the goal of his life. Such a model, then, existed for 'Zacaire', and there would be several more examples of the genre later on, all of which should act as a warning not to treat these 'lives', or even the names attached to them, as necessarily accurate, historical or reliable. If 'Zacaire's' account is true, or even partly true, it is a valuable witness. If it is not, it has a limited value as an insight into the kind of story people were telling or expected to be told about alchemy and its practitioners in the sixteenth century.

What distinguishes 'Zacaire's' account from that of 'Bernardo' is what can be read as its wry tone, its tongue in cheek, such as 'Zacaire's' confession that, after 11 years' pursuit of his goal, he still 'had none of the basic principles of the art', and that even though he had spent a whole year in Paris, studying some of the most obvious books on the subject, because of his ignorance he still did not understand on what he should concentrate. Diddling the King of Navarre, and being diddled by him in return, is an episode of simple humour and a tale with a moral, and one cannot help wondering whether it has been included simply for its entertainment value; and the inclusion of a gullible and greedy abbot, and a sensible, honest monk also smacks of a similar literary balance between 'bad' and 'good' which makes another moral point, as do the claimed achievement of transmutation on the day of Christ's resurrection, and the pious ascription of the alchemist's success to a favour from God.[3]

Mocking tale, entertaining *conte*, moralizing fable – whatever one thinks of these 'lives', they reflect, perhaps, the increasing popularity of the science. 'Zacaire's' 'hundred alchemical operatives' in Paris alone may have been an exaggeration, but alchemists were by no means rare, and quite ordinary people such as the Platter family, whose father ran a school in Basel during the early 1540s, knew two of them: Hans Rust who, so Felix Platter believed, turned mercury into silver, and Martin Borrhaus who frequently went on his travels and got to know the Platters when he settled down for a while in Basel in 1536. Alchemists tended to travel quite a lot. They were usually looking for patrons, or trying to escape officers of the law. Patrons were available in remarkable numbers. Philip II of Spain, for example, encouraged alchemists to come to his court in the 1570s, especially from Italy because alchemy was in good standing there; and Queen Christina of Sweden (1626–89) not only read alchemical works and extended her patronage to several alchemists, she also employed one, Pietro Antonio Bandiera, to run a laboratory for her, may have acted as an assistant to another, Giuseppe Francesco Borri, and practised the science herself with an Italian named Vitebo as her assistant.

Where royalty led, of course, nobility would probably follow, and we find that between February 1565 and March 1567 one Cornelius de Lannoy, a Dutch alchemist who had come to England towards the end of 1564 and been installed in Somerset House to train English workmen in the techniques of glass production, was involved in an unhappy episode with Elizabeth Tudor, the Earl of Leicester and William Cecil over a promise 'to produce for her Highness's use 50,000 marks of pure gold yearly on certain conditions'. De Lannoy wrote to Elizabeth, claiming that he had 'acquired great skill in the transmutation of metals', and was given the chance to prove his claim. But something went awry, because in mid-July 1566 he had to write her a letter of apology. 'As to the business of transmuting metals and gems to greater perfection, either the work has been disturbed, or some wicked man has been present, or I have erred through syncopation [*missing a vital step*].' He was arrested and put in the Tower; but this did not stop him from renewing his offer to make Elizabeth gold by alchemical means, and this plea is the last we hear of him in official records. The débâcle, however, did not put people off similar attempts, and in his *Annals* for the year 1574, John Strype recorded:

> A great project had been carrying on now for two or three years, of alchemy, William Medley being the great undertaker, to turn iron into copper. Sir Thomas Smith, Secretary of State, had, by some experiments made before him a great opinion of it. And for the better carrying it on, and bearing the expenses, it was thought fit to be done by a corporation: into which, by Smith's encouragement, the Lord Burghley and the Earl of Leicester entered themselves, with others: each member laying down an £100 to go on with it . . . But the thing underwent delay, till in December this year, that lord, according as Smith advised him, for his better satisfaction, to send some able person to Medley,

to see his method, and by discourse to understand his ability, sent William Humfrey, assay-master of the Tower mint, and a chemist, with some other learned in that science, to see what Medley could do, or pretend [*claim*] to.

A conversation ensued between Humfrey, a Mr Topcliff and Medley in the presence of Sir John Ebots, and Medley then undertook to produce a richer type of copper than could be obtained naturally, and to do so in Sir John Ebot's presence. This was agreed, whereupon Medley became awkward and started complaining that 'some went about to deprive him of his art and labours':

> March was now come; and yet little or nothing was done in this pretendedly advantageous project. But the pretence of the delay was the great expense required for lead, iron, cask, workmen, vessels, housing, building, casting up of earth, and other necessaries; which the undertaker of himself could not bear. Therefore the said Earl and the Secretary (who were earnest in it) and, by their persuasion, the Lord Treasurer, did assist with round sums of money. And Smith determined to send down his servant with Medley, ready to go down to the works; who might make a calculation, whether it would turn to account. Which however they themselves were in some doubt of, yet were resolved, upon some probabilities, to make the trial.

But, try as they might, neither they nor Medley made any progress, and eventually he was forbidden to 'multiply or make any gold or silver contrary to law' under penalty of £5,000, an immense and crippling sum of money. Were his patrons the dupes of a deliberate fraud, or did he and De Lannoy genuinely believe they could change one metal into another? The Jesuit Martín del Rio who considered the matter in 1599–1600 was of the opinion that while some operations might be fraudulent – such as those of Bragadino of Venice who was punished in 1591 – it was still entirely credible that some alchemists had been and were successful in their endeavours, and he cites testimony to the transmutation of gold in the presence of the Doge and leading patricians in Venice, and three Venetian patricians who were likewise witnesses of a demonstration in 1550. Unless we have strong evidence to the contrary, therefore, we should try to give practitioners the benefit of the doubt instead of assuming they *must* have been cheats and con-merchants. Their position was a difficult one. If they believed they really could achieve transmutation of metals if only they tried long enough and hard enough, and if they were able to find a patron who would pay for their experiments, and if those experiments kept on failing, they must have been aware that there was a thin line between being able to explain their failures and retain their patron's loyalty long enough to be given yet another chance to prove their worth, and failing once too often for their patron's patience which might well take an unpleasant turn if he decided he had been duped from the very beginning. Hence De Lannoy's imprisonment and Medley's discomfiture.

These, however, were nothing in comparison with the dangers which could and did attend alchemists elsewhere in Europe. On 14 September 1570, for example, Pietro Apolloni, a parish priest, was interrogated at the instance of the Bishop of Siena about his possession of chemical substances, minerals and apparatus for the practice of alchemy. The list of equipment is long, so Apolloni was obviously a serious practitioner, but when interrogation was renewed on 20 September, he admitted possessing alchemical books but said he did not know the practice of alchemy was forbidden. Meanwhile, other charges had come to light, including possession of books dealing with magic; but the main thrust of questioning concerned alchemy – which he admitted he practised – and alchemical books, in particular the *Testamentum* attributed to Raimund Lull. Again, during a third interrogation on 12 December, he pleaded ignorance, this time saying he did not know Lull's book was suspect material. Finally, on 20 February 1571, sentence was pronounced. Apolloni was to cease practising alchemy under pain of suspension from holy orders and loss of his benefices – personal ruin, in fact.

By August that year, however, he was in prison again on separate but related charges: possessing a book of political lampoons and a book of divinatory astrology. In addition to questions about these the bishop's representative wanted to know what kind of phenomena could be produced by powdered bat and a powder which burned in water. Questioning in September concentrated on alchemy, on procedures whereby 'white gold' was extracted from silver and then coloured so that it looked like real gold (a clear accusation of fraud). A week later, Apolloni was pressed for details about other people who practised alchemy – a monk, a perfumier, and 'a certain Vincenzo da Fermo' – a pressure he obviously found too much to bear, as he made a clumsy attempt to run away by saying he needed to pee. But his liberty was short-lived and he was brought back into court to hear a résumé of charges of possessing books on alchemy, books on divinatory astrology, a book of lampoons, and a new one of having a manuscript leaf which contained a spell to make spirits appear. He was also accused of selling counterfeit silver and gold, possession of alchemical apparatus as well as alchemical books, attempted simony, and trying to escape during interrogation. Apolloni denied everything, and witnesses came forward to say that he did not practise alchemy in order to make money but to provide medicines for the poor – in effect, that his alchemy concentrated on elixirs rather than transmutation. At this point, unfortunately, the record comes to an end. We do not know the outcome of this second set of interrogations, but since Apolloni had already had one chance to redeem himself and seems, quite signally, to have failed to take it, and since the new set of charges contained serious accusations of various kinds of fraud, the likelihood is that he would have been found guilty and punished severely.

This certainly was the case for Anna Maria Zieglerin. In 1574, she and two other alchemists (one her husband), employed by Duke Julius of Braunschweig-

Wolfenbüttel, were prosecuted by their patron on charges of murder, attempted poisoning, intended theft and failure to keep their promises of success in alchemy. Anna was one of several female alchemists at the time, although she is better known, perhaps because, unlike them, she published and published voluminously. She and her husband, Heinrich Schombach, arrived in Wolfenbüttel in 1571 and worked for the Duke for fully three years until their prosecution for murder and fraud. Anna quite evidently knew what she was doing and was given her own laboratory and assistant. She detailed her experiments and intentions in private letters and in a small booklet, *The Noble and Precious Art of Alcamia*, which she sent to the Duke in 1573, and it is clear from these that her principal interest lay in the practical side of the science. She described two processes for obtaining the stone, and recommended using the result not only to make good gold but also to encourage growth of fruits out of season, produce a range of gemstones and act as a remedy against various kinds of illness.

Her most unusual claim, however, was that the stone could be used to 'ripen' children in the womb, and she boasted to her husband that with the help of the stone she herself would bear children every four weeks, since their natural growth would be stimulated and hastened by contact with the stone. The father of these prodigious infants would not be her husband, though, but the supposed son of Paracelsus, the Count Karl von Öttingen (who in fact did not exist), the man by whom she further claimed to have been instructed in alchemy. Was she insane? Not necessarily. Her claims may have been fabrications, but they could have been fabrications with a purpose: to gain Duke Julius's attention; to offset the possible disadvantage of being a woman by acquiring the extra cachet of having a notable alchemical teacher who would lend authority and glamour to her claims to be a competent alchemist; to fulfil some personal ambition to make a mark on the world by suggesting that she, as a woman, could manage an alchemical achievement obviously impossible to men.

Unfortunately for her and her husband and their colleague, however, torture was employed after their arrest, and they confessed to the crimes with which they had been charged. Then they were executed, all three with the barbarities to be expected. Does the fact they were tortured mean they were innocent? Again, not necessarily. It does not follow that because they were tortured, their confessions were *ipso facto* lies or fantasies. People do tell the truth under torture. It depends what they are asked. Still, innocent or guilty, Anna's death and those of her husband and colleague were gruesome and must have served as a dreadful warning to others who might be thinking of following in their footsteps. Alchemy may have had its attractions, but failure or proven fraud brought death in its wake. For it was not only Duke Julius who pressed for the ultimate penalty. When one of the alchemists in Braunschweig-Wolfenbüttel was shown to be a fraud, red-hot pincers mutilated his body, he was drawn and quartered, and his remains were then hung from a gibbet beside the main road from Braunschweig to Goslar. The Duke of Württemberg, on the other hand, preferred the sardonic humour of having such failures hanged on a gold-plated gallows; and to these examples one can add the case of Hans Heinrich Nüschler in 1601, who signed a contract to demonstrate the art of transmutation but failed to do so by legitimate means. Desperate to retain his patron, he resorted to fraud and was, almost inevitably, found out, after which he was put on trial, adjudged guilty and hanged.[4]

These English, Italian and German episodes, then, are good examples of the way in which earnest pretension or deliberate fraud not only presented danger to alchemical practitioners but also proved to be frequent obstacles in the path of those rulers and nobles who hoped to benefit financially from their investment in and encouragement of alchemy. Yet still they persisted. In the German states alone the Elector of Brandenburg and his son, the Margrave of Brandenburg-Ansbach, the Duke of Württemberg, the Landgrave of Hessen-Kassel and his son were all keen to finance alchemical experiments, not to mention Wolfgang II, Count of Hohenlohe, who conducted alchemical experiments himself. But none was as great a patron as Rudolf II, the Holy Roman Emperor, to whose laboratories in Prague a large number of alchemists were invited in the last decades of the sixteenth century and the opening years of the seventeenth; and it is important here to note that the intellectual circles operating in Prague provide a reminder that alchemy did not exist *in vacuo*, but alongside various kinds of magic, astrology, astronomy, mathematics, natural philosophy and theology, with one person frequently practising several of these arts and sciences, since the boundaries between them were entirely fluid and knowledge had not yet been separated into self-contained compartments after the modern fashion.

Thus, for example, the Danish natural philosopher Tycho Brahe, who became Imperial Astronomer to Rudolf II, wrote to him in advance of his appointment a kind of curriculum vitae including the information that, 'from my earliest years I have given myself assiduously to the study [of iatrochemistry] no less than to astronomy, and I have pursued it with diligence and at considerable expense'. He had been introduced to alchemy while he was a student in Germany but refused to practise the transmutational side of it, preferring instead that aspect of the science which concentrated on the production of 'spagyric' medicines, in other words elixirs (which eventually killed him in 1601 soon after he had come to Rudolf's Court, because of their heavy content of mercury). His friend and later brother-in-law Erik Lange, however, was obsessed with transmutation and was keen to reveal to Rudolf the method he used for the purpose, largely (Tycho suspected) because it was appallingly expensive and Lange was hoping to gain for himself an imperial patron. Tycho's extraordinary establishment of *Uraniborg*, a place which amounted to a 'scientific' complex of museum, extensive library, laboratories, aviaries and observatories on the island of Hven, seems at first glance to be nothing more than that – a complex of buildings in which 'scientific' work was done. But, as John Christianson points out, 'in Tycho's day, some philosophers built elaborate curiosity cabinets with many drawers and compartments, suitably decorated with emblematic designs, and within these cabinets, they arranged objects – mineral, animal, vegetable, and artificial – to create magical microcosms with the power of talismans. On Hven, this manipulative scheme had been enlarged into the whole complex centred on the museum.'

A similar combination of 'scientific' and occult interests informed the work of the Englishmen John Dee and Edward Kelley, who came to the Imperial Court in 1584. Both were well versed in alchemy, but both actually spent most of their initial time in Prague engaged in having and recording conversations with spirits who appeared to Kelley, the sensitive, in a ball or mirror, and had their messages and instructions relayed by him to Dee who sat in a corner of the room and wrote them down; and it was these activities rather than alchemy which engaged Rudolf's attention, although alchemy was never far from Kelley's thoughts, and he turned exclusively to this for his Czech patrons once his scrying period with Dee came to an end.

Politics, however, were never far away. Since the most obvious basic principle of alchemy was to eliminate the baser parts of metals so that they were enabled to change, at extraordinary speed, into their most noble form of gold, it is not difficult to see that success in alchemy, which was constantly being trumpeted as a gift from God and therefore a sign of divine favour, could be interpreted as an overt message that the successful practitioner – or, more likely, his or her royal or noble patron – was especially pleasing to God who had confirmed His approbation in this particular way. At a time of confessional division, then, a sign that God favoured a ruler of one religious persuasion over another could furnish powerful propaganda for the cause, not to mention extra material wealth to pay for war on the one hand and charitable deeds on the other. Successful alchemy also promised command over the processes of Nature, and this too had its symbolic connotations which could be translated into both religious and political terms. Hence, as Pamela Smith explains it:

> The interest at the Rudolfine Court arose within an educated world view that sought an intellectual reconciliation between the contraries of Catholic and Protestant confessions as well as among the growing divisions in the territories of the Holy Roman Empire. This reconciliation was to be achieved through a metaphysical rendering of the multitude of contraries in the temporal world into a unified and meaningful whole. Alchemy, in particular, provided a material demonstration of a superior power and made intelligible the degeneration and decay of the visible world by showing these processes to be part of the divine plan.

We may expect, therefore, to find that at least some of the alchemists who visited Rudolf's Court during the 1580s and 90s – Michał Sediwój (Sendivogius), Michael Maier, Ewald Hoghelande, Nicolas Barbaud, Oswald Croll and Heinrich Khunrath – were, in one way or another, exponents of more than the purely practical or operative side of alchemy.

This is certainly true of Heinrich Khunrath (1560–1605) whose engraving of the alchemist in his oratory-laboratory we have mentioned before. Khunrath had originally been physician to the richest of the Bohemian princes, Vilém Rozmberk (1535–92), whose house in Prague, castle at Reichenstein in Silesia and huge palace at Krumlov in southern Bohemia constituted the other great centre of alchemical learning and experimentation in Rudolf's empire, and was attended at various times by the great Czech alchemist, Bavor Rodovsky, the Englishmen John Dee and Edward Kelley who included the prince in their conversations with spirits, the German Karl Widemann who, together with others, was working to produce the stone and the elixir of life, and the Frenchman Nicolas Barnaud who compiled a number of alchemical books and may have done some alchemical work himself.

After Rozmberk's death, however, Khunrath moved to Prague. For the past 20 years, as he explains in his *Confessio* (1596), he had been engaged in alchemical work. The experience was practical as well as theoretical. 'I have had to put my hands in the lime and coal,' he wrote, 'in order to know, or get to the bottom of something properly. I have had to build stoves and tear them down again, and have broken many large and small glasses for distilling, and suchlike vessels and retorts. I have travelled far after many an expert in order to learn some good from him, and have spent much over it, before I became really acquainted with what alchemy and chemistry are. Before I received this spirit and gift of distinction in this art of God, without praising it too much, in the oratory through prayer, and in the laboratory through working, I had to learn to distinguish the bad and lies, and to maintain the good and truth, many a wonderful and strange thing had come under my nose.'

It seems to have been through (or perhaps in spite of) this individual approach to the science that he managed to gain Rudolf's favourable attention to the extent that in 1598 he was granted a copyright licence to protect his works for a period of ten years, 'writings and pictures', from plagiarism, whether those works dealt with medicine, alchemy, Kabbalah or 'many other, more secret things'. Mention of the Kabbalah here is a timely reminder of the great range of esoteric subjects explored under Rudolf's patronage, and Khunrath lists them for us in his most famous work *The Amphitheatre of Eternal Wisdom* (*Amphitheatrum Sapientiae Aeternae*, 1609): magic, physiognomy, metoscopy, chiromancy, the doctrine of signatures – by which it is meant that every created thing has its particular character, peculiar to itself and yet related in some way to all other signatures – alchemy, astrology, geomancy and Kabbalah, all 'handmaids of true wisdom'. Condemned by the Sorbonne in 1625 in the most virulent terms, largely because of its roots in the teachings of Paracelsus who had been more or less canonized by a number of his more enthusiastic supporters, the *Amphitheatrum* proposes that humans were created in order actively to express their astonishment at God's creation by investigating it further to the benefit of themselves and their neighbours. The way of investigation was, as we have seen from what Khunrath said in his *Confessio*, through prayer and contemplation – this is what the alchemist is doing in the famous engraving, so often reproduced, from Khunrath's work – and during this contemplation and prayer revelation of creation's secrets will be given either directly by God Himself in a vision or some similar state, or indirectly through the teachings of an angel or an adept in the laboratory, or via the observed and observable actions of Nature herself. 'I have', Khunrath said, 'thanks to God, knowledge of the Catholic Trinity, entirely through the mercy of God, and partly from a wise and good master, from his Kabbalistic tradition, and in part from the practice I have spoken of already, and my industrious reading of many philosophic writings and a wise consideration of the good book of Nature.' Thus taught, he maintained, the alchemist will not only achieve greater knowledge of God's creation, but will be able to work wonders him- or herself, becoming a kind of thaumaturge in the divine scheme of things, an ambition or outcome made explicit in the detailed engravings which accompany Khunrath's text.

Khunrath himself denied that any of this amounted to magic, but many did not believe him and he was attacked for gross impiety by several people: by another alchemist, for example, Andreas Libavius, who had been a fellow student with him at the University of Basel. Libavius's argument was that Khunrath approved the teaching of Hermes Trismegistus, an assertion which implied that Khunrath looked favourably upon magic. It was an implication he made again later, in somewhat more overt form, by saying that magicians take pleasure in dogs and that Khunrath carefully added his own dog to the engravings in his *Amphitheatre*. It is the kind of criticism one can see again in Gabriel Naudé's earlier *Instruction à la France sur l'histoire des Frères de la Roze-Croix* (1623) with its references to those who claimed to be following the lead of Paracelsus and reviving a tradition of magic, Hermeticism, and Kabbalah, along with the deceitful tricks of magicians, alchemists, astrologers and [other] charlatans – namely Khunrath, Oswald Croll and Johann Hartmann.[5]

Hartmann (1568–1631) had a distinguished university career in Germany and is often lauded as the first person to be appointed a Professor of Chemistry, although this is not entirely accurate unless one appreciates the considerable overlap in the early modern period between chemistry as we now understand the word, alchemy and chemical medicine (iatrochemistry) so closely allied to alchemy. This alliance, indeed, Hartmann himself emphasized in a public lecture he delivered at the University of Marburg on 4 April 1609, claiming that alchemy 'revealed more than [was done] by all the regular physicians combined', and he promised his listening students that, among other things, he would make known to them the method of manufacturing the potable gold of the alchemist. His interests were thus principally to be found in the practical side of the science – we know, for example, that he wanted to borrow *The Royal Medicine, A Gift from Heaven* (*De medicina regia coelidonia*) by Michael Maier, published from Prague in 1609, a book which contains descriptions of his laboratory work – so it is likely that Naudé's dislike was centred upon Hartmann's Paracelsianism rather than any impious or blasphemous dabbling in magic or Kabbalah. On the other hand, Libavius, who had started off on friendly terms with Hartmann when they were students together at Marburg, later had no hesitation in lambasting him in print, saying he apparently had little fear of being considered weird, and applying such epithets as 'lying', 'stupidity', 'scurrilous jests' and 'impiety' to his work; and while these were particularly inspired by Libavius's hostility to the Paracelsian theories of medical treatment, which Hartmann espoused, it looks as though the common association of Paracelsianism with Hermetic, magical and unorthodox religious opinions was bound to taint anyone who followed or appeared to follow Paracelsian principles.

Much the same can be said of Oswald Croll (c.1560–1609). Like so many alchemists, Croll had been trained as a physician – he too was an alumnus of Hartmann's University of Marburg – and travelled extensively, like a good Paracelsian, before coming to Prague in 1597, settling there permanently in 1602. Again, like any alchemists at this time, Croll was a Protestant (actually a Calvinist), but with highly unorthodox theological ideas he had got from his reading of Paracelsus. True to one of the prevailing intellectual winds of the period, he was also convinced that the old world was about to be overturned and a new world brought to birth. One can therefore see the parallels with alchemical symbolism. Croll's principal treatise was *Royal Alchemy* (*Basilica Chymia*), published at about the time of his death in 1609, with the telling subtitle, 'The alchemical church' – what a remarkable choice of words that is – 'containing a philosophical description, based securely on personal and practical experience, and containing directions for using very select and special alchemical remedies by the light of grace and Nature'. Harmony between the macrocosm and microcosm was the aim of all his therapeutical treatments, and to achieve this end, he believed, spiritual means were much more effective than material remedies, a view which did not, however, prevent his relying on iatrochemistry for the practical prescriptions he provided in his everyday working life.

His recipes, recorded in *Basilica Chymia*, were very specific (one reason, no doubt, for the book's popularity both during and after his lifetime); but he illustrates remarkably well the frequent connection between alchemy, iatrochemistry, magic and medicine and why people such as Libavius deplored in forthright and sometimes virulent terms his work and influence.

> Material for making amulets or talismans in conjunction with planetary influence:
>
> Two ounces of toads dried in the air and the heat of the sun, and reduced to powder under an open sky with what is technically known as a hanging pestle. Make sure your nostrils are blocked or turned away. Eighteen toads produce about two ounces of dust. The menstruum of young girls: as much as can be got. Crystals of white arsenic. An ounce and a half of red arsenic or the same quantity of orpiment. Three drams of dittany root or an equal amount of tormentil. One dram of unpierced pearls. [One dram of] coral. One dram each of fragments of eastern sapphire and eastern emerald. Two scruples of eastern saffron. Several grains of musk or amber can be added for the sake of their pleasant smell.
>
> Everything must be reduced to as fine a powder as possible and mixed together. Then dissolve gum tragacanth in rose-water until it becomes a viscous fluid. Use this and the powders to make a paste and, when the sun and moon are in Scorpio, or the moon is very new, fashion round amulets and mark them with the two pestles under that same celestial influence. If you prefer, you can prepare these protective discs in the shape of a heart, cover them with red muslin, and then suspend them over your undertunic in the region of the heart.
>
> Uses: hang [the amulet] round the neck by a silk cord on top of your clothing. Hang it in the region of the heart over your undertunic. It not only preserves one from the plague but makes the body less susceptible to venereal or astral diseases. It draws out poison from within, and consumes it from without.[6]

Misunderstanding the degree of unorthodoxy in these theories, opinions and practices is, however, all too easy to do. Sympathetic magic was an integral part of medical diagnosis and therapy at this time – as Croll expressed it in his other famous book, *A Treatise on Signatures*, 'all herbs, flowers, trees, and other things which proceed out of the earth are books and magic signs communicated to us by the immense mercy of God, which signs are our medicine'. So too was astrology, so was religion, and so was natural philosophy, and it was precisely this interpenetration of various sciences and disciplines with each other to which Libavius objected. His attack on the Paracelsian Alexander von Suchten, for example, was stimulated by what he saw as Von Suchten's defence of speculative alchemy which, in his view, amounted to magic and mysticism. 'Nothing is to be taken into chemistry which does not properly belong to chemistry' was one of his stringent observations. In other words, 'chemistry' (as we understand the word now) was to concern itself only with physical matter and nothing else.

The proposition may strike us as obvious, but in fact it was Libavius who was startlingly out of step, not Hartmann or Croll or any of the other occult practitioners who thronged the courts of rulers, princes and nobles during the last decades of the sixteenth century and the early years of the seventeenth; and in the overheated religious and political atmosphere of the period, when dissident religious factions and sects were multiplying and struggling for *Lebensraum* in a Europe already torn by confessional religious wars whose suppurating antagonisms were about to break forth again in the Thirty Years' War, alchemy held out a hope not only that wealth could be created, sufficient to pay for mercenaries and thus for victory, but also that its processes of purification and resurrection of matter could resonate in the spiritual realm, and so prepare humankind for the Coming of Christ, which many in Europe saw as imminent. The alchemist could, according to such hopes, re-enact Christian soteriology in his oratory-laboratory, just as Khunrath's pivotal engraving suggested, for during the last 100 years at least, alchemy had been seeping into the consciousness of Europe in a multitude of ways until it was possible for a Catholic, Nicholas Olahus or Nicholas Melchior of Hermanstadt, to present the alchemical process in the form of a Mass, and a Protestant divine such as John Donne to preach in alchemical terms:

> Therefore David who was metal tried seven times in the fire, and desired to be such gold as might be laid up in God's treasury, might consider that in the transmutation of metals, it is not enough to come to a calcination or a liquefaction of the metal . . . Nor to an ablution, to sever dross from pure, nor to a transmutation, to make it a better metal: but there must be a fixation, a settling thereof, so that it shall not evaporate into nothing, nor return to his former state. Therefore he saw that he needed not only a liquefaction, a melting into tears, not only an ablution, and a transmutation, those he had by this purging and this washing . . . but he needed *fixionem* and establishment.
>
> Or here, where the action of the Stone in transmutation parallels the redemptive mission of Christ and the healing power of His sacrificial blood, as the Philosopher's Stone . . . has virtue by means of its tincture and its developed perfection to change other imperfect and base metals into pure gold, so our Heavenly King and fundamental Corner Stone, Jesus Christ, can alone purify us sinners and imperfect men with His blessed ruby-coloured tincture, that is to say, His blood.

We should not be surprised, then, to find that the old-style constant ebb and flow of the various branches of knowledge in and out of each other's shores had immense and widespread appeal in many quarters and this even though it can be acknowledged that those quarters consisted largely of religious nonconformists with idiosyncratic ways of interpreting the aims of their experiments and discoveries. For the Christianizing of the alchemical process and the imagery derived therefrom, which had begun during the Middle Ages, was now virtually at the height of its influence and allure.[7]

7

The Rosicrucian Episode and its Aftermath

The early seventeenth century continued to see people's constant attempt to produce gold by transmutation, and their ever more intricate experiments with a variety of herbs and minerals, intended to manufacture the one elixir which would cure every disease and ailment – the kind of *omnium remedium* described by the shadowy figure of Johann Isaac Hollandius in terms which are reminiscent of those used by Chinese alchemists talking about their mercury-based elixirs.

> This Stone cures skin diseases, plague and every illness which can dominate the earth. It is the true potable gold, the fifth essence sought by the ancients, of which the crowd of philosophers who have concealed its name and operations, has said so many extraordinary things.
>
> Put one grain of this Stone in half a glass of white wine and it will heat the wine. It dissolves as though it were butter. It makes the wine red, and sweetens it so much that sugar cannot add to the sweetness. Let a sick person drink this wine and he will spend very little time in bed. The Stone will go straight to his heart, expel all bad humours from it, draw them, from all his veins and arteries, and eject them through his sweat. This Stone, you see, opens every pore and drives out the humours through them so that the invalid thinks he has been in water. But this sweat does not weaken him, because the Stone does not drive out anything unless it is contrary to Nature. It guards whatever is essentially natural, and so the sick person is not debilitated. The more he sweats, the more he becomes alert and strong, and his veins become lighter. The sweat lasts until every bad humour is expelled from his body, and then it stops.
>
> Next day, give one grain of the Stone in wine, as you did before. At once it will churn up the stomach and will not stop while anything contrary to Nature remains in the body. The more stools there are, the happier and stronger the sick person will be, for the Stone expels only what is inimical to Nature. On the third day, give a grain of the Stone in warm wine. It will fortify the veins and heart so much that the invalid will think he is not a human being but a spirit, because of the lightness and vigour of his limbs.
>
> If anyone were to take a grain every day for nine days, it would be as though he had been in Paradise for nine days and had eaten the fruits which perfect his appearance, his age and his strength. So use one grain of the Stone in warm wine once a week, and you will live in health right up to the time appointed by God.

But in 1603 there were signs in the sky, confusing and troubling to a Europe made tense by apocalyptic expectation and politico-religious tensions. Three times that year there had been a conjunction of Jupiter and Saturn, a significant phenomenon when it happened only once. Thrice, however, was particularly portentous, especially as both planets had moved into Sagittarius, one of the fire signs of the zodiac, a change of position which took place only at the end of a 960-year period, and which was known as 'the great mutation'. Then in October 1604 a new star – a galactic supernova – became visible in the constellation of Ophiuchus. Galileo noted it in his lecture notes:

> On 10 October 1604 a certain strange light was first observed in the heavens. At first it was quite small, but soon it was visible even by daylight, surpassing in brightness all fixed and wandering stars with the exception of Venus. It was red as well as sparkling. It gave off waves of light, which seemed both to kill and set aflame, more than any of the fixed stars and the Dog Star itself. It had the splendid brilliance of Jupiter and the redness of Mars, which is like fire. The contractive quality of these terrible rays announced destruction, as if from the boiling redness of Mars, whilst the expansive quality of these rays gave forth Jupiter's bright lightning.[1]

Clearly something prodigious was afoot: the birth of Antichrist, the Second Coming, the death of the old world and the birth of the new? Possibly the last of these three. In 1604 Johann Valentin Andreae, a Lutheran pastor from Württemberg, composed what he called a *ludibrium*, a bit of a laugh, called *The Chemical Wedding of Christian Rosencreutz in 1459* (*Chymische Hochzeit Christiani Rosencreuz anno 1459*). This no longer exists, but there was a later version, published in 1616, and as nothing about it suggests it was a revision, we may reasonably deduce that Andreae's youthful *ludibrium* probably dealt with alchemy under the form of a wedding between a king and a queen, to which the legendary figure of Christian Rosencreutz had been invited. As we shall see in a moment, the king and queen in the 1616 version symbolically undergo a series of alchemical processes which are clearly to be interpreted as the mystic marriage of the soul to God; so there is every likelihood the 1604 original, like its 1616 counterpart, belonged to that alchemical tradition of religious allegory which by now constituted quite a large part of alchemical literature, and would have chimed with the current Protestant hopes for that reformed and godly Europe to which many people thought the great conjunction and the new star were pointing. One of these people was undoubtedly Andreae himself, for in 1616 he produced a vision for the future in the form of the perfect city, *Christianopolis*, a utopian vision developed, as he tells us, from his personal experience of strict Calvinist discipline and order during the time he spent in Geneva.

But it was not the *Chymische Hochzeit* which initially had a profound effect on the substratum of religious and political life of Europe during the years before the outbreak of the Thirty Years' War. Impact of this kind belonged to another work attributed to Andreae, *News of the Brotherhood* (*Fama Fraternitatis*), published anonymously in German in 1614. Its full title indicates both its scope and tone: 'Universal and General Reformation of the Whole Wide World: together with the *Fama Fraternitatis*, News of the laudable Brotherhood of the Rosy Cross, written to all the erudite and the leaders of Europe: Also a short reply sent by Herr Haselmayer, for which reason he was held prisoner by the Jesuits and chained on a galley. Now put into print and communicated to all loyal hearts.'

The pamphlet – it is scarcely more, despite the length of the title – therefore promises a worldwide (by which it means European) reformation; announces the existence of a kind of monastic order related to Rosencreutz (the German has *Ordens des Rosencreutzes*, which implies a religious organisation); and appends an anti-Jesuit narrative which is there not so much for confessional propaganda as for alerting the readership to Haselmayer's belief that the Rosicrucian brotherhood had come into existence in order to fulfil certain prophecies related to the purging of Europe by Antichrist and the start of a 'Third Age', the Age of the Spirit, and to spread the teaching of Paracelsus whose effect upon Protestant occult writers in particular was growing ever more powerful, especially as he had predicted the appearance of a kind of prophet or interpreter called Elias who would emerge 58 years after his (Paracelsus's) death. (As so often with such prophecies, however, the key year – in this case 1599 – came and went with nothing remarkable happening; but the notion that a figure of international importance was about to make himself known in one way or another was 'in the air', so to speak, and candidates for such a reformer-cum-saviour were by no means hard to find.)

The *Fama* introduces us to Christian Rosencreutz, German founder of the supposed Rosicrucian fraternity. He travelled widely in the Middle East, we are told, and while in Fez learned secrets from erudite men, magicians, Kabbalists, physicians and philosophers. After spending two years in Fez, he moved to Spain where learned men told him that the Church and indeed the entire structure of moral philosophy should be reformed, a message repeated to him elsewhere on his travels, along with the hint that there might exist a society capable of distributing immense wealth to rulers and governors to pay for their good works. Rosencreutz now came back to Germany, an experienced alchemist – this point is emphasized – and built for himself a house of retirement and meditation where he remained for five years before deciding that he should found a fraternity of talented men who would be sworn to virginity. This fraternity was not to be an enclosed order, however. Its members would travel all over the place, but would be bound together by certain rules to which they all agreed. The rules were simple: (1) brethren would concentrate their efforts entirely upon curing the sick, and would do so free of charge; (2) they would wear the clothes of the country in which they happened to be living; (3) they would assemble once a year in the mother-house or send a written apology explaining their absence; (4) each brother would choose some worthy individual to take his place after the brother's death; (5) 'Christian Rosencreutz' would constitute their seal and mark; (6) the existence of the fraternity would be kept secret for 100 years.

A brief history of the subsequent lives of the key members of the community follows, which brings the narrative up to the present day of the writer. We are now told that the time had come for the fraternity's existence to be made known to the German states and for the hitherto secret burial-chamber of Christian Rosencreutz to be opened. This last is done, the burial-chamber described, the tomb opened, and the perfectly preserved body of Christian Rosencreutz discovered, and the pamphlet closes with a short prophecy looking forward to the general reformation of religion in conformity with Protestant teaching, and a denunciation of practical alchemy:

> Now concerning (and chiefly this in our age) the ungodly and accursed gold-making, which hath gotten so much the upper hand, whereby under colour of it, many runagates and roguish people do use great villanies and cozen and abuse the credit which is given them. Yea nowadays men of discretion do hold the transmutation of metals to be the highest point and summit in [natural] philosophy, this is all their intent and desire, and that god would be most esteemed by them, and honoured, which could make great store of gold, and in abundance, the which with unpremeditate prayers, they hope to attain of the all-knowing God and searcher of all hearts. We therefore do by these presents publicly testify that the true philosophers are far of another mind, esteeming little the making of gold, which is but a work of secondary importance.

Since we have been told that Christian Rosencreutz himself was a talented alchemist, this fulmination against the science may seem odd, especially as it is repeated a few lines later: 'we testify that under the name of *chymia*, many books and pictures are set forth in a manner insulting to the glory of God, as we shall name them in due season, and will give to the pure-hearted a catalogue or register of them; and we pray all learned men to take heed of these kind of books, for the Enemy never resteth but soweth his seeds till a stronger one doth root it out.'

The context of these condemnations, however, suggests that spiritual regeneration, not material gain, was the principal thrust and goal of this call to the learned of Europe, and we are already well acquainted with the esoteric side of alchemy, which pursued precisely such an aim.

Nevertheless, it is notable that the second 'Rosicrucian' pamphlet, 'A Short Review of a Somewhat Secret Philosophy, written by Philipp à Gaballa, a student of philosophy, and now brought to light for the first time at Kassel, together with the Testimony of the Brotherhood of the Rosy Cross', ends its renewed call for reform – expressed much in the form of a sermon – with a condemnation of alchemists, both those who seek transmutation of metals and those who look for the ultimate curative elixir, but again in the context of spurning material riches and comfort in favour of spiritual wealth and enlightenment:

> We must earnestly admonish you that you put away, if not all, yet the most books written by false alchemists who do think it but a jest or a pastime, when they either misuse the Trinity, when they do apply it to vain things, or deceive the people with most strange figures and dark sentences and speeches, and cozen the simple of their money; as there are nowadays too many such books set forth, which the Enemy of man's welfare doth daily, and will to the end, mingle among the good seed, thereby to make the truth more difficult to be believed, which in herself is simple, easy, and naked, but contrarily falsehood is proud, haughty, and coloured with a kind of lustre of seeming godly and of humane wisdom. Ye that are wise eschew such books, and turn unto us who seek not your moneys, but offer unto you most willingly our great treasures. We hunt not after your good with invented lying tinctures, but desire to make you partakers of our goods . . . But those thinking such great riches [of alchemical gold] should never fail, might easily be corrupted and brought to idleness and to riotous proud living, we desire that they would not trouble us with their idle and vain crying. But let them think that although there be a medicine to be had which might fully cure all diseases, nevertheless those whom God hath destined to plague with diseases and to keep under the rod of correction, such shall never obtain any such medicine.

What makes these condemnations of practical alchemy the more noteworthy is that both the *Fama* and the *Confessio* were published in 1614 and 1615 respectively (although the *Fama* had been circulating in manuscript since 1610 or 1611), in Kassel where the Landgrave of Hesse-Kassel encouraged the pursuit of alchemy and other occult sciences, and acted as a patron of several scholars learned in these subjects – he appointed the Swiss Paracelsian and alchemist Raphael Iconius Eglinus lecturer in Hermetic studies at the University of Marburg, for example. It is clear, of course, that the pamphlets condemn only cheats and greedy frauds and urge, if only by implication, a quite different form of alchemy. Even so, issuing as they did from the press of the Landgrave's official printer, their deliberate side-swipe at alchemy (which need not have been included, since the bulk of both works is concerned with other subjects and does not depend on any references to alchemy in order to make its points) strikes one at first glance as a little bold and perhaps a trifle tactless under the circumstances. A closer look, however, suggests that the true meaning of the criticism is somewhat different.[2]

The message itself was commonplace enough, of course. In the words of St Paul, 1 Timothy 6.10, usually misquoted, 'The love of money is the root of all evil', a proverb we can see illustrated in one of the Rosicrucian emblems of Daniel Cramer, published in 1617. Emblem 32, 'Slime: Excrement', shows an elderly man on his knees, hands raised and clasped in an attitude of prayer, in front of a huge open chest filled with gold coins, an over-large heart balanced on top of them; and there is a superscription from Matt. 6.21, 'Where your treasure is, there will your heart be also'. But if Andreae was indeed the author of the *Fama* and *Confessio* (and there are still doubts on this point), his condemnation of practical alchemy and implicit approval of spiritual alchemy embodied in the figure of his 'hero', the alchemist Christian Rosencreutz, makes perfectly good sense with the publication of his youthful fantasy, the *Chymische Hochzeit*, inasmuch as its complex alchemical symbolism is clearly allied to the central messages of the *Fama* and *Confessio*. A new golden age should, must be, will be initiated on German soil under the aegis of Protestantism. People will learn to value the true gold of this invigorated reformation over the false glitter of mere worldly wealth, and the superficially attractive deceptions of fraudulent alchemists will no longer have power to seduce them. So who are these fraudulent alchemists who, together with their books, are to be avoided? On one level, alchemical charlatans, the deliberate deceivers or pretentious claimants we have met quite often already; on another, Catholics – in the words of the *Confessio*, 'Romish seducers who have vomited forth their blasphemies against Christ, and as yet do not abstain from their lies in this clear, shining light', part of a passage which immediately precedes the author's condemnation of 'false alchemists'.[3]

Separating the history of alchemy from that of the Rosicrucian movement is well nigh impossible, but sheer space precludes me from pursuing the idea of the brotherhood in any detail. Did the Rosicrucian fraternity as described by these manifestos actually exist? Almost certainly not. Were there precedents for such a brotherhood? Plenty. Vilém Rozmberk for example, whom we have met as the most important patron of alchemy in Bohemia at the end of the sixteenth century, invited many alchemists to his city of Cesky Krumlov, and there provided a large building (which still stands) to house meetings of his Alchemy Guild, an organization which began in a relatively informal way in 1576 and evolved into an association of alchemical practitioners whose work largely concentrated on the transmutation of metals, the production of elixirs and the refinement of laboratory processes. But in any case, Andreae would have not had to look further than the German states for any number of models for his supposed fraternity, for Germany was awash with secret or semi-secret societies, and informal groups of *eruditi*, such as those who came to stay in, and went from, Prague, providing a network of more or less like-minded scholars and practitioners of the occult sciences, who spread their ideas, often somewhat unorthodox, throughout Europe and provided a ready audience for publications such as the Rosicrucian manifestos. This complex river and its tributaries can be illustrated here by only one or two examples, and perhaps the three most obvious to choose are the Pole, Michał Sediwój, commonly known by the Latin form of his name, Sendivogius, the German Michael Maier, both of whom were for a while protégés of Rudolf II and active at his Court in Prague, and 'Nicolas Flamel', the name attached to a series of hieroglyphic figures which set out to draw direct parallels between alchemical imagery and Christian imagery.

Michał Sediwój (1556–1636) came from a Poland which had a rich tradition of teaching the occult sciences in the Jagiellonian University of Kraków despite an official ban on doing so. The publication in Latin of two of Paracelsus's works in 1569, however, stimulated interest in alchemy even further, to the chagrin and active opposition of the Church, but with enthusiastic royal approval – both Zygmunt II and Zygmunt III supported alchemical laboratories – alchemy flourished in its speculative and its practical aspects. Sediwój came from a noble Polish family and was almost certainly educated in Kraków where he could not fail to come into contact with alchemy. He then travelled extensively in Europe where he met and maintained contact with several scholars who were eager that alchemy be recognized officially as a university discipline, and in 1593 came to Prague where he entered Rudolf's service as a diplomatist while performing a similar function for his own king, Zygmunt III. His enthusiasm for alchemy was enhanced by the contact he made in both countries – indeed, it is believed that alchemical experiments he was conducting in the royal castle in Kraków in 1595 set the place on fire, causing the King (and hence the Polish capital) to move to Warsaw the following year. In Prague Sediwój worked under the patronage of Ludvik Koralek who took a keen interest in alchemy and funded several other alchemists, too, and there in 1604, after having spent nearly four years back home in Poland, he is said to have transmuted a base metal into gold in the presence of the Emperor and many other witnesses. But the following year he made the mistake of visiting the Duke of Württemberg in Stuttgart, and was held under house arrest in the hope he would give the Duke and the Duke's Court alchemist, Heinrich Mühlenfels, his secret; and there he stayed until Rudolf intervened and he was allowed to go home to Poland. The incident seems to have cured him of giving public demonstrations of his alchemical abilities, and he spent the rest of his life in less dangerous pursuits.

As so often happens, legend accrued to him, and fantastic embroidery of his career and discoveries was made after his death, including identifying him and fusing him with a Scotsman, Alexander Seton, and a contemporary Polish alchemist, Alexander von Suchten. Such legends apart, however, it is clear he actually did discover oxygen 170 years before the discovery usually attributed to Priestley and Scheele, and we know he published a number of books, including *The Philosophers' Stone* (*De lapide philosophorum*, 1604), later re-titled *A New Alchemical Light* (*Novum Lumen Chymicum*), and *A Treatise on Sulphur* (*Tractatus de sulphure*, 1616). Our interest in Sediwój at this point, however, lies in his authorship of a set of *Statutes* for a society of 'unknown philosophers', which was first published anonymously in Paris in 1691. Zbigniew Szydło has made a convincing case for their originating with Sediwój; even more interesting,

Rafał Prinke has suggested that Sediwój may, in fact, have provided a model for
the figure of Christian Rosencreutz, and similarities between these *Statutes* and
the *Fama* are immediately obvious. The preface describes someone who, faced
by the dreadful times in which everyone was living, decided to form a society for
the propagation of Hermetic science, whose members would keep their identity
a secret. The *Statutes* themselves lay down the organization of such a society,
qualities required of members, how to recruit new members, and how to make
use of the stone. In this last, however, lies a major overt difference between the
Statutes and the *Fama*, for 'Sediwój's' society is clearly one in which alchemical
work in the laboratory is to occupy the members, not Paracelsian medicine.
Otherwise, secrecy, strong religious convictions, lamentation for conditions in
contemporary Europe, and the desire to use wealth acquired from the brethren's
activities for a wider social good, are the notable points they have in common.

Sediwój thus rescues practical alchemy from the defamation it suffered at
the hands of Andreae (or whoever wrote the *Fama* and *Confessio*), as does his
contemporary, Michael Maier (1568–1622). Maier trained as a physician, getting
his doctorate in medicine from Basel, and then returned to Germany where
he went into practice for a while and discovered an interest in alchemy. Both
disciplines took him to Prague in 1608 where, a year later, he became physician
and counsellor to Rudolf II. Between 1611 and 1616 Maier visited the Court of
James VI and I in England, and while there took the opportunity to meet Sir
William Paddy, President of the College of Physicians, to whom he dedicated
his first publication, *Mystery of Mysteries* (*Arcana arcanorum*, 1614), and the
alchemist Francis Anthony who claimed to have discovered how to make potable
gold; and it is likely he also met one of Sir William Paddy's friends, Robert Fludd,
another physician with alchemical and mystical interests, whose red elixir, he
said, was to all intents and purposes the body and blood of Christ in alchemical
form, an effectual Catholicizing of alchemy which was by no means peculiar
to him and which can be seen underlying the older conception of Christ as the
philosopher's stone. Maier was thus part of that loose network of Protestant
and dissenting individuals bound together by their interest in and practice of
the occult sciences, who behaved as a kind of leaven to the apocalyptic hopes for
change and reform in Europe, and to whose aspirations the various Rosicrucian
manifestos acted as a stimulant; and although Maier himself never claimed to
be a member of the Rosicrucian fraternity, he defended it in his *Silence after
Shouting* (*Silentium post clamores*, 1617), and purported to reveal further details
about it in his *Golden Order* (*Themis Aurea*, 1618).

Both appeared during a remarkable period of about four years during which
Maier produced six other books dealing with alchemy in one way or another.
De circulo physico quadrato draws a parallel between the human heart, gold and
the sun; *Lusus Serius* contains an allegory about Mercury (the pagan god) and

mercury (the alchemical substance), and associates them with Christ; *Symbola aureae mensae duodecim nationum* is a history of alchemy from its supposed origins to Maier's time; *Examen fucorum pseudochymicorum* criticizes the pretentious mountebanks, among whom he includes John Dee's companion, Edward Kelley, who had stayed on in Bohemia to concentrate on alchemical work after Dee's departure, and had come to a bad end after being arrested and imprisoned for fraud; and *Viatorium* is a practical guide for the laboratory alchemist. But the work which has won him most fame is *Atalanta in Flight* (*Atalanta Fugiens*, 1617), a book of emblems which take the reader, via the emblem itself and the Latin verse which accompanies it, through the growth of metals, the operation of male and female principles in creation, the death and resurrection of the alchemical 'King', and the production of the stone itself, using a series of Greek myths on which to base his illustrations.

What makes *Atalanta Fugiens* particularly interesting is the music which is meant to accompany the Latin epigrams. As John Read has pointed out, music had long been considered an important part of the alchemical interpretation of the universe, partly because it saw a mystical relationship between numbers – we have noted this already in Muslim alchemy, too – a perception stemming from Pythagoras and reinforced by Kabbalah, which manipulated the numerical values of Hebrew letters for magical purposes. Music set moods according to the mode which was being played, and it is possible that some working alchemists used music in their laboratory to induce effects within themselves and thus affect the various stages of their experiments. One notes, for example, that in Khunrath's engraving of the oratory-laboratory, the central table bears several musical instruments and a Latin motto, 'Sacred music disperses sadness and evil spirits because the spirit (*spiritus*) rejoices cheerfully in a heart filled with devout joy'. *Spiritus* is, among other things, a technical term for various kinds of particles which travelled through the bloodstream, and were expedited from the liver to the heart and thence into the brain. Alchemical distillation manipulated these *spiritus* in the substances it used, and they were thus open to change and alteration, and it is therefore interesting to find that, according to an illustration from the *Révélation des mystères des teintures essentielles des sept métaux* (1668), attributed to 'Basil Valentine', the steps to wisdom consist of a series of seven: seven metals, the seven planets, seven masters of the science, including 'Hermes', Geber, and Basil Valentine himself, the musical scale represented by seven organ stops, and the seven strings of the viol, which is accompanied by the motto, 'Sacred harmony puts evil spirits to flight and is medicine for insanity'. Maier's canons, therefore, may have had a practical purpose within the laboratory, although James Haar has drawn attention to the possibility that such music may have had a part in intellectual games played at the Imperial Court: an emblem would be shown to the participants and audience, its accompanying epigram sung, and then selected speakers would display their learning and wit in disquisitions (perhaps extempore) on the subject matter. Neither suggestion, of course, precludes the other.[4]

These years of Maier's productiveness coincided with the heyday of the alchemical emblem book. In 1616, for example, Stefan Michelspacher, a Tyrolean physician, published *Cabala, Spiegel der Kunst und Natur*, whose illustrations depict themes from the biblical Apocalypse in alchemical terms; in 1622, Johann Daniel Mylius, yet another student of medicine, published *Philosophia Reformata* in which 60 pictures, arranged in blocks of four, show the separate stages of the Great Work leading to the production of the stone; and in 1624, Daniel Stoltzius von Stoltzenberg, a Bohemian alchemist and physician, reproduced many of the emblems from both Maier and Mylius in his own *Viridarium Chymicum*, a piece of plagiarism so successful that he and his publisher, Lucas Jennis who had been responsible for Maier's and Mylius's books, decided to plunder them yet again for another book along the same lines, *Hortulus Hermeticus*, which appeared in 1627. To these we should add the earlier *Exposition of the Hieroglyphicall Figures* attributed to Nicolas Flamel, which was first published in a French edition in 1612. Flamel was a real historical figure who was born in 1330 and died in 1418. Together he and his wife, Pernelle, practised the art of transmutation, reputedly with great success, and this of course was sufficient to have all kinds of rumours and legends cluster about his name, many derived from the introduction to the *Exposition*, which claims to be autobiographical.

The images now published with the *Exposition*, however, did not appear with the text until the 1670s. But they are described by the text, and what we have there consists of an introduction, two chapters giving the reader instructions on how to read the emblems, first according to theological interpretation, then according to Hermetic philosophy, and seven representing the seven stages of the Great Work, each of which chapters summarizes its emblem in a few phrases and adds the colours which are meant to accompany the drawing, instructions which remind us that colours are not to be applied to these pictures in accordance with personal whim, but in harmony with the schemes appropriate to the subject matter and significant of the themes represented by the individual emblem. The seven chapters go as follows.

1 Two dragons, to be painted yellowish, blue and black on a black background. This is the *nigredo* stage in which putrefaction and the purging of the *prima materia* set in. The yellowish and blue colours indicate that the process is under way; the black is a sign of the intended goal.

2 A man and a woman clothed in orange upon a light blue and darker blue background. They are encircled by a scroll bearing the two sentences, 'Humankind will come to the judgement of God. Truly that day will be

dreadful'. Here the four elements represented by contrary sexual natures are to be united. The references to the Last Day show the violence attendant upon this process out of which will emerge the hermaphrodite child, the cleansed result of its parents' 'death' in putrefaction. The predominant orange of this emblem, however, shows that the stage is not yet finished.

3 A figure like St Paul, wearing white and yellow bordered with gold, holds an unsheathed sword. A man kneels before him, clothed in orange, black and white, and holds a scroll which says, 'Destroy the evil things I have done'. Putrefaction is still continuing, the process a violent one, as shown by the naked sword. But the appearance of several colours, and especially the white and yellow of St Paul's robe, shows that the purification is proving successful because, as the text explains, 'Nature always tends to perfection, which thou shalt accomplish by the apposition of virgin's milk and by the decoction of the matters which thou shalt make with this milk, which being dried upon the body, will colour it into this same white yellow which he who takes the sword is clothed withal'.

4 On a green field appear three people, two men and a woman, who have been raised from the dead on the Day of Judgement, all in white. Above them are two angels playing musical instruments, the bagpipes and a lute, and, dominant above them all, the figure of Christ clothed in perfect citrine. Here unmistakably Christ is identified as the philosopher's stone – an allegorical conjunction we have met before – while the presence of music at this stage of the process suggests a harmony of what is above with what is below, as well, perhaps, as hinting at the use of music in the laboratory.

5 Two angels in golden citrine red upon a field of violet and blue. They carry a scroll saying, 'Come, ye dead, to the judgement of the Lord'. This is the *rubedo* stage, the process of reddening, with the angels representing sulphur and mercury. The variety of colours shows that we have reached the moment of the peacock's tail when the matter in the alchemist's vessel passes through a variety of colours in quick succession.

6 A figure like St Peter clothed in citrine red, with a key in his right hand, lays his left hand on the shoulder of a kneeling woman who is wearing a dress of the same citrine red. Her scroll says, 'Christ, I pay that you be just'. St Peter holds a key because St Peter is the guardian of Heaven, and (if we remember that he is described as a figure *like* St Peter) he is the alchemist who holds the key to successful production of the stone and accomplishment of transmutation.

7 Finally, a man wearing imperial crimson is surmounted by a winged red lion against a dark violet field. He holds the foot of the lion which looks as though it is about to seize him and carry him off, and we are told that the lion (i.e. the stone) is in fact the woman who has cast off her disguise and is now capable

of raising the man out of poverty and sickness and taking him to realms far above the mere physical and material. From her mouth issues the word, 'Mine', as she accepts what appears to be the man's complete surrender.[5]

This fusion of religion and laboratory process, however significant it was in certain widespread intellectual circles in Europe during the early years of the seventeenth century, should not make us forget that alongside these refined and esoteric exercises there still existed the 'puffer', the practical alchemist whose aim was simply to produce alchemical gold in such quantities as to win him a patron, make him rich and give him access to more lucrative and more socially respectable ways of making a living. Playwrights, for example, continued to mock him as a cheat and incompetent. The Englishman Ben Jonson, as is well known, wrote his satire on practitioners of the science, *The Alchemist*, in 1610 and published it two years later. Herein he pokes fun at the extraordinarily various substances alchemists used as their basic matter, and concludes:

> That alchemy is a pretty kind of game,
> Somewhat like tricks o' the cards, to cheat a man
> With charming . . . What else are all your terms,
> Whereon no one o' your writers 'grees with other?
> Of your elixir, your lac virginis,
> Your stone, your med'cine, and your chrysosperm,
> Your sal, your sulphur, and your mercury,
> Your oil of height, your tree of life, your blood,
> Your marchesite, your tutie, your magnesia,
> Your toad, your crow, your dragon, and your panther,
> Your sun, your moon, your firmament, your adrop,
> Your lato, azoch, zernich, chibrit, heautarit,
> And then your red man and your white woman,
> With all your broths, your menstrues, and materials
> Of piss, and egg-shells, women's terms, man's blood,
> Hair o' the head, burnt clouts, chalk, merds, and clay,
> Poulder of bones, scalings of iron, glass,
> And worlds of other strange ingredients,
> Would burst a man to name? (Act 2, scene 3).

Likewise, in 1616 Johann Andreae wrote a comedy, *Turbo*, in which the feckless youth of the title indulges himself with one daft scheme after another, including alchemy. Needless to say, he is swindled by a conman called Beger (i.e. 'Geber'), who is mocked by Harlequin, Turbo's companion throughout the play. Harlequin is given to passing satirical comments on what he sees and the foolish people he meets. 'I know a good poem about alchemy,' he says to the charlatan alchemist:

1. Wei Po-Yang and a disciple. Wei Po-Yang wrote the first surviving Chinese book on alchemy (c.AD 142). The dog and the pupil were essential to his experiments.

FIGURE 2 – *The preparation of the pill of immortality according to Shang-yang-tzu.*

Yang is represented by the man, dragon, and fire; *Yin* by the woman, tiger, and water in the forms of clouds, rain, and hail. The tortoise and the serpent, symbolizing the material embodiments of *Yang* and *Yin*, further represent the combination of the Two Contraries.

(Reproduced from the Ming edition of the Chin Tan Ta Yao [*Essentials of the Gold Medicine*], *written by Shang-yang-tzu, otherwise Ch'ên Kuan-wu, during the Chih-shun reign of the Yüan dynasty* (A.D. 1330–33).)

2. Preparation of the elixir of immortality. The man, the dragon, and the fire represent *yang*, the male balancing power within the universe. The woman, the tiger, and the water represent *yin*, the female balancing power.

3. *Right:* Nāgārjuna. There were several authors of this name, and a number of them had alchemical works attributed to them. Their dates range from the second century AD to at least the tenth.

4. *Below:* Maria the Jewess. She was credited with inventing several pieces of alchemical apparatus, including the bain-marie for the distillation of liquids, and the tribikos, a still with three funnels and receivers in which distilled vapours are condensed. This picture shows her pointing to the white herb growing upon a mountain, a herb which is mentioned several times in teachings attributed to her.

5. *Above:* Avicenna: Abu Ali al-Husain ibn Abdallah ibn Sinā. Along with al-Razī (Rhazes), Avicenna was one of the best known of the Islamic alchemists from the late tenth and early eleventh century, a period when Islamic alchemy was at its height. The postage stamps show his continuing fame in the Islamic world.

6. *Left:* A table of alchemical symbols, from Basil Valentine's work. It shows not only those for the seven planets but also for the four elements, essential ingredients, and the principal stages of the Work itself.

OPVSCVLE
TRES-EXCELLENT,
DE LA VRAYE PHILOSOPHIE
naturelle des Metaux.

Traictant de l'augmentation & perfection d'iceux.
Auec vn aduertissement d'euiter les folles despenses
qui se font par faute de vraye science.

Par Maistre D. Zacaire Gentilhomme Guiennois.

Plus le traitté de M. Bernard Allemand Compte
de la Marche Treuisane.

Derniere edition reueu & corrigé de nouueau.

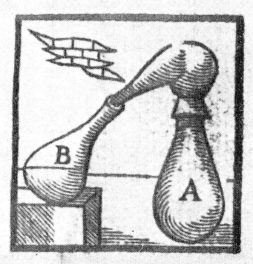

A LYON,
Chez Pierre Rigaud, en ruë Merciere, au coing de ruë
Ferrandiere à l'enseigne de la Fortune.

M. DCXII.

---

7. Title page of Denis Zacaire's supposed autobiography, the account of an alchemist's trials and misfortunes in his pursuit of the alchemical goal of transmutation.

A particular Experiment.

8. An alchemical recipe from an eighteenth-century manuscript, now kept in St Andrews University Library.

9. A nineteenth-century version of an alchemist at work. It is clearly derived from sixteenth and seventeenth-century engravings, none of which should be taken as photographs, but rather impressions appealing to a general public view of what an alchemist ought to look like.

10. One of the fifteen engravings from the seventeenth-century *Mutus Liber*, a book which formed the basis for experiments in alchemy during the twentieth century.

It is an art without art,
Whose sum total is a part without a part,
Whose truths are to tell tall stories,
Whose mother is to take a holiday,
Whose prayer is to be blackened,
Whose reputation is to be chronicled,
Whose proof is to lie,
Whose method is to be obstructed,
Whose task is to fill with wind,
Whose reward is to beg,
Whose end is to despair,
Whose payment is not to settle down anywhere,
Whose punishment is to perish
And to die on a cross.

Sarcasm and invective are to be found plentifully scattered in non-dramatic works, too. Thomas Lodge produced a portrait of poor puffers in his *Anatomie of Alchymie* (1595):

Old, clotheless, meatless, smelling brimstone still,
Besmeared with coal dust from their furnace brought,
Plagued with the palsy (lechers common ill),
By temp'ring of quicksilver quickly caught;
Their riches are the droppings of their nose,
Where else beside, the slaves are brought so low,
That for three farthings they will beg and glose,
And sell their souls, and teach whate'er they know.

And it was against just such social oddities that Gabriel Plattes issued his warning about 50 years later in his pamphlet 'A Caveat for Alchymists, or, a Warning to all ingenious Gentlemen, whether Laicks or Clericks, that study for the finding out of the Philosophers Stone: shewing how that they need not to be cheated of their Estates, either by the perswasion of others, or by their own idle conceits'.

But we must not run away with the idea that literature as a whole was hostile to alchemy. On the contrary, both the verse and prose of the late sixteenth and early seventeenth century took advantage of their readers' ready familiarity with much of the theory and technical vocabulary of the science, and played upon that with as many variants as they could manage. In English, Donne, Herbert, Vaughan and Milton all use alchemical images, similes and metaphors in the confident belief that their allusions will be understood at once; and it is striking that, by and large (there are exceptions to every rule), they employ alchemy, not for purposes of satire or invective, but in order to convey a sense of the sublime, of refinement, of higher aspiration and attainment. Donne's *Anatomie of the*

World (1633), for example, contains a eulogy of Elizabeth Tudor, expressed in just such terms:

> She of whom th'ancients seem'd to prophesy,
> When they call'd virtues by the name of 'she';
> She in whom virtue was so much refin'd,
> That for allay unto so pure a mind,
> She took the weaker sex; she that could drive
> The poisonous tincture, and the stain of Eve,
> Out of her thoughts and deeds; and purify
> All by a true religious alchemy. (vv. 175–82)

Likewise, Abraham Cowley praised Charles I in 1636:

> Where, dreaming Chymics, is your pain and cost?
> How is your oil, how is your labour lost?
> Our Charles, blest alchemist (though strange,
> Believe it, future times), did change
> The iron age of old
> Into an age of gold.

Novels or romances, too, happily used alchemy or the figure of the alchemist and his or her quest for transmutation either as elements in their tales, or as their subject matter, often linked (as one might expect) with love and sex. Thus, *Le cabinet de Minerve* (1596) by François Béroalde de Verville uses alchemy as a vehicle for reflections upon the moral and spiritual advancement of the individual, while his *Voyage des princes fortunez* (1610) seizes upon the current hope for a transformation of contemporary Europe into an ideal state; and *La Carithée* (1621) by Marin Le Roy de Gomberville, which is essentially a love story and travelogue, is filled with passages which depend entirely on alchemical imagery or associations, as when the hero recounts a journey he once made in Arabia Felix where he discovered a fantastic garden with seven streams, each of which represents one stage of the Great Work. To get to this garden, the hero and his companion had to cross a big, deep ditch filled with black water, but once arrived they saw that the seven streams had different colours: the first red, the second white, the third whitish, the fourth merely dirty, the fifth likewise. The sixth, bubbling and foul, was reminiscent of the ancient quarrel between Jupiter and Saturn; and the seventh was filthier and more stinking than any of the others. So the hero and his companion are seeing the stages of the Work in the reverse order in which these actually happen.

If writers of all kinds were thus able to call upon alchemy to illustrate their various themes, it was because practical alchemy continued to be widespread and therefore familiar. The composer Monteverdi, for example, wrote to Ercole

Marigliani in August 1625 about a slightly odd experiment with gold and lead, in which fumes from the heated lead were supposed to reduce the gold to a state where it became almost too thin to feel, and an attempt to make mercury from unrefined matter; and further letters dated September that same year and February 1626 indicate that the two men were continuing to work with mercury. In England, the Welsh landowner, Sir Owen Wynne, whose family had lead and other mineral deposits on their land, which they were keen to exploit, was very interested in the possibility of transmuting lead into copper, and in 1629 bought a large collection of alchemical and metallurgical manuscripts and books to help advise him in the necessary techniques. Adriaen Metius, a Dutch physician and Professor of Mathematics at the University of Franeker, is said to have spent a fortune on alchemy; and one even finds alchemy carried over the Atlantic into the New World where John Winthrop the Younger (1606–76), later a Fellow of the Royal Society of London, conducted alchemical experiments in an effort to find the philosopher's stone.[6]

But alchemy did not confine itself to literature or the theatre, whether laudatory, satirical or occasional. Laurinda Dixon and Petra ten-Doesschate Chu have argued that it may be the key to interpreting a number of pictures hitherto presenting puzzles to the viewer, and they give as an example the *Royal Repast in a Cave*, painted in 1660 by Gerbrandt van den Eeckhout who had been one of Rembrandt's students in the mid-1630s. The picture shows an old king dressed in a red robe and a golden cape, seated in a cave at a table on which are placed a goblet of wine, a loaf of bread and a peacock. Three male attendants clad in dark blue, white and yellow, offer him a sheaf of wheat, a dead hare and a dish of stones, and they are accompanied by two dogs, one russet-coloured, the other grey and white. Towards the back of the cave can be discerned four winged figures chained together. One is a black boy with a glowing halo; another a pale, thin old man; and a third has red highlights in his hair and along his wings. Alchemical interpretation of these features sees the four figures as representations of the four elements, the dogs as dualities in the alchemical process – hot-dry, cold-moist, sulphur-mercury, and so forth – the three attendants as body-soul-spirit, or mercury-sulphur-salt, or Father-Son-Holy Spirit, and their offerings as emblems of the three material realms, animal-vegetable-mineral. The items on the king's table remind us of the bread and wine of the Mass, the ultimate transformative action, and the rapid changes of colour, which show that the transformation is reaching its critical but successful stage. The old King himself is the basic material which is to be changed into the stone, and the firelight which illumines the cave tells us that this change will be worked by the violent action of fire. An axe and a flail on the floor of the cave represent this violence, and the cave itself is a reminder that metals, stones and minerals grow within the womb of the earth.

The picture has been interpreted in other ways, although perhaps not so convincingly, but if one asks why a painting probably intended at first for private rather than public viewing should embody such a wealth of esoteric emblems, the answer is that to its original audience the subject matter was not especially esoteric. If theatre audiences could pick up alchemical allusions without difficulty, so could onlookers of art. A similarly rich painting, dense in occult symbolism, is an altar-piece from Bad Teinach in Germany, dated to 1673 and apparently painted for one of the family of Frederick I, Duke of Württemberg, whose interest in and encouragement of alchemy we have met before. The painting's central panel shows a garden in the centre of which stands the resurrected Christ at the nub of 12 flower beds arranged so as to form a kind of wheel, with 12 figures attended by a mass of complex symbols clearly representing the tribes of Israel, the Apostles and the signs of the zodiac. Beyond Christ rises a domed temple approached by seven stages, with two pillars each carrying a helix of seven turns – and so on and so forth. The picture is one of immense detail comprising symbols of both Kabbalah and alchemy, and yet these are all perfectly comprehensible to anyone who has rudimentary knowledge of both, and rich enough to provide matter for endless meditation.

If literature, theatre and art could draw upon the amalgam of Hermetic, Kabbalistic and alchemical emblems, vocabulary and theories with which intellectual life in the seventeenth century was imbued, one can expect to find them elsewhere, too, and sure enough architecture also bears their imprint in various ways. The walled garden at Edzell Castle in Scotland was probably built, as a plaque over its entrance suggests, in 1604, and its walls contain three sets of seven carved panels representing the seven planets/ liberal arts/ cardinal virtues, with seven pointed stars set in bays between these images. The lairds of Edzell were the Lindsays, and Sir David Lindsay, Earl of Balcarres (1585–1641), was a practising alchemist with an interest in and possible connection to the Rosicrucian movement elsewhere in Europe; and so Adam McLean has tentatively suggested 'that the Edzell Garden of the Planets should be seen as an early seventeenth-century Mystery Temple connected with the Hermetic revival'. He likewise draws our attention to an alchemical gate in Rome, dating to the late seventeenth century, which carries signs of six of the planets on its jambs and the seventh upon the doorstep itself. Ten Latin inscriptions have been carved into the frame, seven of which clearly refer to the seven stages of the alchemical process.[7]

During the first half of the century, all this managed to flourish in spite of the Thirty Years' War (1618–48) which brought to an end the largely Protestant hopes for a Church and Empire reformed and renewed through application of Hermetic and alchemical philosophies such as those which had flourished under Rudolf II, and in spite of an intellectual atmosphere increasingly tinged by the proposition of Descartes that creation was nothing more than a mechanism, and humans and animals mere automata. The usual explanation for the origin of this notion is that when Descartes joined the Dutch army in 1618 as a gentleman volunteer, he watched the soldiers being trained in the use of firearms, and noted that after a while they began to act and drill as though they were automata, without minds or wills of their own, although Paul MacDonald has suggested that this impression may have been assisted in part by a different experience.

Rudolf II, as is well known, had accumulated an immense collection of marvels which were set out for display in a labyrinth of rooms in Prague Castle. MacDonald argues that Descartes saw this collection in November 1620, just before it was dispersed, and that the sight of the mirrors and false walls which helped to create optical illusions, the alchemical laboratories and (perhaps most suggestive) the mechanical automata, set in motion what turned out to be his most distinctive hypothesis. His followers, however – or, at any rate, those who followed him – found it difficult, although not always impossible, to carry on alchemical work when assailed by doubts about the underlying natural philosophy of their science, and we find a renewal of that intellectual battle between proponents and opponents of alchemy which, in different terms, had been waged earlier during the Middle Ages. Thus, the Dane Ole Borch (1626–90), wrote in his *Dissertation on the Rise and Progress of Alchemy* (*De ortu et progressu chemiae dissertatio*, 1668):

> This subtle philosophy of Descartes is quite useful for penetrating the mysteries of alchemy/chemistry in as much as it makes one think about everything, including the three little particles, like a stone to sharpen [al]chemical spirits and a path leading to more sublime realities. However, one cannot deny that while his demonstrations make him dominant in mathematics, Descartes has found himself brought to a halt in the realm of metals, vanquished by the diversity of phenomena, and has dearly longed for experiments which could direct his subtle mind during its meditation, and that runs counter to the character of many Cartesians for whom nothing is more familiar today than to consider everything from assumed axioms and to do without experiments.[8]

The 'little particles' referred to here were regarded as the smallest parts of the various elements and as fundamentally different from one another. They derive from the notion that the elements act as repositories or wombs for 'seeds' – Libavius thought these seeds were the equivalent of Democritus's atoms – and that together the seeds and elements produce the 'bodies' of created things, the seeds giving each thing its essential characteristics and particular qualities. It is a theory which, at first reading, seems to lend itself to the new mechanist philosophy, since it seems to suggest that everything can be conceived simply in terms of size and weight and shape – a reductionist view, in fact. But we need to bear in mind that by the mid-seventeenth century it was clear that alchemy had, as Bruce Moran puts it, 'entered a phase of cultural metamorphosis', and there was an increasing tendency for 'chemistry' to be separated from 'alchemy'. This was partly because recent experience of alchemy had located it in royal and noble courts in which it almost invariably rubbed shoulders with other occult sciences, especially astrology and Paracelsianism; and partly because it was so easily and commonly associated with fraudulent gold-making and wild claims about the benefits of its elixirs. (Margaret Cavendish, for example, could toss into her autobiography (1656) the offhand remark that her husband occupied his time with horses and swordsmanship, 'and though he hath taken as much pains in those arts ... as [al]chemists for the Philosopher's Stone, yet he hath this advantage of them: that he hath found the right and the truth thereof and therein, which [al]chemists never found their art, and I believe never will'.) French academics in particular, as might be expected, tended to follow Descartes and his deep scepticism with regard to any knowledge inherited from the past. Hence 'chemistry' needed to be purged of its increasingly embarrassing associations with alchemy which leaned upon that past since, perhaps most difficult for the modernists to swallow, it had philosophical and spiritual as well as practical agenda, and in consequence 'was laundered', in Moran's words, 'so as to have an untraceable history' and provided with a claim 'to be a distinct and unprecedented form of knowledge possessing its own rational mode of discovery'. Only thus could it be rendered respectable and conformable to the new and fashionable Cartesianism. Of such considerations are academic careers and reputations made.[9]

8

Theology Wearing a Mask of Science: The Later Seventeenth Century

The growing distance between past-informed and present-inspired disciplines was expressed by Johannes Baptista van Helmont (1579–1644), a Flemish physician, in his *Magnetic Cure of Wounds* (*De magnetica vulnerum curatione*, 1621). 'Nature', he wrote, 'did not call theologians to be her interpreters, but desired only physicians to be her sons', and 'the theologian should inquire about God and the natural philosopher about Nature'. Yet van Helmont, in spite of several notions which took him over the verge of religious unorthodoxy, was by no means a man of the new intellectual order, and when it came to alchemy, for example, he accepted the validity of transmutation and indeed used a sample of the stone given to him by a stranger to transform some mercury into gold, a feat he managed, according to his own account, on more than one occasion. There are notable parallels here with Johann Friedrich Schweitzer, known as 'Helvetius' (1625–1709), a Dutch physician, who also left an account of being visited by a stranger who engaged him in conversation about the philosopher's stone and showed him three samples of it, 'sulphur-coloured, almost transparent lumps of stone about the size of a walnut'. Schweitzer examined the stones carefully and managed to scrape off a little of their substance with which he later tried a transmutation, but without success. A second visit from the stranger revealed that the stone had to be covered in yellow wax to protect its powers from the vapours given off by melting lead, and when Schweitzer followed this instruction, he found it worked. He melted lead, threw in a ball of wax-covered stone, and within 15 minutes the lead had been transformed into gold which, when tested by the mint master of his province, turned out to be true gold indeed. A third account with much the same set of details and with the same outcome was told of Robert Boyle (1627–91) and is dated to 1702, so we have more than one narrative purporting to involve a genuine transmutation, and directly involving witnesses or participants whose credibility and reliability are clearly intended to be unimpeachable.

Not that these are the only examples. In 1644 and 1646, Christian IV of Denmark minted coins from gold he said had been transmuted from base metals by his Court alchemist, Gasper Harback; in 1647, one J.P. Hofman transmuted base metal into gold in the presence of the Holy Roman Emperor, Ferdinand III; and the following year another equally obscure alchemist called Busardier had some powder (presumably the stone, as it turned out), stolen virtually from his deathbed by a friend, recorded only as 'Richthausen' who then used it to perform a transmutation of mercury in the presence of Ferdinand III and the Count von Rutz, the Imperial Director of Mines. Every precaution, we are assured, was taken to prevent fraud, and at the conclusion of the demonstration the Master of the Imperial Mint declared that the gold was the finest he had ever tested. The Emperor was impressed and had a medal struck to commemorate the occasion: Prague, 15 January 1648. Two years later the Emperor himself carried out a successful transmutation with some of Richthausen's powder, and in 1658 the experiment with mercury was repeated, again successfully, in the presence of the Elector of Mainz. In 1675 Emperor Leopold I witnessed the transmutation of a copper vessel into gold by a monk from Bohemia, Wenzel Seyler – a man, however, who was discovered cheating and sent back to his cloister for a couple of years; and in 1704 the Emperor was treated to further demonstrations, this time by a Neapolitan, Domenico Caetano, who had astonished the Court of Madrid in a similar fashion. But Caetano also turned out to be a fraud, and was hanged in 1709, just like the official alchemist to the Margrave of Bayreuth, who had successfully swindled his master for nine years between 1677 and 1686 before being uncovered at last and ending on the gallows.

What this mixture of eyewitness account, suspension of disbelief, willingness to trust and clever sleight of hand reveals is that even while some people were seeking to separate alchemy from chemistry in such a way as to boost the reputation of the latter while killing that of the former, fascination with and eagerness for the gold-making side of the science continued unabated; and while it is true that the effort at distancing was increasingly effective in the field of iatrochemistry or alchemical medicine, it is also a fact that spiritual as well as transmutational alchemy seemed scarcely aware of the hostility each could arouse. Pierre-Jean Fabre (1588–1658), for example, was both a physician and an alchemist and, like many doctors, prescribed iatrochemical medicine for the plague. His *Alchymista Christiana* (1632) provided, in the midst of the religious savagery of the Thirty Years' War, a powerful plea to take alchemy seriously as a system in which close parallels could be drawn between the Christian sacraments and alchemical operations:

> Baptism, the first sacrament of the Church, simply means in Greek 'immersion in water' and 'tingeing', because therein by the grace of the Spirit a person is changed into something better and is made something very different from what he or she was ... Nature by means which closely match this instructs and teaches alchemists that they must use water and fire in the rudimentary stages of purifying and purging everything, because calcinations and washing purge everything and make it gleam.

Similarly, confirmation corresponds to fixation; the Eucharist to the stone itself; penance to calcinations, putrefaction, and dissolution; marriage to the union of the sun and moon from which may be expected several issue; and extreme unction to an amazing oil possessed by alchemists produced from 'the ashes of the metal's "body", or those of a salt completely exhausted and destroyed by its final death', which they use to manufacture 'an oily cleansing substance whereby everything is made to gleam and shine and pour forth wonderful rays'. This oil also corresponds to the oil used during ordination since, 'just as the Church has orders which are sacred and divine, whereby Christians are elevated to the highest honour, authority, and power of the Church and are appointed fathers, shepherds, directors, and spiritual governors of our souls', so this alchemical oil 'blesses and elevates a number of [natural] philosophers to a supreme knowledge of Nature with the power and ability to bring everything in Nature to perfection and purge it of all its dross, in such a way that these [natural] philosophers, furnished with the spirit of alchemy, can be called the real fathers, directors, and governors of things in Nature'.

Summarizing his elevated view of alchemy in *L'abrégé des secrets chymiques* (1636), Fabre maintained that this particular science was, in fact, more important than any other precisely because it was not bound to physical matter and did not regard creation and created things as mere pieces of machinery:

> Alchemy is not only an art or science for teaching metallic transmutation, but is also a true and solid science which teaches us the central core of all things and this in divine language one calls the Spirit of life. God infuses this Spirit among all the elements for the production, nourishment, and maintenance of natural things. It is to be found at the centre of all things, making a body incorruptible, permanent, and fixed, able to resist all sorts of changes which it will have to endure for the benefit of the diverse generations which will be hatched from its centre. Alchemy then teaches us about this divine and spiritual substance in all things; and it demonstrates by its chemical operations how to extract and separate it from the elementary entanglement and corruption, in order to free its powers and virtues which are nearly infinite and God-given. [Alchemy then] merits truly the name of unique natural philosophy since it shows the basis, foundation, and root of all created things and it teaches the purification and exaltation of the same; whence comes the metallic transmutation of metals, the fertility of vegetables, and the prolongation of life.

It was in just such an atmosphere that Johann Moriaen, George Starkey, Robert Boyle and Isaac Newton laboured to conduct their alchemical experiments. By 1648 the Thirty Years' War was over, with devastating economic and demographic consequences, especially for the German states and the Low Countries. In England, however, a period of bellicose upheaval was about to begin and, by a curious conglomeration of religious and political theories, alchemy and its daughter iatrochemistry began to look as though they were to be associated with radical rather than conservative opinion. For alchemy, as we have seen often, easily translates its goals of perfecting lesser metals into gold and producing elixirs which will banish ill health and prolong life into spiritual ideals of perfecting the individual and his or her soul. England, it so happened, was awash with these and similar or related notions at this time, partly bred at home, partly gained from translations now made available to an eager readership. Thus, the German mystic Jakob Böhme (1575–1624) – another visitor to the Prague of Rudolf II – had visions which convinced him that, in order to restore humankind's relationship with God, people must undergo a kind of violent separation from Him so that they could evolve into a new condition of harmony with Him, more perfect than before. The ease with which parallels can be drawn between this notion, kept in spiritual terms or translated into political, and the alchemical process is obvious. More overt are the views of the Welsh alchemist Thomas Vaughan (1621–66), a Royalist clergyman, who died while conducting an experiment in his laboratory. 'Eugenius Philalethes' (Vaughan's authorial pseudonym), 'died as 'twere suddenly when he was operating strong mercury, some of which by chance getting up into his nose marched him off'. Vaughan Englished the Rosicrucian manifestos *Fama* and *Confessio*, and produced in his *Anthroposophia Theomagica* (1650) – dedicated to 'the most illustrious and truly reborn brethren of the Rosy Cross' – an alchemical account of Creation, which he was to repeat and expand in his *Lumen de lumine* (1651). That the intentions of alchemists should be of an elevated sort, he makes clear in his postscript to the reader in a version of the old exclusive claim of secret and superior knowledge vouchsafed to the relatively few.

They should not, he says:

> Conclude anything rashly concerning the subject of this art, for it is a principle not easily apprehended. It is neither earth, nor water, air, nor fire. It is not gold, silver, Saturn, antimony, or vitriol, nor any kind of mineral whatsoever. It is not blood, nor the seed of any individual, as some unnatural, obscene authors have imagined. In a word, it is no mineral, no vegetable, no animal, but a system as it were of all three. In plain terms, it is *sperma maioris animalis*, the seed of Heaven and earth, our most secret, miraculous hermaphrodite. If you know this, and with it the hydro-pyro-magical art, you may with some security attempt the work. If not, practice is the way to poverty. Essay nothing without science [knowledge], but confine yourselves to those bounds which Nature hath prescribed you.

Claims of a personal revelation of higher truth meant that it was also not difficult to make connections between what Andrew Mendelsohn calls 'the chymist's luminous, spark-like principle or tincture, and the private illumination of radical Protestant theology'. One of the forms this might take can be seen in the notion that, just as the alchemist could seek to recreate the first six days of Creation in his laboratory, so the political idealist might be encouraged by consideration of certain aspects of alchemical theory to try to create a perfected form of society. Not that alchemy influenced the aspirations of only one side during the Civil Wars. Bassett Jones, for example, Welsh author of *Lithochymicus* (1650), published his extensive alchemical poem in Oxford, a Royalist stronghold, and, while his views are clearly occupied more by the Paracelsian debates of the turn of the previous century and an enthusiasm for the fraternity of the Rosy Cross, as far as the contemporary religious and political situation was concerned, he seems to have avoided overtly identifying himself with either extreme although, as Robert Schuler points out, 'such views as Jones expresses were, in fact, perfectly compatible with high-church royalist beliefs'.[1]

Royalists, Puritans, Levellers, sectarians of all kinds alike, then, were prepared to steep themselves in the crapulent brew which a mixture of alchemy and millenarianism offered because alchemy was, in Mendelsohn's words, 'an especially powerful metaphor for the problem of uncertainty and its resolution, because alchemy's history was in such a large part the history of its contested credibility', and the establishment of an English republic coincided, not altogether by accident perhaps, with widespread active interest on all sides of the religious and political divide in the possibility of transmutation, however that was to be interpreted. So when Charles II was restored to his English throne in 1662 (he had been acknowledged King of Scots since 1 January 1651), we should not be surprised to find that he happily brought with him Nicolas le Fèvre, a French alchemist, who now effectively became a royal alchemist-in-residence and set up his laboratory in St James's Palace.

With Böhme, Vaughan and Charles II's French alchemist, we begin to catch a glimpse of those international circles of scholars and practitioners of various sciences, which had characterized intellectual exchange at the beginning of the seventeenth century and continued to do so even after the disastrous Thirty Years' War. Samuel Hartlib (c.1600–62) was a Polish-Prussian polymath who studied in Germany and in England, fleeing to London in 1642 from religious persecution at home. His multifarious learning attracted the interest of many like-minded people with whom he kept up a voluminous correspondence, a network often referred to as the 'Hartlib circle' – a forerunner, in fact, of the Royal Society. It may have been the dreadful harvests during the late 1640s and early 1650s which stimulated him not only to look for ways to improve agriculture, but also to prolong human life and ameliorate standards of health by looking at alchemical medicine to help achieve this aim, while millenarian speculations and prophecies were also of keen interest to members of the 'circle', who discussed them constantly as stimuli to the great reforms and improvements they had in mind for society.

These plans often sprang from unusual soil. One of these many acquaintances of Hartlib, for example, was the Dutch-German alchemist and clergyman, Johann Moriaen (c.1591–1668). His religious views were unorthodox, though not altogether unusual or unacceptable in the circles in which he moved, and, while regarding himself as a Christian, he went through a phase of interest in pansophy as defined by Jan Amos Comenius, another of the Hartlib circle – everyone, said Comenius, should be taught everything as a basis for his or her better qualification as a citizen – before deciding that this would not work. Disillusion made him turn to alchemy as a means (in the words of John Young), 'of returning Creation itself to its original status as a blank page . . . [on which] alchemists would rewrite Creation in better accord with the original divine intention'.[2]

Hartlib's circle also included George Starkey and Robert Boyle. George Starkey (1628–65) was an American alchemist who created for himself an interesting double life by writing as the alchemical author 'Eirenaeus Philalethes', and creating a separate existence for him by including in his tracts sufficient information about this doppelgänger to enable later writers on alchemy to build fantasies which linked him to the Rosicrucian fraternity and gave him a much expanded physical life. Eirenaeus, in fact, is the subject of what we might call an alchemical novel. He discovers the philosopher's stone at the age of 23 but wanders all over the world as an outcast from society, constantly in danger from persecution and torture. Even when he uses his extraordinary knowledge to cure the sick, he is greeted by violent ingratitude and forced to run away in disguise. It is all part of the millenarianist psychology of the period. The Golden Age will be preceded by the Age of Antichrist, when the harbinger of the New Jerusalem is persecuted. Real gold – and the art of transmutation which produces it – is ultimately valueless, and humankind must be brought to understand this. Only a purging and renewal of the world will transform the age of (moral) dross into the age of genuine gold, and those who realize this will be granted, by God's favour, the secrets of Nature which not only reveal to humankind some of the intimate workings of God's mind, but also present in concrete metaphors the transmutation which God intends for His creation. Thus, the story of the 'life' of Eirenaeus Philalethes combines the practices of the laboratory with a chiliastic vision of the future in a way which owes much to Paracelsus and his particular followers.

George Starkey was born in Bermuda and educated at Harvard where the theory that the world is a machine and all its inhabitants automata held sway. Disillusioned by his experience of this teaching, however, Starkey rejected his education and turned to alchemy and iatrochemistry as subjects more fruitful and more worthy of attention. His working methods, revealed in the laboratory notebooks he kept during the 1650s, show that he read existing literature, made conjectures, did experiments, and then drew conclusions from them. This sounds remarkably straightforward, as indeed it was, but when he came to write extensively on alchemy, Starkey resorted to elaborate allegories, metaphors and conceits which hide rather than reveal his meaning. In this, however, he is typical of alchemical authors in general. But perhaps there is a reason for his apparent retreat into complexity – that the way in which he received some of his inspiration left it unsayable by its very nature. For one of the more profound influences on him, according to his own account, was the revelation of natural secrets in dreams. In January 1652, for example, he had been working hard one day and was exhausted. He fell asleep with his head on his arm:

> Behold! I seemed intent on my work, and a man appeared, entering the laboratory, at whose arrival I was stupefied. But he greeted me and said, 'May God support your labours'. When I heard this, realising that he had mentioned God, I asked who he was, and he responded that he was my Eugenius. I asked whether there were such creatures. He responded that there were . . . Finally I asked him what the alkahest of Paracelsus and Helmont was, and he responded that they used salt, sulphur, and an alkalised body, and though this response was more obscure than Paracelsus himself, yet with the response an ineffable light entered my mind, so that I fully understood. Marvelling at this, I said to him, 'Behold! Your words are veiled, as it were by fog, and yet they are fundamentally true'. He said, 'This is so necessarily, for the things said by one's Eugenius are all certain, while those just said by me are the truest of all'.

Was this the result simply of extreme tiredness, or are we to infer that Starkey thought he was inspired to discover such things, and indeed to write under the name of Eirenaeus Philalethes, in a state of heightened consciousness during which a kind of spirit-guide opened his understanding and transmitted hitherto elusive or secret information? His play on the name 'Eugenius' and the Graeco-Latin *eu-genius*, 'well-disposed spirit of place or inspiration', suggests that at the very least he was trying to explain in metaphorical terms the experience of sudden revelation; but we should be chary of assuming that this *must* have been his meaning, for the mid-seventeenth century largely accepted the existence of non-human entities of innumerable kinds, assumed that they could and did interpose themselves in human affairs, and that forces beyond human, sent by God or Satan or acting of their own volition, were capable of influencing the material world and its inhabitants in ways which were little understood (though people tried), and for motives which might often be obscure. Starkey's revelatory dream was not a single instance. On at least two other occasions, he recorded that God had revealed or communicated secrets to him, a view of alchemy as a body of secret knowledge passed on to a relatively few elect by means of divine or at any rate more-than-natural illumination, which he got from intimate acquaintance with the works of van Helmont, the other most notable influence on his work.

For van Helmont was clear that knowledge in the laboratory came via acts of divine favour:

> Led thus by divine will (which others might think a chance event), I found part of that which I had long been seeking anxiously with much expenditure. Hence I praised God that He had given understanding to one who was small and poor. For if He had not commanded that I be called away from the work, nor detained me in festivities until the Duelech congealed on the receiver, and if the receiver had not been so clear and precious, indeed, if I had completed the whole operation in one go, then I would have done all in vain. Therefore God has considered the needs of mortals, and has not spurned the prayers of the lowly.

It is well known that van Helmont contradicted the ancient conception that everything consisted of four elements. Fire, he said, was not an element; water was the fundamental element of all things. Water itself was composed of the alchemical principles of mercury, sulphur and salt, and when water was heated, its salt was forced upwards, and was followed by the mercury and the sulphur, all in the form of a vapour; and when this vapour passed into higher regions still, the result was an attenuation of the three constituent parts which thereby turned into a 'gas', the word van Helmont coined from Greek *khaos*. It was not gas, however, but van Helmont's alkahest which perhaps especially intrigued Starkey. In *Imago Fermenti*, van Helmont described it thus in typical rococo style:

> Chemistry is intent on discovering a body that would play a symphony with us of such purity that it could not be destroyed by a corrupter. And finally religion is stupefied by the discovery of a liquid which, reduced to the smallest atoms possible in Nature, would chastely spurn the marriages of any ferment. The transmutation of it is despaired of, as it may not find a body more worthy than itself to which it might be married. But the work of wisdom has created an anomaly in Nature, which has arisen without the commixture of any ferment diverse from itself. This serpent has bitten itself, recovered from the venom, and henceforth cannot die.

The revelation which told Starkey the basic composition of this remarkable substance resulted in a book, *Liquor Alcahest*, published several years after his death. Herein we learn that Starkey derived his alkahest from urine to which he added ethyl alcohol, the result being a white substance on which Starkey conducted a series of experiments in order to produce the alkahest itself. We are here in the realm of iatrochemistry, of course, not transmutation of metals, and it was in this realm that Starkey's reputation lay, although 'lay' is perhaps the wrong word since the orthodox physicians of London and their Helmontian colleagues whose theories and practice were at variance with them had begun a series of skirmishes with each other during the 1650s, when Starkey was resident in London. The latter banded together in a Society of Chymical Physicians which claimed to be an institutional counterpart of the College of Physicians, and Starkey joined the pamphlet war between them, as virulent in his denunciations of orthodox Galenic medicine as anyone.

Starkey died during the great plague of 1665. He appeared to be fearless and administered remedies – toad powder, and a toad amulet to be hung round the neck – to his friend and colleague, George Thomson, who had been the moving force behind setting up the Society of Chymical Physicians. Thomson survived, but Starkey himself then fell ill and his remedies had no beneficial effect. Perhaps, as Thomson later wrote, the excessive amount of beer he had drunk before contracting the disease had subverted the natural ferment of his stomach, exalted the poison, debilitated the ruling faculty which controlled his constitution, congealed the blood, obstructed the pores, and thus locked in the plague so that it could not escape.[3]

The friends and acquaintances of Samuel Hartlib, as we said, included Moriaen and Starkey, and Robert Boyle (1627–91). Boyle is often portrayed as the person who finally distinguished between alchemy and 'chemistry' (in the modern sense of the word), and as an important advocate of the mechanistic theories originating with Descartes. In fact he was much more complex than this simplified figure implies. While rejecting Paracelsian notions that the human body was analogous to the macrocosm, for example, he retained the possibility that non-human entities or forces could be present in Nature, and that certain failings in or illnesses of the body could be cured by sympathetic magic; and he was wedded to the possibilities behind some of the key ideas expressed by van Helmont, while ultimately rejecting some of the ideas themselves. Thus, having tried (like Starkey) to reproduce van Helmont's alkahest, he finally came to the conclusion he could not do it, although he did not dismiss van Helmont's claim to have done so. He also rejected van Helmont's proposition that 'seeds' – that is, transformative powers in Nature – were responsible for the creation of individual bodies. Observation and experimentation led him to write his major work, *The Sceptical Chymist, or, Chymico-Physical Doubts and Paradoxes touching the Spagyrist's Principles commonly called Hypostatical; as they are wont to be Propos'd and Defended by the Generality of Alchymists* (1661), which objects to those [al]chemical claims which rest upon assumptions and traditions rather than close scrutiny of what actually goes on in the laboratory. More importantly, however, he argued that confusion of language among [al]chemical practitioners led to misunderstanding and mistaken hypotheses, and Lawrence Principe has pointed out that it is a touch of misunderstanding (and perhaps wilful thinking) on the part of earlier historians of science which credits Boyle with making a distinction between alchemy and chemistry. In fact he did not do so. What he did was to distinguish between cheats, puffers and adepts.

'There lies concealed in the world', he wrote, 'a set of spagyrists of a much higher order than those who are wont to write courses of chemistry or other books of that nature; being able to transmute baser metals into perfect ones, and do some other things, that the generality of chemists confess to be extremely difficult; and divers of the more judicious even among the spagyrists themselves have judged impossible.'

Rather than denying or disposing of the possibility that some alchemists might be capable of transmuting substances into gold, Boyle accepted the notion. His fire was concentrated elsewhere. By the seventeenth century, practitioners of alchemy had become quite remarkably diverse. The figure of Paracelsus looms large over the science, but neither his theories nor their development by his followers had so taken it over that 'alchemy' and 'Paracelsianism' had become synonymous. On the other hand, it was difficult to ignore him entirely, and alchemists absorbed very little or a great deal of his influence according to their individual inclinations and developing experiences in the laboratory. Far from existing as a multitude of self-contained groups, therefore, seventeenth-century [al]chemists floated freely in a sea of ideas, tending to metallurgy, glass-making, chemistry, iatrochemistry and medicine, and gold-making as the demands of their chosen métier suggested, and practising one or more or all in accordance with a variety of personal preference and economic need. What concerned Boyle were such matters as the assertion that all bodies consist basically of precisely three substances – mercury, sulphur, salt – a criticism which immediately put him at odds with Paracelsians who insisted that salt was one of the three prime principles: and what he regarded as the unnecessary and damaging obscurity of language and secrecy of intention which characterized so much writing on alchemy.

What he meant, of course, was the obscurity of charlatans and puffers, not that of adepts such as Raimund Lull or Basil Valentine. Both these examples get to the heart of the business. Was alchemy a vehicle for ideologies of one kind or another, world-reforming and spiritually transforming in ultimate intention, or was it a series of physical experiments confined to the laboratory, whose aim was to produce specific preparations and provide insights purely into the composition and working of matter? Boyle's answer was not to choose or favour one rather than the other – and so from this point of view he cannot be regarded as providing a break between 'alchemy' and (modern) 'chemistry' – but to take forward elements of both and what he hoped was a more defensible version of the discipline. In the words of Lawrence Principe, 'much of the apparent conflict between Boyle as a seeker of the Stone and Boyle as an architect of early modern chemistry vanishes as an artefact of an historiographic mistake. There is no conflict; Boyle was simply a seventeenth-century chymist – some of his chemical activities have potential counterparts in modern chemistry while others continue the traditions of chrysopoeia and spagyria'.[4]

Boyle's later years saw him pursue his interest in the philosopher's stone as part of a profound religious concern over what the age called 'atheism'. It was founded upon a much older puzzle: what exactly is the relationship between spirit and matter, and how is it possible for the two to interact? The sixteenth century and the early seventeenth had devoted much time and effort in attempts to elucidate these points in relation to witchcraft. By what means, for example, can spirits have sexual intercourse with human beings, and what is the nature of the apparently physical appearance of any non-human entities? Now, however, such questions shifted themselves from witchcraft to alchemy. We have already come across the intervention of spirits in alchemists' dreams which have been used by the spirits as vehicles for transmitting arcane knowledge. Could the stone itself act as a kind of magnet to attract spirits and were these spirits the cause of any subsequent transmutation? Merely posing these questions, of course, challenged the mechanistic and deterministic view of creation, which led towards atheism, and again Boyle occupied the middle ground, refusing to accept some of his contemporaries' arguments against mechanism, while suggesting that the philosopher's stone potentially offered a demonstration that the angelic and spirit world was real since the stone attracted its inhabitants into the world of matter.

This, then, was one of the important strands of thought which might go to make up the mindset of anyone undertaking laboratory work during the last part of the seventeenth and early years of the eighteenth century, and it therefore needs to be taken into account as we come to the most famous of the Hartlib circle, Sir Isaac Newton (1642–1727). Sometimes presented as a lone genius who worked by himself and made his discoveries without help from other people, Newton actually belonged to a milieu in which extensive correspondence between scholars was the norm, and exchange of views thereby – or via the more hostile route of critical pamphleteering – the most frequent way of seeding inspiration, sowing doubt, or influencing the direction of one another's thoughts.

Thus, Starkey (Newton's favourite alchemist) and Boyle, with whom Newton conducted a fruitful exchange of letters, both helped to formulate and extend his views not only on alchemy but on other branches of science as well. Boyle, for example, believed that the shapes and natures of individual 'corpuscles' – that is, atoms – created differences in chemical behaviour. Newton read this and took notes on Boyle's book *Origine of Formes and Qualities* (1666) which discussed the behaviour of two different corpuscularian mechanisms which might bring about transmutation, and from this he deduced that what was needed was to get these 'corpuscles' to do their work was to open up metals so as to extract their basic 'mercury', by which he (and other alchemists) meant the innermost quality of the metal, released when a metallic ore or compound was subjected to heat. Betty Teeter Dobbs explains the thought behind the experimentation:

> Newton's concept of the 'mercury' of metals probably never was *exactly* based on the 'chymical' theory that the principles of metals were 'mercury' and 'sulphur' – or at least his conception was not *limited* to that approach. In later years he published material indicating that he thought that the large corpuscles, which by cohering formed massy bodies, were themselves composed of complex arrangements of smaller particles. There are indications in his later writings that his conception probably included a 'mercurial' particle within the largest corpuscle of the metal, one step down the hierarchical ladder from the largest particles, and *inside* them. Thus the 'mercury' of which he spoke, although having mercurial chemical characteristics certainly, was made of relatively complex particles of matter and was obtained when the largest particles of the metal were 'opened', allowing the smaller component parts to exit.

Newton's work in the laboratory, then, did not come entirely out of his own head but was suggested, if only implicitly, by that of others whose theories he was testing or whose prescriptions stimulated him to go in certain directions. There is, however, a major obstacle in the path of understanding Newton's alchemy. His alchemical manuscripts, which are held mainly in Cambridge, Jerusalem and Massachusetts, have never been put in order and in consequence it is extremely difficult to tell which contain his original thoughts and experiments, and which are his transcriptions or résumés of other authors. So there is no reliable telling how his alchemical ideas developed. Discoveries, or rather rediscoveries, are also being made – a collection of his alchemical notes, for example, which disappeared after their sale in 1936, came to light again in 2005 during cataloguing of the Royal Society's miscellaneous manuscripts – and there are scattered individual items, such as a single leaf in the University of St Andrews.

Nevertheless, what studies of Newton's manuscripts make quite clear is that there is no clean break between 'alchemy' and 'chemistry' during the seventeenth century, a realization which was beginning to dawn in the 1970s when Charles Webster observed, 'We have been misled by the subtle philosophical reasoning of Hobbes, the rigorous experimentalism of Harvey or Boyle, and the abstract mathematical analysis of Newton, into believing that the natural philosophers before 1700 thought in essentially modern terms, differing merely in lacking our considerable resources of experience and information.' Theology and alchemy were, in fact, Newton's predominant interests, and the latter he pursued throughout most of his 35 years in Cambridge; for alchemy in his eyes provided evidence of God in the form of an active, animating spirit which contradicted Descartes' picture of a universe which was little more than a closed mechanical system. His assistant, Humphrey Newton (no relation), provided John Conduitt, who intended to write a biography of Sir Isaac but never did so, with a portrait of Newton the alchemist:

> He very rarely went to bed till two or three of the clock, sometimes not until five or six, lying about four or five hours, especially at spring and fall of the leaf, at which times he used to employ about six weeks in his [e]laboratory, the fire scarcely going out either night or day, he sitting up one night and I another, till he had finished his chemical experiments, in the performances of which he was the most accurate, strict, exact. What his aim might be I was not able to penetrate into, but his pains, his diligence at these set times made me think he aimed at something beyond the reach of human art and industry ... On the left end of the garden was his [e]laboratory, near the east end of the chapel, where he at these set times employed himself with a great deal of satisfaction and delight. Nothing extraordinary, as I can remember, happened in making his experiments: which, if there did, he was of so sedate and even temper, that I could not in the least discover it ... About 6 weeks at spring and 6 at the fall, the fire in the [e]laboratory scarcely went out, which was well furnished with chemical materials as bodies, receivers, heads, crucibles, etc., which was [*sic*] made very little use of, the crucibles excepted, in which he fused his metals. He would sometimes, tho' very seldom, look into an old mouldy book which lay in his [e]laboratory, I think it was titled *Agricola de Metallis*, the transmuting of metals being his chief design, for which purpose antimony was a great ingredient.

Why did Newton spend so much time in pursuit of alchemical ends? The production of gold through transmutation was certainly not a consideration. Wedding alchemy and the mechanical philosophy then prevalent was one of his aims, but this does not really explain the source of his motivation. What did matter to him was the omnipresence of God, and if alchemy could demonstrate that there was some kind of universal spirit which caused the diverse substances of Creation to come into being, and if active principles ('seeds') could be shown to operate within the interstices of the separate pieces of matter which made up the physical universe, and thus reveal in and through themselves the existence of such a universal spirit, then alchemy would have provided evidence for God's active presence in the universe, His agency setting in motion and guiding to their conclusion the forces of attraction which made the workings of Nature coherent by constituting bonds between the smallest and the largest of created bodies. It is a notion which can be glimpsed in Query 31 of his *Opticks*:

> Have not the smallest particles of bodies certain powers, virtues, or forces by which they act at a distance, not only upon the rays of light for reflecting, refracting, and inflecting them, but also upon one another for producing a great part of the phenomena of Nature? For it's well known that bodies act upon one another by the attractions of gravity, magnetism, and electricity, and these instances show the tenor and course of Nature and make it not improbable but that there may be more attractive powers than these. For Nature is very consonant and conformable to herself.

Newton's alchemy, in fact, and the other discoveries for which he is better known and honoured, at bottom sprang from his theology. Gravity was part of this alchemically-inspired interest in attraction and affinity between bodies, just as his work on the spectrum can be traced back via alchemical 'illumination' to Gen. 1.3, 'And God said, Let there be light, and there was light.' As 'Eirenaeus Philalethes' expressed it in *The Marrow Of Alchemy* (1654–5),

> There must be an inward agent granted,
> Else would a thing unchanged still remain.
> This agent is the form that water wanted,
> While it its proper nature did retain.
> This form is light, the source of central heat,
> Which, cloth'd with matter, doth a seed beget.

Heinrich Khunrath had envisaged Creation as 'the wonderful laboratory (i.e. workshop) of wonderful God, the macrocosm, everlasting, universal, with Nature watching over it, superintending it, and toiling at it'. Similarly, Newton saw God sending out His animating breath or spirit over the waters which preceded His creation of light, a breath which, alchemy revealed, used as its medium an ethereal mercury which brought life to this watery chaos.

Perhaps, then, we may say that while scientists have tended to claim Newton as one of their own in spite of his divagations into alchemy and sacred numbers, the opposite stands a chance of being somewhat closer to the truth: that Newton was essentially a somewhat unorthodox theologian who divagated into some of the sciences and produced insights from, not in spite of, his quest for evidence of God's active creation of and intervention in Nature.[5]

9

Alchemy in an Age of Self-Absorption: The Eighteenth and Nineteenth Centuries

Denunciation of alchemists and the threat of physical violence to them had by no means disappeared during the late decades of the seventeenth century and the opening years of the eighteenth. Giuseppe Borri, an alchemist with a flamboyant past, the facts about whose life are buried in a mass of legend, met Queen Christina of Sweden in 1655 and spent two years with her in Rome, performing alchemical experiments, before fleeing the plague in 1657 and going back to his birthplace, Milan. During the next 34 years he acquired even more notoriety for his heretical opinions as much as for his professional activities, and while his reputation and abilities attracted several royal and influential patrons, his career slowly began to fade until, in 1691, he ended up imprisoned in Castel Sant'Angelo where he died of a fever in 1695. Fame and patronage, then, were no protection, and the old charges of greed, ineptitude and charlatanry which had for so long dogged alchemists' heels did not go away or even diminish in vigour. The French were especially dismissive, perhaps because they were acutely aware that Paracelsus had had his greatest influence in France. An anonymous *Explanation of Several Doubts Regarding Medicine* (1700) denied the possibility of producing potable gold and denounced iatrochemists as mountebanks. The Duc de Saint Simon records in his *Memoirs* for 1710 that during the last days of that December, 'a fraudulent alchemist appeared, who claimed to possess the magic formula for making gold'. One of Louis XIV's physicians, Jean Boudin, took him under his wing, partly because he himself dabbled in alchemy, but was thoroughly swindled, not only by this man but by others as well, who knew a dupe when they saw one. In 1711, François Pousse took a line very similar to that of the anonymous author of the *Explanation of Several Doubts*, in his *Examination of Alchemists' Assumptions about the Philosopher's Stone*; and in 1722, Etienne Geoffroy published a paper in the *Memoirs of the Académie Royale* in which he fulminated against the deceits practised by alchemists, especially in relation to making or increasing the weight of gold by means of hollow stirring rods, amalgams, acids and double-bottomed cupels; and one may compare with this Georg Wegner's polemical treatise, *Adeptus Ineptus* (1744), in which he sarcastically describes alchemists as thieves to themselves and to their needy neighbours.

It is therefore interesting to follow, briefly, the activities of one or two practitioners of the period to see what it may have been that gave rise to such continued suspicions and dismissals. Giuseppe Borri was a prototype Cagliostro, an adventurer and fantasist as well as a physician and alchemist. His published work – and several books bearing his name were actually written by other people eager to profit from his notoriety – is filled with magical spirits, the salamanders and undines of the elemental world, and a type of Kabbalah more magical than Kabbalistic. In a period which is usually called the Age of Reason but would more accurately be called the Age of Theatricality, this kind of heady mixture was almost bound to repel as well as attract. Its mysteries and histrionics appealed to people's sense of adventure and thirst for diversion, but proved distasteful to scholars and academics, who wanted to divest themselves of learning or belief in or reliance upon earlier conceptions of God and Nature, and clothe themselves in the modernism of post-Cartesian philosophy and 'scientific' enquiry, while enjoying the mental frisson of what the age called 'atheism'.

But Borri was not the only forerunner of Cagliostro. The man who called himself the Comte de Saint-Germain (1676? –1784) and may have belonged to the noble House of Ránóczy, created a sensation when he appeared in various courts of Europe. Wild stories about him proliferated. He had been born in the time of Christ – 'I knew Him intimately. He was the best man in the world, but romantic and reckless. I always told Him He would come to a bad end' – and owed his immense age and youthful looks and vigour to a very strict diet and an elixir made of sandalwood, senna leaves and fennel seeds. He gave the impression of being very rich and perhaps let people think this was the result of his possessing the philosopher's stone, although his money is more likely to have come from his skills in dyeing and tincturing. He also claimed to be able to remove flaws from diamonds and to possess a formula which would take away stone from the bladder. Tales continued to be told of him long after his death in 1784. It was said he appeared to Madame du Barry as she was about to be guillotined during the revolution, and to the Duchesse de Lamballe on the point of her being murdered – a testimony to the impression he had made during his lifetime.

Multiple impressions, in fact. The Courts of France, England, Russia and Berlin were well acquainted with him, and many of their principal figures, including Louis XV and Frederick II, were prepared to take him with a degree of seriousness. But the same can be said of his younger contemporary, the Sicilian Giuseppe Balsamo, otherwise known as 'Cagliostro' (1743–95). Alchemy, prophecy, magic, Freemasonry and miracles of healing were all part of his repertoire, and he too appeared in many of the European capitals: Paris, London, St Petersburg and Rome. Like Borri, he fell foul of the Inquisition and, like Borri, died in prison. Meanwhile, however, he experimented with beauty creams and elixirs, setting up the first of his laboratories in 1773 in a garret he rented in Naples. Four years later he was changing silver into gold, enlarging precious stones, and performing necromantic rites in The Hague before going to Venice where he tricked a merchant into paying a large sum of money for a red powder which sounds (or is supposed to sound) like the philosopher's stone. In 1779 he was in St Petersburg where he had a mixed reception. Baron Heyking, the chief officer in the imperial palace guard, was an enthusiastic chemist, but Cagliostro snubbed him. 'Chemistry', he said, 'is child's play for anyone who knows alchemy, and alchemy is nothing for someone who commands the spirits.' He thus made a powerful enemy who eventually managed to chase him out of Russia in spite of the great reputation he had acquired as a healer. From Russia he went to Warsaw where Prince Adam Poninsky, a passionate alchemist, threw open to Cagliostro his personal laboratory and put him in charge of it. But Cagliostro lasted only two months in Warsaw before having to flee, along with his wife. He should have been content to work on alchemy. Instead, he seems to have devoted himself to magic – and so the sad story of opportunities given, bungled and lost goes on.

Clearly none of these thespians was a genuine alchemist or, shall we say, practised alchemy with any degree of seriousness. For them it seems to have been merely one among an array of dazzling claims and performances which they used to divert, mystify and titillate their patrons and audiences. We may also care to note that in 1784 Cagliostro founded a pseudo-Masonic order, the so-called 'Egyptian Rite', with himself residing as Great Copt and his wife Serafina as the Queen of Sheba, by no means a unique act. For at much the same time, Antoine Pernety, a one-time Benedictine monk with an early interest in alchemy and physiognomy who had defended Nicolas Flamel's reputation as an alchemist against doubts being expressed during a controversy of the 1760s, founded his own Hermetic rite which practised ritual magic in order to contact, speak to and learn from angelic spirits. His views on alchemy were equally singular, since he maintained that Classical mythology was derived from ancient Egypt and that alchemy provided the key to reading the true meaning of its symbols and allegories. This, however, was not enough, and in 1786 he founded the Illuminati of Avignon, who were to achieve individual enlightenment through trans-figuration both spiritual and physical in rites essentially magical and Kabbalistic, and in this he seems to have been following in the footsteps of Adam Weishaupt, a Professor of Law at the University of Ingoldstadt, who, ten years previously, had founded the Illuminati of Bavaria, a society devoted to establishing a universal utopia through occult means. What these orders or societies have in common is the membership which found them appealing – royalty, nobility and those scholarly circles in which alchemy was either supported or derided or treated with delicate caution, the same circles which provided the readership for Hermann Fictuld's *Aureum Vellus oder Goldenes Vlies* (1749) which set out to explain the noble Order of the Knights of the Golden Fleece in terms of alchemy.

So it is with this kind of pantomime forming a notable thread in the occult tapestries of Europe that we should consider not only the expressed hostility to alchemy we have seen from certain writers, but perhaps more importantly the continued vigorous interest in the science, which pressed ahead with public and patronly approval regardless of the play-acting which gained the headlines. Germans, for example, were happy to defend alchemy as a valid if difficult branch of knowledge. Konrad Horlacher, in *Geschichte des Alchemie*, takes the familiar line that alchemical understanding comes through the specific favour of God, while Johann Creiling, to whom *Die Edelgeborne Jungfer Alchymia* (1730) is attributed, devotes much space to discussing whether alchemy-as-transmutation is sinful or not. He also reviews the most common objections against alchemy and dismisses them; provides plentiful testimonies, largely from German sources, of successful transmutations; relates a number of alchemical experiments, including his own; gives a somewhat fuzzy account of iatrochemical remedies; and finally asks whether alchemy should be regarded as a gift of God. Creiling's is not a work without its share of doubt. Statements from various alchemists about the possibility of transmutation were sometimes full of discrepancies, as Creiling acknowledges, and he notes the long history of failure in the science as well as alleged successes. So although he is prepared to defend alchemy as a valid science, he vacillates between acceptance and doubt in a way which seems to reflect that general situation among eighteenth-century 'scientists' we have noted already. '*Die Edelgeborne Jungfer Alchymia*', says Vladimir Karpenko:

> belongs to those works that allow deeper insight into the final stage of European alchemy. In the closing chapter of his book, Creiling, a believer in alchemy, did not search for causes of its failures within alchemy itself. In his opinion, the cause was not in this science, but in the supposed results of alchemical activities, in promised material riches, and longevity. No wonder that anybody who knew the Art was not willing to reveal its secret to those not familiar with alchemy. Therefore, the only way was to study on one's own and try to understand the secret of the Great Art.[1]

Trying on one's own meant experimentation, and we find this encouraged, without the trappings of theatricality, by patrons such as Peter the Great of Russia. He visited Hermann Boerhaave, the Dutch Professor of Chemistry at Leiden, for example, who regarded chemistry as an important discipline precisely in so far as it kept to experimentation and did not seek to develop a universal system of explanation for matter, whether animate or inanimate. It is interesting, therefore, that he accepted the possibility of transmutation – 'we don't see why this art should be absolutely pronounced false' – and did not demur at the alchemical proposition that metals grow in the earth and require their own peculiar nourishment to be able to do so. Tsar Peter also collected a number of alchemical books for his private library, and invited to his Court enthusiasts for the science, such as Feofan Prokopovich, Archbishop of Novgorod, who was learned well beyond the confines of theology and confidently looked forward to the time when alchemists, who had not yet succeeded in making gold, would be able to do so in addition to the many discoveries and inventions their efforts had produced already. Peter's Field Marshal and Master of the Russian Artillery, Jacob Bruce, a Russian of Scottish descent, was fascinated by alchemy, as his library demonstrates, and seems to have understood both alchemical and chemical processes as a result of personal experimentation; and a Scottish physician, Robert Erskine, who first came to Russia in 1704, amassed one of the most extensive private alchemical libraries in Europe and was clearly an iatrochemist in the tradition of Paracelsus, was happily accepted by the Tsar who was treated by him on more than one occasion. Erskine also seems to have been interested in the Rosicrucians, since he possessed a fine copy of Andreae's *Chymische Hochzeit* and another of Daniel Cramer's book of Rosicrucian and alchemical emblems. In this he was similar to the Englishman General Charles Rainsford (1728–1809), a distinguished army officer, Fellow of the Royal Society and Member of Parliament, who put together quite a collection of alchemical and Hermetic manuscripts (his entry in the *Dictionary of National Biography* says he 'dabbled', but the evidence points to something more than that) and translated many of them into English.

But it was another Fellow of the Royal Society, James Price (who had changed his name from Higginbotham), who not only set out to conduct experiments with a view to achieving transmutation, but ended a victim either of his own over-ambition or of others' suspicions. The change of name had been made to satisfy the wishes of a relative who had left him a large sum of money, which he used to build himself a private laboratory in a new house near Guildford in Surrey. It was there, he said, that he succeeded in transmuting mercury into gold, and he demonstrated the operation twice before an invited audience, once adding a white powder to his crucible and producing silver, once adding a red powder and turning out pure gold. Both ingots were assayed, proved genuine and shown to George III. Price thereupon published a detailed account of what he had done and what had happened: *An Account of Some Experiments on Mercury, Silver, and Gold, made in Guildford in May 1782, in the Laboratory of James Price MD, FRS.* Curiously enough, Price denied in print that his powders were the philosopher's stone – perhaps a necessary repudiation in the face of stern dismissal of alchemy by well-known chemists of the day, such as Joseph Black, President of the Royal Society at the time – and in view of this kind of intransigent opinion, it is perhaps not surprising that Price's experiments were thought to have reflected badly on the Society's honour, and so he was required to repeat them in front of some of the Society's Fellows as a test of his integrity. Price expressed himself reluctant to do so. His stock of powders had run out and he was given only six weeks to prepare another batch, a length of time which seems not to have been sufficient, for at the end of that period of grace, when the three designated Fellow-witnesses came to his laboratory to scrutinize his procedure, Price left the room, drank a solution of prussic acid, came back, and died in front of their horrified eyes.

Holmyard speculates on the reasons for his suicide. It is too easy to suggest that Price 'must' have been a fraud, or (as the inquest concluded) that he was of unsound mind, and it is interesting that a letter from London to the *Göttingisches Magazin*, dated 30 September 1783, informed its readers that Price was actually alone when he took the poison, no one having turned up to witness his experiments. If this was indeed the case (and the writer gives every impression of being well informed), then the suicide becomes explicable as a matter of personal honour, for the non-appearance of the Fellows could suggest they had no faith in his integrity and were treating him with contempt. So why was it suggested he killed himself in the presence of witnesses? This version strongly implies that Price was a fraud, and that is exactly the impression which would have suited the closed minds of some of the Society's Fellows. So we are left with a choice to make between the two versions, as our various dispositions will dictate.[2]

The hostility which Price met from certain quarters, however, was by no means universal in academic circles. In the USA, as we have seen, practical alchemy was a lively issue at Harvard and continued to be so in more than one university into the eighteenth century. Charles Morton, for example, produced a handbook for undergraduate instruction, *Compendium Physicae*, which contains references to the real possibility of transmutation; a Master's thesis at Yale upheld alchemy in 1718; and Samuel Darnforth who graduated from Harvard in 1715, was later ridiculed, so Arthur Versluis tells us, as 'Madam CHEMYIA (a very philosophical Lady) who some years since (as is well-known) discover'd that precious Stone, of which the Royal Society has been in quest a long time, to no purpose'. But Darnforth clearly thought he had the stone, for he offered some of it to Benjamin Franklin in 1773, and Franklin replied by thanking him for a gift 'which, curing all diseases (even old age itself) will enable us to face the future glorious state of our America'. Ezra Stiles (1727–95), a clergyman and President of Yale from 1778 until his death, kept a diary in which he noted, among other things, the interest of Dr Aeneas Munson, a remarkable physician and chemist, in alchemical experiments, and it is worth pointing out that between March and August 1789, Stiles changed his opinion on the subject from dismissive scorn to respectful curiosity as he detailed Munson's attempts to turn mercury into silver. We may also care to consider the interest in the science shown by Virginia's learned élite. Ralph Wormeley, for example, owned the collected works of the German alchemist Johann Glauber and Richard Mathew's book on iatrochemical remedies, *The Unlearned Alchymist in his Antidote*, while Richard Lee (died 1715) owned the alchemical works attributed to Albertus Magnus.

Even the French *philosophes* were unwilling to dismiss alchemy as entirely foolish, provided it was supported by 'chemistry'. 'Alchemy draws some lights from philosophical and analytical chemistry,' wrote Diderot in 1756,

> and gives some in her turn. Several alchemists have thought [chemistry] useless for their work: but true adepts recognise its full worth and pay heed to it, especially that part of chemistry which deals with metals. With the help [of chemistry], the [al]chemist will be diverted from the tiresome and fruitless search for the Philosopher's Stone: or, if he does look for it, he will do so better informed and with greater caution, and he will spare himself a mass of useless, ridiculous processes and will pursue only those which lead more directly to the goal.

For many, that goal consisted increasingly of unravelling the workings of Nature for the sake of the unravelling, although God was not necessarily left out of the process altogether, as in the case of Georg Stahl (1660–1734), a physician who rejected the remedies of the iatrochemists, but remained sympathetic to the idea of transmutation and attributed success in the alchemist's laboratory to 'the divine will which, without all dispute, governs and directs the thing itself and its success'. But while 'chemistry' sailed into a nineteenth century more and more fascinated by the expanding capabilities of technological invention, alchemy found itself (along with the other occult sciences) on the one hand marginalized in the public academic consciousness, but on the other wedded to unorthodox aspects of the century's chosen spiritualisms and obliged thereby to give birth to unexpected offspring. Thus, Karl von Eckartshausen (1752–1803), a Christian Theosophist (if that is not a contradiction in terms), embraced alchemy as an expression of the inner chemistry which was required to bring about the destruction of a sinful substance present in everyone's bloodstream, a substance he called *gluten*, after which the individual could be regenerated by the tincturing power of Christ's blood, and so become one with Him and thus divine. Von Eckartshausen went into more detail about this process in a book, *Chemical Essays* (*Chemische Versuche*, 1802), in which he described Nature and the Bible, along with God's grace, as the three great lights which would help humankind along the path of this higher chemistry – all a remarkably far cry from those practical uses to which some people were clearly putting their alchemical efforts, as can be seen from a recipe for an alchemical fertilizer which uses nitre, urine and salt, among other ingredients, and subjects them to repeated applications of heat to produce the final 'fructifying liquor'.[3]

It cannot be emphasized too strongly, however, that although many eighteenth-century writers were keen to pretend that their 'chemists' were a new breed, unconnected with the foolish, misguided and superstitious 'alchemists' of earlier periods – a repudiation which would have the effect of shielding chemists from the opprobrium often inflicted on practitioners of alchemy – and while one can

understand and perhaps sympathize to an extent with this desire to keep the
new chemistry pure and untainted, one must not forget the role of snobbery in
history. Alchemists more often than not claimed for themselves a special, elect
status and looked down on the common puffers and charlatans who laboured
in their laboratories. Now alchemists were being hoist with their own petard as
the new 'chemists' did the same. The only problem occurs when one takes either
claim seriously.

As we can see from Von Eckhartshausen's example, however, it is not really
surprising if the nineteenth century lumped alchemists together with magicians,
astrologers, diviners and other such practitioners. Looking back over the past 100
years must have been a somewhat disconcerting experience for those devoted to
and fascinated by the onrush of the new technology. Visionaries and millenarianists
with both feet in the supernatural seemed to be swarming wherever they looked.
In the American state of Georgia, John De Brahm, an engineer and cartographer,
published four works with alchemical significance during the 1780s and 90s, and
wrote another (never published) which synthesized alchemical, Rosicrucian and
chiliastic beliefs. In France, Louis-Claude de Saint Martin, in Sweden Emmanuel
Swedenborg, and in Germany Friedrich Oetinger developed their own particular
strands of Christian esotericism. Oetinger, indeed, went so far as to praise magic
as the loftiest of the sciences which studied relationships between earthly and
non-earthly states of existence, while Martinez de Pasqually founded a magical
order with the aim of enabling members to call upon spirits to help human
reintegration with the divine. Even 'scientists' were not always reliably free
from speculation which took them beyond the untrammelled consideration of
matter, as the case of Franz Mesmer illustrated; his doctoral thesis, intended to
research the cause of universal gravitation, was entitled 'The Influence of the
Planets on the Human Body' (*De influxu planetarum in corpus humanum*, 1766),
where 'influence' retained its Latin sense of a 'pouring into', and proposed the
existence of an invisible fluid which could be found everywhere and acted as the
vehicle for interaction between everything in Creation, animate and inanimate.
Perhaps reassuringly material in its tone at first, this notion quickly developed
a life of its own and ended in typical eighteenth-century fashion in 1783 with
the founding of an initiating society (in this case a Society of Harmony) using
symbols borrowed from Freemasonry.

But if the nineteenth century thought it had freed itself from these embarrassing entanglements, it was much mistaken. John De Brahm had been a military
man; so was Ethan Hitchcock (1798–1870), a figure prominent in the American
Civil War, especially as an adviser to Abraham Lincoln. But Hitchcock, along with
his enormously active public life, led an interior life of study and voluminous
reading. He was particularly interested in alchemy and published a book on the
subject. *Remarks upon Alchemy and Alchemists* (1857) defends the reputation of

alchemists and their science, and makes it clear that Hitchcock considered that the significance of alchemy lay in its being a spiritual discipline, not a laboratory activity. Indeed, he goes so far as to say that the writings of alchemists consist entirely of symbols, and that the chemical or mineral or metallurgical terms to be found therein do not actually refer to material substances but to aspects of humankind itself. Such a wholesale sweeping aside of the laboratory is interesting in view of the nineteenth century's educated psyche which usually placed great store by practicalities; but in another way Hitchcock betrays his nineteenth-century origins, because during the book he draws attention to parallels between the Indian school of Vedanta and the alchemy he is describing, and thus reminds us of the westward flow of Eastern esotericism which was increasingly influential during the middle years and second half of the century in the West's construction of syncretistic philosophies.

But, regardless of this individual contribution to the interpretation of alchemy, the older view of it as a means of spiritual regeneration for the individual and humankind dominated the 1800s. From Francis Barrett's *The Magus* (1801), whose account consists largely of a lengthy anecdote attributed to Van Helmont, and a series of instructions to the alchemist on the best way to prepare himself for the work – be serious-minded, discreet, generous, merciful, patient, studious and sober – to the *Book of Mormon* (1829) which has alchemical themes and connotations running through it; to Brigham Young's sermon on true and false riches, which he delivered at Salt Lake's Temple Square in August 1853, and which likewise contains alchemical allusions; to François Cambriel's *Cours de la Philosophie Hermétique ou d'Alchimie* (1843) which interprets Notre Dame as a kind of alchemic temple; to Mary Anne South's *A Suggestive Inquiry into the Hermetic Mystery* (1850), the nineteenth century concentrated its attention on those esoteric aspects of alchemy which chimed best with the prevailing psychology – separating alchemy from the laboratory so that 'science' could flourish uncontaminated by its own past: using alchemy as an illustration of and exercise in spiritual evolution which, in the second half of the century, would parallel the theory of physical evolution; and seeing (if subconsciously) the message of esoteric alchemy as one which agreed with the underlying tenet of the century's passion for technology, since technology seemed to promise a way to transcend the normal limitations of human life, just as did religious millenarianism and the alchemical pursuit of elixirs on the one hand, and spiritual regeneration on the other.[4]

Most of these considerations can be found in the work and influence of Sigismund Bacstrom. Probably Scandinavian by birth, he was a doctor by training and, after travelling all over the world as a ship's surgeon, settled in London and got to know a number of like-minded people among whom he circulated his own translations from a variety of alchemical authors. In September 1794,

he was initiated into a Rosicrucian society by the Comte de Chazal, an old
man who, it has been suggested, was taught the science by none other than the
Comte de Saint-Germain. Members of this society swore, on their admission, to
be worthy of their membership, to keep the society's secrets and to undertake
the Great Work, by which was clearly meant the practice of alchemy; and it is
obvious from Bacstrom's annotations to the *Aphorisms of Urbiger*, for example,
that he himself had a detailed practical knowledge of laboratory work. Now
since, as Adam McLean points out, 'at the time when Bacstrom was collecting and
translating alchemical material, there was little available in the outer world . . .
Bacstrom's material and his access to sources was of the greatest import'. Hence
his influence upon later developments of the science in the nineteenth century,
as his manuscripts passed from occultist to occultist.

But if Bacstrom provided a conduit for transmission of what one might call
laboratory workings, Mary Ann South, later Atwood (1817–1910) and her father
Thomas South, are important for influences of a quite different kind. Mary
Ann's education was patchy, but her reading was extensive and so she benefited
in particular from Lorenz Oken's *Elements of Physiophilosophy* which covered
Nature, science and the arts, and propounded a version of the old theory that
there was a correspondence between the human body and the rest of Creation
– the microcosm and the macrocosm – a theory which would help her make sense
not only of alchemical theory, but also of the mesmerism, animal magnetism,
trances and clairvoyance which were the staple of conversation, journals and
romances of mid-nineteenth-century genteel society. That Mary Ann eagerly
availed herself of opportunities to swim in these occult waters and to take part
(if only as a spectator) in experiments designed to demonstrate their truth and
their innate worth, we know from her correspondence. So it is not surprising to
find Mary Ann and her father collaborating on a book, published in 1846, called
*Early Magnetism in its Higher Relations to Humanity as Veiled in the Poets and
the Philosophers*. It did not take them long to turn their interest in mesmero-
mysticism to a study of alchemy, and the result – apart from a second venture
which did not see the light of print, an epic poem called *The Enigma of Alchemy*
– was the book which made Mary famous, *A Suggestive Inquiry*.

It is divided into parts and chapters, and begins with 'An exoteric view of the
progress and theory of alchemy', itself beginning with 'A preliminary account of
the Hermetic philosophy, with the more salient points of its public history'. In this
chapter we are treated to an idiosyncratic view of the development of alchemy
from its earliest times to the late seventeenth century, with special praise being
given to Thomas Vaughan and Jakob Böhme. Chapter 2 then tells us about 'The
theory of transmutation in general, and of the first matter', and chapter 3 deals
with 'The golden treatise of Hermes Trismegistus concerning the physical secret
of the Philosopher's Stone'. Part 2 provides 'A more esoteric consideration of

the Hermetic art and its mysteries'; part 3 discusses 'The laws and vital conditions of the Hermetic experiment'; and part 4 looks at 'Hermetic practice'. The book as a whole weaves together comments, translations and lengthy observations from a wide variety of alchemical sources – it is clear that Mary Ann and her father were well read in the subject – and her overall view of alchemy seems to be (a) that the alchemist's *prima materia* is a kind of non-material ether, and (b) that the alchemical vessel in which the operations of the science are to take place is the alchemist him- or herself. By attracting into himself, in some fashion akin to the action of a magnet, the prime ether, he can then afford the right conditions for the creation of the philosopher's stone (here understood as 'pure ethereality of Nature'), which will then act as the agent of fundamental change in the alchemist himself. Magnetism, Mary Ann's first interest, thus seems to have had a profound effect on her view of what alchemy is and how it works, while her description of the alchemical process leading to the individual practitioner's exaltation 'to a higher plane of existence' seems to have been a precursor of that theory of evolving humanity which would find its most concrete expression in Darwin's notorious publication nine years later.

A short passage on the *prima materia* will give a fair notion of the style and substance of the Mary Ann's *Inquiry*:

> Thus obscure, after all, is the true Matter of the Alchemists; and if we presume to add here, that it is the simple generated substance of life and light, immanifestly flowing throughout nature, and define it as that without which nothing exists is able to be, we are not for this yet wiser how to obtain or work it apart; nor are words sufficient to convey a just notion where there is no ground of apprehension; and whether a thing be most like water, earth, fire, quicksilver, azote, or ether, is indifferent to the mind, needing actual experience to fix its idea. This the art promises to a patient and true philosopher, but as a reward of individual labour and perseverance only. We may content ourselves thus early, therefore, with the exclusive assurance that it is not one of the many things with which sense brings us acquainted; that it is neither water, nor earth, nor air, nor fire, though it contains in principle the nature of all these; neither gold, nor silver, nor mercury, nor antimony, nor any alkali, or gas, or vitriol of the vulgar; though these titles are found interspersed abundantly with others, equally deceptive, in the pages of the adepts. Neither is it animal absolutely, or vegetable, or mineral, or any natural particular whatever; but the alone Laelia Aelia latent in and about all, which the Enigma celebrates as comprehending all; but which the alchemists alone teach experimentally to expound.

The prose is opaque, not in the manner of mediaeval or early modern alchemical writing whose obscurities are largely those of terminology, and take the form of allegories and symbols which can be interpreted by reference to a rich and complex tradition handed down from early times, but opaque in a manner peculiar to nineteenth-century occultist writing in which the sense turns out to be a will o' the wisp flitting hither and thither among thickets of abstract nouns and the tangled roots of pseudo-biblical cadences. It is a specimen of the 'higher blather', its intricacies promising much more than they actually deliver. Still, the book was excellently attuned to its period and started to sell well, although no sooner had it appeared than Mary Ann and her father suffered a crisis of conscience and tried to recall or buy up as many copies as they could. These they burned on the lawn of their own house. Apparently they were afraid they had revealed all too clearly the secrets of a sacred art, a fear which the density of Mary Ann's prose should surely have put to rest.[5]

Her conviction that alchemy contained esoteric truths about the nature of matter and the means whereby individuals could set about and achieve spiritual regeneration was, however, typical of a long-standing belief, and one which gathered assent from a wide variety of men and women all over Western Europe and the USA during the second half of the nineteenth century. In France, for example, there was a notable burgeoning of interest in all the occult sciences at this time, the principal and most influential exponent of which was Alphonse Louis Constant, better known under his pseudonym Eliphas Lévi (1810–75). A series of books on magic, which he published between 1855 and 1861, established his reputation as an important adept, and although all contain remarks on alchemy, it is his *Dogme et Rituel de la Haute Magie* (1855–6) which provides the most comprehensive expression of how to understand the science:

> The Great Work is, before all things, *the creation of man by himself*, that is to say, the full and entire conquest of his faculties and his future. It is especially the perfect emancipation of his will, assuring him universal dominion over Azoth and the domain of Magnesia, in other words, full power over the universal magical agent. This agent, disguised by the ancient philosophers under the name of the First Matter, determines the forms of modifiable substance, and we can really arrive by means of it at metallic transmutation and the universal medicine. *This is not a hypothesis. It is a scientific fact already established and rigorously demonstrable* . . .
>
> The Great Work of Hermes is therefore an essentially magical operation and the highest of all, for it supposes the absolute in science and volition. There is light in gold, gold in light, and light in all things. The intelligent will, which assimilates the light, directs in this manner the operations of substantial form, *and uses chemistry solely as a secondary instrument*. The influence of human will and intelligence upon the operations of Nature, dependent in part on its labour, is otherwise a fact so real that all serious alchemists have succeeded in proportion to their knowledge and their faith, and have reproduced their thought in the phenomena of the fusion, salification, and recomposition of metals. Agrippa, who was a man of immense erudition and fine genius, but pure philosopher and sceptic, could not transcend the limits of metallic analysis and synthesis. Etteilla, a confused, obscure, fantastic but persevering Kabalist, reproduced in alchemy the eccentricities of his misconstrued and mutilated Tarot. Metals in his crucibles assumed extraordinary forms which excited the curiosity of all Paris, with no greater profit to the operator than the fees which were paid by his visitors. An obscure bellows-blower of

our own time, who died mad, poor Louis Cambriel, really cured his neighbours and, by the evidence of all his parish, brought back to life a smith who was his friend. For him the metallic work took the most inconceivable and apparently illogical forms. One day he beheld the figure of God Himself in his crucible, incandescent like the sun, transparent as crystal, His body composed of triangular conglomerations . . .

Raymond Lully, one of the grand and sublime masters of science, says that before we can make gold we must have gold. Out of nothing we can make nothing; wealth is not created absolutely; it is increased and multiplied. Hence let aspirants to knowledge understand and realise that neither miracles nor jugglers' feats are demanded of the adept. *Hermetic science, like all real sciences, is mathematically demonstrable.* Even its material results are as exact as a well-worked equation. Hermetic gold is not only a true doctrine, a shadowless light, truth unalloyed with falsehood; it is also material, actual, pure gold, the most precious which can be found in the veins of the earth. But the living gold, living sulphur, or true fire of the philosopher, must be sought in the house of Mercury. This fire feeds on air. To express its attractive and expansive power, a better comparison is impossible than that of lightning, which primally is a dry and terrestrial exhalation united to humid vapour, and afterwards, assuming an igneous nature, in virtue of its exaltation, acts on its inherent humidity, which it attracts and transmutes into its own nature, when it falls rapidly to earth where it is drawn by a fixed nature similar to its own.

These words, enigmatic in form but clear in essence, express openly what the philosophers understand by their mercury fructified by sulphur, which becomes the master and regenerator of salt. It is Azoth, universal magnesia, the great magical agent, *the astral light, the light of life*, fertilised by animic force, by intellectual energy, which they compare to sulphur on account of its affinities with divine fire. As to salt, it is absolute matter. All that is material contains salt, and all salt can be converted into pure gold by the combined action of sulphur and mercury, which at times act with [such] swiftness that transmutation can take place in an instant or in an hour, without labour for the operator and almost without expense. At other times, when the tendencies of the atmospheric media are adverse, the operation requires several days, months, and occasionally even years.

'Azoth' is further explained in Lévi's *La Clef des Grands Mystères* (1861): 'Azoth . . . is the vital element which manifests itself by the phenomena of heat, light, electricity and magnetism, which magnetises all terrestrial globes and all living beings.' Key phrases and sentiments in these passages mark out Lévi's views as those common among and peculiar to occult practitioners of this period. There is the appeal to science – the universal magical agent is a proven fact; alchemy can be demonstrated by the arts of measurement and number. Laboratory chemistry, however, is an art subordinate to its spiritual counterpart; human beings can be in complete control of their own development and destiny; and there exists within the universe an agent which produces transformative miracles, an agent both magnetic in its action and illuminating in its final manifestation

– 'astral light', a concept which harks back to Isaac Newton and beyond him to the 'light' of the original creative act recorded by Genesis. Was this creative act performed by a blind chance, or by a divinity with deliberate intentions? It was a question which dominated intellectual debate midway through the century, and various people tried to solve it in their various ways. 'Agnosticism', a word most characteristic of the period, teetered between 'science' on the one hand and 'creationism' on the other, unhappily aware that 'science' in effect constituted the fundamentalism of the day. It brooked no argument, no compromise, no question. The forces of unbelief and of anti-clericalism were on the march, soon to break out in particularly virulent strains, and reformulations of society, inspired by a combination of French revolution and economic growth, exercised a strong appeal over those very social strata which were also prepared to take to occultism. Spiritualism, Mesmerism, Clairvoyance, Nordic cults, Theosophy, Christian Science – a welter of alternatives to undiluted materialism rose and prospered during the course of the century. So to have Lévi proclaim that alchemy could be proven, and hint that this demonstrable science had weighable certainties to offer in connection with the 'light' which permeated everything and from which everything had originally risen, was both comforting and seductive to many.

Lévi's works were made available in English by Arthur Waite (1857–1942), who also translated a large number of the classics of alchemical literature and provided a history of alchemists and another of the science, *The Secret Tradition in Alchemy* (1926). '[It] completes', he wrote in his preface, 'my examination of the Secret Tradition transmitted through Christian Times, Alchemy being the one branch so far unexplored of that which has claimed to constitute Theosophy in Christ, illustrated in experience rather than by formal doctrine.' Waite's interest in the occult sciences extended far beyond alchemy, however, and in January 1891 he became a member of the Hermetic Order of the Golden Dawn, more or less a university of training in the magical arts and their related subjects, of which alchemy was one. Its symbols and terminology played an important role in some of the Order's rituals, and actually formed the basis of other rituals which were not part of the Order's regular grade system. These alchemical rites are an interesting fusion of laboratory process and ritual magic, and although they are too long to reproduce here in their entirety, a brief extract from one will give a notion of what they are like:

> The curcurbite or Egg Philosophic being hermetically sealed, the alchemist announces aloud that all is prepared for the invocation of the forces necessary to accomplish the work. The matter is then to be placed upon an altar with the elements and four weapons thereon; upon the white triangle and upon a flashing tablet of a general nature, in harmony with the matter selected for the working. Standing now in the place of the

Hierophant at the east of the altar, the alchemist should place his left hand upon the top of the curcurbite, raise his right hand holding the lotus wand by the Aries band (for in Aries is the beginning of the life of the year), ready to commence the general invocation of the forces of the divine light to operate in the work.

The aim of this rite is to produce a distilled liquid which is then subjected to heat for seven days and becomes an elixir 'for use according to the substance from which it was prepared'. This operation leaves a residue which is treated again for another seven days, and so becomes 'either a precious stone or a glittering powder, and this stone or powder shall be of magical virtue in accordance with its nature'. It is interesting to note that the practical side of alchemy had not been neglected during the decades of theorizing and spiritualizing, and we have evidence that members of the Golden Dawn would indeed try their hand at producing elixirs in this ritual fashion, for on 10 April 1890, the Reverend W.A. Ayton wrote to another member of the Order, Frederick Gardner, that he had been seeking the elixir of life for 50 years but had got nowhere because he was not properly prepared:

> There are the initial difficulties as to the furnaces. If you look into this part of the subject, you will see how difficult it is. All the old writers tell you, 'The regimen of the fire is the most important part'. From my experience, I believe that without a personal preparation, it is vain to attempt it. A friend of mine who is upon this line was making experiments in a room next to that in which were his wife and children, and it did not succeed. He is also in communication with intelligences in or out of the flesh, and gets the most extraordinary knowledge given him. One of these intelligences told him that the reason he did not succeed was because of the too great contiguity of his family. There are conditions necessary of which the generality of seekers have no idea. If I felt sure you were in right earnest in seeking the necessary personal conditions, I should be very glad to give you the benefit of my experience and practice, but I dare not do it in writing, nor except under the most inviolable secrecy. The difficulties in the practice are immense and inconceivable except to those who have made attempts at it.

Another Golden Dawn member who sought the elixir and claimed to have made it successfully was Aleister Crowley. His success was achieved, however, through a German magical order, the Ordo Templi Orientis, founded by a wealthy industrialist, Karl Kellner, some time between 1895 and 1906. Crowley records his preparation of the elixir and the effect it had on him:

> In the bosom of the Sanctuary of the Gnosis of the OTO is cherished a magical formula, extremely simple and practical, for attaining any desired object. It is, however, peculiarly appropriate to the principal operations of alchemy, most of all the preparation of the Elixir of Life and the Universal Medicine. At first I used this method casually. It was only when various unexpectedly and even astoundingly successful operations compelled my attention, that I devoted myself systematically and scientifically to the serious study and

practice of it. For some two and a half years I had conducted a careful and strenuous research into the conditions of success . . . Just before leaving New York I had prepared by this method an elixir whose virtue should be to restore youth, and of this I had taken seven doses. Nothing particular happened at first; and it never occurred to me that it might be imprudent to continue. I was mistaken. Hardly had I reached my hermitage before I was suddenly seized with an attack of youth in its acutest form. All mental activity became distasteful. I turned into a mere vehicle of physical energy.

It is probably best not to enquire too closely into what ingredients Crowley used for such an elixir, but his well-known predilection for sex magic suggests that he would have had no qualms about employing a variety of bodily fluids, such as had been recommended and used by earlier alchemists, too; and so his elixir brings us back, after its fashion, to those of imperial China. Crowley's interest was by no means peculiar to a tiny coterie. According to one account, for example, by 1894 there were about 50,000 alchemists in Paris alone, and whether one chooses to believe the claim or not, it is an indication that, on the verge of the twentieth century, in one of Europe's most sophisticated capitals, some people were prepared to accept that alchemy was more popular than at any time in its previous history. Certainly, if one considers the extent of the occult demi-monde in Paris – and it can be replicated in most of the other great cities across the continent – the insistence of the 'scientific' establishment that scientists, and scientists alone, had a unique access to and hold on Truth, a claim to which the twentieth century was to pay much more than lip service, was constantly being undermined by the widespread belief among the class from which scientists regularly drew their numbers, that mathematics alone were not enough and that worlds which could not be weighed or measured or even detected by man-made instruments not only existed but also penetrated the physical fabric of Creation, which scientists were so keen to preserve inviolable.[6]

10

A Child of Earlier Times: The Twentieth Century

'I believe it is useless for anyone to waste time on purely chemical experiments,' wrote William Westcott, a member of the Golden Dawn. 'To perform alchemical processes requires a simultaneous operation on the astral plane with that on the physical. Unless you are adept enough to act by will power, as well as by heat and moisture: by life force as well as by electricity, there will be no adequate result.'

Stephen Emmens (1844/5–c.1903/21) would not have agreed. Described by George Kauffmann as 'an unconventional, flamboyant, iconoclastic scientific and pseudoscientific entrepreneur of wide interests with dubious academic credentials and with more than a touch of paranoia and megalomania', Emmens had migrated from Britain to the USA at some time in the late 1880s, and there set up a number of companies dealing with metallurgy and mining. He himself certainly understood these and related subjects, and was at various times a member of the American Chemical Society, the American Institute of Mining, Metallurgical and Petroleum Engineers, and L'Association Alchimique de France, although he kept his membership of this last very quiet. But in 1896 he let it be known he had succeeded in transmuting a quantity of silver into a substance intermediate between silver and gold, and was immediately attacked by divers learned parties in a controversy which continued for the next two years, fuelled by Emmens' published claim that, given a million ounces of silver, he would make 60,000 ounces of gold at a profit of $2,700,000. Challenged to let qualified people see his process at work, Emmens first agreed, but then raised difficulties such that the offer was not taken up; and yet while suspicions about his claims and honesty can be raised by these circumstances, sufficient doubt remains to make one pause a little before dismissing him outright as a fraud. One is reminded somewhat of the Comte de Saint-Germain or Cagliostro, about whom it may have been possible to say that there was more than met the eye, however much one might want to resist their outrageous boasts.

Emmens was going to provide a pattern which would become common in the twentieth century, but the legacy of the nineteenth century had no intention of going away. As early as 1854, Louis Figuier had constructed a dialogue between proponents and opponents of the metaphysical tendencies to be found in alchemy and had put in a plea for greater tolerance of pre-nineteenth-century alchemists, whose work was underrated because it was not properly understood;

and understanding and explaining alchemy's metaphysical tendencies was to be a major strand in the work of the Swiss psychologist Carl Jung (1875–1961). He began his studies as early as 1913, but it was not until the 1920s and 1930s that he began to publish some of his best-known interpretations of the subject. One of these saw a parallel between the images some of his patients saw in their dreams and those of alchemical illustrations, a key idea which itself came to him in dreams:

> Before I discovered alchemy, I had a series of dreams which repeatedly dealt with the same theme. Beside my house stood another that is to say, another wing or annexe, which was strange to me. Each time I would wonder in my dream why I did not know this house, although it has apparently always been there. Finally came a dream in which I reached the other wing. I discovered there a wonderful library, dating largely from the sixteenth and seventeenth centuries. Large, fat folio volumes, bound in pigskin, stood along the walls. Among them were a number of books embellished with copper engravings of a strange character, and illustrations containing curious symbols such as I had never seen before. At the time I did not know to what they referred; only much later did I recognise them as alchemical symbols. In the dream I was conscious only of the fascination exerted by them and by the entire library. It was a collection of Mediaeval incunabula and sixteenth-century prints.
>
> The unknown wing of the house was a part of my personality, an aspect of myself; it represented something that belonged to me but of which I was not yet conscious. It, and especially the library, referred to alchemy, of which I was ignorant, but which I was soon to study. Some fifteen years later I had assembled a library very like the one in the dream.

His theories then rapidly developed, and Jung came to the conclusion that 'the alchemical *opus* deals in the main not just with chemical experiments as such, but with something resembling psychic processes expressed in pseudochemical language'. The individual is thus treated to a sight of his own unconscious mind receiving images from the collective unconscious of humanity, and the experience is akin to that of a mystic or visionary. This experience, he said, is what has been recorded by alchemical writers, some of whose accounts are more worthwhile than others, inasmuch as some writers were merely charlatans penning the equivalent of gibberish, whereas others were doing their best to express genuine insights and experiences which by their very nature were almost incommunicable in words. Hence the ambiguities and obscurities constant in alchemical texts. Moreover, said Jung, there had been a rift in alchemical literature at the end of the sixteenth or the middle of the seventeenth century, after which the science began to diverge into what would become 'chemistry' and what would become a kind of mystical theology.

(Compare Grillot de Givry's remarks, made in 1929 in *Le Musée des Sorciers, Mages, et Alchimistes*:

My readers are already familiar with the names of various operations of the Great Work, and will henceforth be able to form a conclusion of the highest importance – namely, that from the fifteenth century onward alchemic science, or that manifestation of it which adepts claim as the true science, is presented as a complete doctrine, unalterable, never clearly expounded, but defined under a symbolism the forms of which were to remain invariable down to our own day; a mysterious doctrine which could not progress, since it had reached its point of perfection in one stride, and could not undergo a modification for which there was no necessity. Adepts who have comprehended the science are in agreement on this doctrine, and, deaf to the recriminations of modern chemistry – which they very well understand – repeat the same traditional expressions, veiled in the same traditional allegories. It is by virtue of this unchanging agreement that we find Cyliani and Cambriel, for instance, two alchemists who operated about 1830, speaking exactly the same metaphorical language as Nicolas Flamel or Basil Valentine, who lived in the fourteenth and fifteenth centuries respectively.

The timescale is slightly different, but the sentiments are much the same.)

Jung's delving into the self, however much stimulated and coloured by late nineteenth-century occultism, is part of that more or less continuous tradition of spiritualizing alchemy, which we have observed in several of its manifestations. But Jung plays down the importance (even the existence) of laboratory work in a way that Robert Boyle and Isaac Newton, for example, never did, and while Jung's influence can be seen in later histories or accounts of the science – those of Mircea Eliade, Titus Burckhardt and Johannes Fabricius immediately spring to mind – it is a characteristic of twentieth-century interest in alchemy that it returns very firmly to the workshop and tries to understand alchemy in its practical as well as its spiritualizing side.[1]

Thus, Isabella and Richard Ingalese, an American couple living in Los Angeles from 1912 onwards, became interested in the philosopher's stone as a way of adding another 20 years or so to their active lives. It took them six years of trial and error, but in 1917 they were able to produce the white stone and by 1920 had discovered the red, a success they shared with a coterie of investors who had financially supported their endeavours. This 'sharing' – that is to say ingesting the material – was done with caution, but those who took it, along with the Ingaleses themselves, reported the expected benefits of renewed vigour and cure of diseases including at least one case of cancer, and one remarkable (and unexpected) resurrection from the dead. Richard Ingalese described the incident. The wife of a notable physician had died:

> Half an hour had elapsed and her body was growing cold. A dose of the dissolved White Stone was placed into the mouth of the corpse without perceptible results. Fifteen minutes later a second dose was administered and the heart commenced to pulsate weakly. Fifteen minutes later a third dose was given and soon the woman opened her

eyes. In the course of a few weeks the woman became convalescent, after which she lived seven years.

Without independent verification of any of these details, it is difficult to know how to assess their worth; but the incident does indicate that practical alchemy was alive and well in the 1920s United States, and that some people were willing to take the Ingaleses seriously.

By contrast in France in 1925, Eugène Canseliet, who claimed to be a pupil of the alchemist 'Fulcanelli', published the first edition of his master's *Le Mystère des cathédrales*, in which 'Fulcanelli' promulgated an alchemical interpretation of France's Gothic cathedrals. Certain alchemists, he said, had chosen to record their secrets in the carved figures, emblems and inscriptions which decorate the exteriors and interiors of a number of monumental buildings, each of which 'should not be regarded as a work dedicated solely to the glory of Christianity, but rather as a vast concretion of ideas, of tendencies, of popular beliefs, a perfect whole to which we can refer without fear whenever we would penetrate the religious, secular, philosophic, or social thoughts of our ancestors'. Thus, in a prominent place in the central porch of Notre Dame in Paris, 'alchemy is represented by a woman with her head touching the clouds. Seated on a throne, she holds in her left hand a sceptre, the sign of royal power, while her right hand supports two books, one closed (esotericism), the other open (exotericism). Supported between her knees and leaning against her chest is a ladder with nine rungs – *scala philosophorum* – hieroglyph of the patience which the faithful must possess in the course of the nine successive operations of the Hermetic labour' – and so on and so forth.

This kind of interpretation had been attempted before, by Esprit Gobineau de Montluisant (c.1591– post 1651), whose *Very Curious Explanation of the Enigmas and Hieroglyphical and Physical Figures which are in the Great Porch of the Metropolitan Cathedral of Our Lady of Paris* offered similar, equally unconvincing observations on the same range of Gothic statuary. Regarding 'Fulcanelli', of course, we have to bear in mind that by his time the legend that the mediaeval cathedral builders possessed secret knowledge which they passed on to their descendants the Freemasons was taken more or less as fact in occult circles (indeed, it still infects the writing of some Masonic histories today) and so his winkling out alchemical allusions in the highly complex stone imagery of mediaeval cathedrals is not in the least surprising.

What may be surprising is 'Fulcanelli's' possible identity. Christer Böke and John Koopmans have suggested he may have been an aristocratic French engineer and chemist, the Comte de Chardonnet (1839–1924), inventor of rayon and member of the Académie de Science, a highly respected and respectable member of nineteenth-century French society, whose public career gave no indication of his private interests. Whether he founded or re-founded an Hermetic fraternity, as De Pascalis says, is perhaps open to doubt. Certainly remarkable tales congregated around his name and person, as they have always tended to do round supposed alchemical adepts; and so we are told by his pupil, Canseliet, that he looked no more than 50 years old at the age of about 110; that 'Fulcanelli' entrusted the publication of *Le Mystère des cathédrales* to him and then disappeared; that during the 1920s 'Fulcanelli' had transmuted some lead into gold in the presence of two witnesses in a laboratory of the Sarcelle gasworks; that he had 'appeared' in 1937 to Jacques Bergier to offer a warning about the impending atomic bomb; and that he had been seen during the 1950s and 60s, looking younger than he had when Canseliet had met him decades earlier. Like 'Fulcanelli's' interpretations of Gothic stone imagery, however, none of this is essentially new and in fact is rather annoying, as it gets in the way of an historical figure who had something interesting to say which reveals – or could reveal, given careful, judicious treatment – fascinating insights into the workings of a late-nineteenth-century educated, scientific but occult-attracted mind.[2]

Likewise, perhaps, we should note the occult obsessions of the Swedish playwright, August Strindberg (1849–1912), stimulated by his arrival in Paris in 1894. As soon as he took up residence there, he began a series of chemical experiments with sulphur, which convinced him he could succeed in the alchemical production of gold. Sulphur fumes and absinthe, however, began to work their curious magic, and he started to see visions which he put down to clairvoyance: 'he saw not only Zeus and the Devil in a pillow, he saw human faces in pansies, and above the Pantheon floated Napoleon and all his marshals'. Nevertheless, he was able to publish his work, enter into correspondence with Mercellin Berthelot whose own interest in alchemy had led him between 1885 and 1889 to publish many of its classic texts, a history of the science and an introduction to the 'chemistry' of the ancients and the Middle Ages. By 1895, Strindberg's alchemical fame had spread, and he received the enthusiastic support of François Jollivet-Castelot, a young alchemist who in 1897 went on to found the Société Alchimique de France, found and edit more than one occult journal and, after a long series of experiments begun in 1908, claim to have produced alchemical gold in 1925 by heating to a high temperature a compound mixed with silver oxysulphide and antimony. The highly influential Gérard Encausse, known as 'Papus', was equally enthusiastic about Strindberg the alchemist and published the following note about him in *L'Initiation*:

Our eminent author, August Strindberg, who combined vast knowledge with his great talents as a writer, has just achieved a synthesis of gold from iron. August Strindberg has an absolute contempt for riches and has never kept any of his methods secret, consequently he immediately gave us his procedure, which confirms all the assertions of the alchemists. We are carrying out control experiments, which are all giving us absolutely conclusive proof.

Meanwhile in Germany, alchemical societies and their journals rose and fell and rose again: *Alchemistische Blätter*, begun in 1927, with Jollivet-Castelot contributing to the first two numbers; the *Alchemistische Gesellschaft* founded in 1928 with two branches, one in Berlin and one in Hamburg; and *Spagyrische Gesellschaft* founded in 1929, the year in which *The New York Times* reported, 'German Produces Gold in Synthetic Test. Denies Swindling Ludendorff and Others'. The German in question was Franz Tausend who claimed to have developed a process for extracting gold from base metals, a claim which interested the young Nazi Party and ultimately led to Tausend's disgrace. Having raised huge sums of money to underwrite the cost of his experiments, Tausend and his partners spent most of it on high living and were eventually obliged to flee abroad to escape the fury of their creditors. Tausend, however, was arrested in Italy and brought back to Munich for trial in 1929. Indignantly, he demanded to be given an opportunity to demonstrate his methods, and so he was taken to the Bavarian State Mint where, in the presence of the Mint's director, two detectives, the state advocate and his trial judge, and after every precaution had been taken to obviate fraud, Tausend set about his work. The official announcement afterwards said, 'After experimenting for two hours, Tausend produced a grain of the finest gold weighing one tenth of a gram, which was smelted from 1.67 grams of lead. Experts described the result as surprisingly favourable and contradictory to scientific knowledge.' Next day, however, it was said that fraud had been uncovered after all, as gold had been smuggled into Tausend in a cigarette whose ashes, along with the gold, he had presumably managed to drop into his crucible at an appropriate moment. It is possible, of course, since the amount of gold is tiny, but one cannot help wondering about 'surprisingly' and 'contradictory to scientific knowledge'. Was it in someone's interests to have Tausend convicted, regardless of the results of his demonstration?

That way lies conspiracy theory, of course, so one had better be very cautious. But the fact of the matter is that the 1920s were alive with attempts to produce or reproduce alchemical transmutations, stimulated by experiments conducted by two German chemists, Adolf Miethe and Hans Stammreich in 1924, and inevitably these attempts ran the risk of coming up against entrenched theories and attitudes which might not take kindly to being challenged, especially in relation to what the scientific community in general had dismissed as nonsense and superstition. Nevertheless, in 1919 Ernest Rutherford had announced a successful transmutation of one element into another – nitrogen into oxygen – so the possibilities of going further were not entirely without foundation, and we find that the pages of such journals as *Nature* and *Scientific American* frequently report and comment on gold-making attempts in non-alchemical laboratories. In general their comments vary between sceptical and dismissive. A.S. Russell was cautious: 'There are ... two pairs of elements, lead and thallium, mercury and gold, in which the transformation of the type under discussion may occur' – but the more usual tone was that of an anonymous contributor to *Nature* in 1926: 'Claims to have effected "the great work" of transmutation have been made at frequent intervals since alchemy fell into disrepute, and their ignoble fate must make us sceptical of more recent contentions; but if these are proved to be baseless, it will be admitted that modern research into the constitution of the atom gave them a rational basis of possibility such as was never dreamed of by the mediaeval alchemist, even in his most fantastic flights of imagination.' The spirit of academic condescension, it seems, was alive and eager to patronize.[3]

If political eagerness for cash combined with personal curiosity to pursue the aim of transmutation during the interwar years, as the Second World War loomed we find Archibald Cockren establishing an alchemical laboratory in London during the 1930s. He had originally qualified as a physiotherapist in 1904 and set up in private practice which he continued for the rest of his life, apart from a period during the First World War when he was attached to military hospitals. His principal alchemical interest had its starting point in the organo-metallic compounds common in the medical pharmacopoeia of the time, about which he had this to say:

In the administration of a metal ... it must be understood that the body of a metal is worthless, as a medicine, it cannot heal: it is the *essence alone* that is curative. Only too often the body is poisonous, and until that gross part of the metal be broken up, its administration is definitely *harmful*. Probably one of the most common forms of metallic poisoning is that of mercury, but remove the harmful parts of the metal and the healing essence is free to do its work thoroughly. Nitrate of silver is a caustic poison, but remove the gross part of the metal and the essence of the silver is a cure for diseases of the brain. Lead salts are poisonous, it is true, and in many cases their administration has resulted in death from lead poisoning, but remove that poisonous matter and the remaining essence, which is clear, sweet-smelling, and aromatic in taste, forms a cure for all diseases of the spleen. Copper, when the gross body of the metal is removed and the essence unlocked, is invaluable for the nervous system and the kidneys; likewise, tin for the liver, iron for all inflammatory diseases, and the bile, and gold for the heart and general circulation. But gold, too, is suitable for a medicine only when the salts of gold are reduced into the oil of gold and distilled into a golden liquid; then and only then is gold tolerated and utilised by the human body. The salts of gold used at the present day can never be assimilated, for by their present method of preparation they can never be properly distilled and purified. From the foregoing paragraphs it will be seen that the whole principle of cure rests on the proper separation of this quintessence to which alchemy, and alchemy alone, provides the key.

Cockren's book *Alchemy Rediscovered and Restored*, which he published in 1940, takes us through a number of his experiments as he searched for and discovered curative oils made from each of the planetary metals, and gives an account of a eureka moment when his long labours came to an unexpected fruition:

I realised that without the alkahest of the philosophers the real oil of gold could not be obtained, and so again I went back and forth in the alchemists' writings to obtain the clue. The experiments which I had already made considerably lightened my task, and one day while sitting quietly in deep concentration the solution to my problem was revealed to me in a flash, and at the same time any of the enigmatical utterances of the alchemists were made clear . . .

Here, then, I entered upon a new course of experiment, with a metal for experimental purposes with which I had had no previous experience. This metal, after being reduced to its salts and undergoing special preparation and distillation, delivered up the Mercury of the Philosophers, the Aqua Benedicta, the Aqua Celestis, the Water of Paradise. The first intimation I had of this triumph was a violent hissing, jets of vapour pouring from the retort and into the receiver like sharp bursts from a machine-gun, and then a violent explosion, whilst a very potent and subtle odour filled the laboratory and its surroundings. A friend has described this odour as resembling the dewy earth on a June morning, with the hint of growing flowers in the air, the breath of the wind over heather and hill, and the sweet smell of the rain on the parched earth . . .

And now to the final goal, the Philosopher's Stone. Having found my two principles, the Mercury and the Sulphur, my next step was to purify the dead body of the metal, that is, the black dregs of the metal left after the extraction of the golden water. This was calcined to a redness and carefully separated and treated until it became a white salt. The three principles were then conjoined in certain exact quantities in a hermetically sealed flask in a fixed heat neither too hot nor too cold, care as to the exact degree of heat being essential, as any carelessness in its regulation would completely spoil the mixture.

On conjunction the mixture takes on the appearance of a leaden mud, which rises slowly like dough until it throws up a crystalline formation rather like a coral plant in growth. The 'flowers' of this plant are composed of petals of crystal which are continually changing in colour. As the heat is raised, this formation melts into an amber-coloured liquid which gradually becomes thicker and thicker until it sinks into a black earth on the bottom of the glass. At this point (the sign of the crow in alchemical literature) more of the ferment or mercury is added. In this process, which is one of continual sublimation, a long-necked, hermetically sealed flask is used, and one can watch the vapour rising up the neck of the flask and condensing down the sides. This process continues until the state of 'dry blackness' is attained. When more of the mercury is added, the black powder is dissolved, and from this conjunction it seems that a new substance is born, or, as the early alchemists would have expressed it, a son is born. As the black colour abates, colour after colour comes and goes until the mixture becomes white and shining; the White Elixir. The heat is gradually raised yet more, and from white the colour changes to citrine and finally to red – the Elixir Vitae, the Philosopher's Stone, the medicine of men and metals.

We are told that Cockren was killed when a bomb fell on his house during the Blitz. We are also told he escaped and went to Brighton where he died in c.1950. We are also informed that he used to trace a form of the pentagram during his alchemical experiments, an indication of magical as well as purely chemical working, which was the kind of practice a member of the Golden Dawn might well have observed. Now, there is no indication that he was a member of that order, and it had actually folded in Britain by the time Cockren was devoting himself seriously to the Great Work. But a surprising number of alchemists in the twentieth century did mix magic or other occult interests with their alchemy – Aleister Crowley bears witness to that, as do several others – and although Cockren gives no real indication of having what one might call a magical frame of mind, he does make one intriguing remark at one point. 'I fully realized,' he wrote, 'when commencing this work that my only hope of success was to put on one side for the time being any knowledge of chemistry that I might possess and to study alchemystical writings in a sincere attempt to understand the alchemist's language and reasoning, and then, by following out his instructions faithfully step by step, to prove the practicability of this science.' Cockren's spelling of 'alchemystical' seems to be deliberate. Is this a hint that, in spite of his apparent concentration on practical laboratory working, he brought other faculties to bear in the course of his experiments?

Practicability, however, is what he emphasized, and practicability was also one of the starting points for the French alchemist Armand Barbault (1906–82), an engineer by profession, who also worked in the biological department of the Armand Carrel Institute. He had considerable expertise as an astrologer, and could have made his living from it, and this, combined with his particular interest in developing elixirs, meant that he was especially keen to make sure that the dew and plants he gathered for alchemical processing were taken at the astrologically appropriate time of day, season and planetary configuration. He began his search in 1948, re-working, in fact, the process described in the seventeenth-century *Mutus Liber*. This book's 15 engravings take one through several stages of an alchemical operation. They begin with prayer, and then show one how to gather dew that has been deposited on cloths suspended from pegs on the ground and spread out as though on an invisible table. Next, the dew is subjected to distillation, the residue is collected, and the process repeated. A second stage shows six shallow open vessels set upon open ground to collect precipitation, and this too, when gathered, passes through similar distillation, evaporation and purification in the laboratory. Plate 14 of the book shows the process complete, with the lunar tincture in one vessel over a fire, and the solar in another. It is notable that the work is conducted throughout by a man and a woman. This may be an indication that the male alchemist does in reality require a female assistant or companion – in spite of the fact that there are few recorded instances of female alchemists, alchemical engravings constantly show women present during the various stages of the alchemical operation – or the woman may be symbolic, a reminder that a balance between male and female forces is necessary to achieve success. An inscription in the body of the first engraving also reminds us that the whole operation must begin and end with prayer, since God presides over it and is the source of the knowledge contained in it. '[This is a] book which makes no sound, but in which the entire Hermetic system of philosophy is represented by means of symbolic images. [The book] is attributed to God the Merciful, three times best and greatest, and is dedicated to the only sons of the Art by an author whose name is "Altus".'

Barbault followed these steps in a modified way. He took literally the injunction to collect dew as his medium, and did so under advice from his second wife who was a psychic and used her special abilities to help him locate the places from which to take his material. 'My companion', he says of one occasion, 'was at this time in a state of high exaltation. She existed for long periods in a trance-like condition and carried out her functions as guide in the fullest possible way.' Astrology, too, was most important – 'astrology is only one step from alchemy, alchemy only one step from medicine' – and so when Barbault and his wife went for the first time, on Sunday 3 August 1947, to examine the ground from which they proposed to extract their *prima materia* – a 'germ' which Barbault refers to as 'Philosopher's Peat' – Barbault drew up an astral chart to check whether or not the time was favourable for such an inspection. When it came to gathering his sample, he repeated the exercise and found thereby that he should dig the ground several months later, after midnight on 15 February 1948. What was it he dug up, then? 'Is it not – at least as far as the layman is concerned,' he answered, 'plain ordinary earth? For the initiated person it is something quite different. It is a *living* earth, seized from the ground by a very special process belonging to the sphere of High Magic, which allows the adept assigned to the task to gain possession of an entire collection of physical and metaphysical principles.' Some of the vocabulary used here is strongly reminiscent of the nineteenth century – 'initiated', 'High Magic', 'adept' – and reminds us that, through his wife, Barbault seems to have been closely associated with occultists of a quite different kind, such as Jacques Breyer, who thought he was a reincarnation of the last Templar Master, Jacques de Molay, and carried out a necromantic rite on 12 June 1952 to raise the ghost of a Templar, Guillaume de Beaujeu. It is said that M. and Mme Barbault were present and gave assistance at this rite, but even if one refrains from giving credence to anecdotes of this kind – although they could, of course, be true – the association of alchemy with magic is by no means unusual and, as in Cockren's case, an open mind about Barbault's involvement in other types of occultism is probably best.

The bulk of his book, however, is given to a description, illustrated by photographs, of the processes he followed over several years before achieving his 'golden elixir' (golden in colour, not in content), for which he claimed remarkable cures. Not that this vegetable-based elixir was the only one possible, for Barbault concludes by discussing three tinctures derived from gold, silver and antimony, and explains the correspondences between the planets, metals and human organs, correspondences and connections which come from a very old alchemical (not to mention medicinal) tradition, but which should not perhaps be dismissed entirely. For during the 1920s and 30s, in reference to these metal-planet connections – and 'planets' here refers to the old-style seven: Mercury, Venus, Mars, Sun, Moon, Jupiter and Saturn – Lily Kolisko conducted experiments to investigate the workings of etheric forces in material substances and claimed it was possible to show that astronomical events can be linked to observable changes in the pattern of planetary metals.

So with Barbault we return to one of the primary quests of ancient alchemy, the search for elixirs possessing near-miraculous properties, a search which many subsequent twentieth-century alchemists have also undertaken. This, for example, was the main alchemical interest of one of the most influential of these individuals, Albert Riedel (1911–84), known also as 'Frater Albertus', whose *Alchemist's Handbook* (1960) describes not only the preparation of a herbal elixir, but also the astral relationship between herbs and the seven planets. Riedel founded the Paracelsus Research Society – the title tells us the principal source of his inspiration – which attracted large numbers of students eager to learn and pursue alchemical research. But in addition to his alchemical pursuits, Riedel was a member of AMORC – Ancient and Mystical Order Rosae Crucis – a society claiming links with the seventeenth-century Rosicrucians, and this extension into other spheres of occult or unorthodox knowledge can also be seen in one of his contemporaries, Roger Caro, a record of whose laboratory work is available in a remarkable set of colour photographs, taking us beyond the elixir stage to that of the philosopher's stone itself. Caro, too, was intimately connected with modern Rosicrucianism. During the 1960s he was a member of the alchemical-religious Temple Initiatique d'Ajunta, which Caro reorganized into a Rosicrucian order once he became leader of the society. Its activities, as far as one can tell, seem to have consisted of a combination of actual laboratory practice and rituals faintly reminiscent of those of the Golden Dawn – the grades and titles of its officers are certainly borrowed thence. Another French alchemist, Jean Dubuis (1919–), was also a Martinist and a Rosicrucian. For him, alchemy is essentially an initiatic system which will lead the initiate to higher realms of understanding and therefore of self-development, and in 1979 he co-founded a society, *Les Philosophes de la Nature*, designed to promote research into alchemy, Kabbalah and other esoteric disciplines. Similarly, the American Hans Nintzel (1932–2000) promoted not only alchemy but also ritual magic, astrology and Kabbalah. So if these interconnections sound familiar, it is partly because Barbault, Riedel, Caro, Dubuis and Nintzel are clearly in their various ways children of the nineteenth century for whose occultists alchemy was only one among several esoteric interests, and a vehicle to take them towards other goals, rather than an end in itself, and partly because magic is frequently to be found hovering on the borders of alchemy, as evidenced by Robert Boyle's hope that the stone might provide him with a gateway to 'the attainment of some intercourse with good spirits'.

Alchemy, then, far from being a defunct preliminary to the 'rational' investigations of modern chemistry, is as vigorous as ever it was. Laboratories may be found everywhere, although the traditional secrecy or discretion of the alchemist still obtains, and so these workplaces may not be obvious, as Peter Marshall found when he went in search of them. Nor are they confined to the eastern half of the globe. They flourish in Western Europe, too, and in North America, where the pretensions of modern science can be heard at their most vociferous and its claims most loudly trumpeted. But if attempts to make gold still continue, they are perhaps less frequent than the search for an elixir (or various elixirs) which will cure safely and quickly those diseases and debilities still reluctant to yield to other forms of medicine or surgery. An elixir which will restore youthful zest and prolong active life is also much desired, and we can see from this how alchemy is capable of adapting itself to the prevailing ethos of a time and place. Modern obsession with juvenescence gives the search for elixirs precedence over the quest for gold; and yet during times of war or those periods of tension in which war is contemplated, a ready illimitable source of gold may become especially attractive, as the sixteenth and early seventeenth centuries, not to mention the 1920s and 30s, illustrate. Perhaps, then, the twenty-first century will see a resurgence in this branch of alchemy. But if the spiritualizing side of the science continues to exert its influence – and this aspect of alchemy has remained more or less constant in its appeal throughout the centuries, if differently expressed at different times – then it will be interesting to see whether the self-absorption of the eighteenth and nineteenth centuries, aided and abetted by the speculations of Freud and Jung, directs that influence, or whether there will be a return to the specifically religious awe with which alchemists approached their investigations of the created universe, in which case the observations of Jean D'Espagnet may be considered pertinent:

> Lest man should dream fancies to himself, glory in divers privileges, assume to himself as proper only to him the name of Microcosm, or the world's lesser draft, because there are discernible in his material workshop an analogy of all the natural motions of the Macrocosm, or the larger volume of the world: let him consider that every creature, even a worm, that every plant, even the weed of the sea, is a lesser world, having in it an

epitome of the greater. Therefore let man seek for a world out of himself, and he shall find it everywhere; for there is one and the same first copy of all creatures, out of which were made infinite worlds of matter, yet in form differenced. Let therefore man share humility and lowliness of spirit, and attribute to God glory and honour.[4]

Notes

Notes to Chapter 1: China: The Golden Road to Immortality

1 On etymology, see Needham, pt 4, pp. 339–45. Dubs, 'The beginnings of alchemy', p. 81, n. 113. On the difference between China and the West, Davis, 'The Chinese beginnings of alchemy', p. 154. Wu Lu-Ch'iang and Davis, 'An ancient Chinese treatise', pp. 222–3, 224. In referring to alchemy as a science, I use the word 'science' in its Latin sense of 'a branch of knowledge'.

2 Needham, pt 2, p. 54. Quotation from Ko Hung in pt 3, pp. 1–2. A similar contempt for the monetary value of gold can be seen in St Thomas More's *Utopia* where it is used for the manufacture of objects intended for base usage, such as manacles or chamber pots.

3 Needham, pt 3, pp. 26, 187–8. Dubs, 'The beginnings of alchemy', p. 67.

4 Needham, pt 2, pp. 273–81, 209. Waley, 'Notes on Chinese alchemy', p. 15. Quotation Needham, *op.cit.*, p. 62. The caveat regarding natural gold was repeated by Chhen Tshang-Chhi in c.AD 725.

5 Needham, vol. 3, p. 640. Quotation from Liu An in Thompson, *Alchemy and Alchemists*, p. 52. Marshall, *The Philosopher's Stone*, p. 30. Dubs, 'The beginnings of alchemy', p. 73. Sivin, 'Chinese alchemy and the manipulation of time', p. 22.

6 Needham, pt 3, pp. 105–6. Cooper, *Chinese Alchemy*, pp. 49–50. On female alchemists, see Needham, *op.cit.*, pp. 169–70, 191–2, 38.

7 Needham, pt 2, pp. 283, 243.

8 Needham, pt 2, pp. 81–5, 11. Lady of Tai, ibid., p. 304. Marshall, *The Philosopher's Stone*, pp. 3–4. On *hsien*, Needham, *op.cit.*, pp. 96–7. Cooper, *Chinese Alchemy*, pp. 23–32. Quotation from Waley, 'Notes on Chinese alchemy', p. 11. It is also quoted by Eliade, *The Forge and the Crucible*, p. 115 where the poem is dubiously attributed to the alchemist Wei Po-Yang.

9 Ying-Shi Yü, 'Life and immortality in the mind of Han China', pp. 81, 87, 88–9, 93, 115. Cooper, *Chinese Alchemy*, pp. 33–45. Dubs, 'The beginnings of alchemy', p. 65. Quotation from Ying-Shi Yü, *op.cit.*, p. 85.

10 Cooper, *Chinese Alchemy*, pp. 37–40. Needham, pt 2, pp. 1–2 and ibid., pt 3, pp. 147–8. The story about Wei Po-Yang comes from the fourth-century AD *Lives of the Divine Hsien* (*Shen Hsien Chuan*). See Needham, pt 2, p. 295.

11 Needham, pt 3, p.149. The aludel is an earthenware or glass pot in the shape of a pear, open at both ends so that several such pots can be fitted together to form a series. It is used

during the process of sublimation. See Needham, pt 4, pp. 18–19. There is a picture of an aludel made from silver, ibid., p.25.

12   Wei Po-Yang, *The Secret of Everlasting Life (Tshan Thing Chhi)*, trans. R. Bertschinger (Shaftesbury: Element Books, 1994), pp. 91–2.

13   Trans. Waley, 'Notes on Chinese alchemy', p. 2. Date of the passage, ibid., p. 3.

14   Eliade, *The Forge and the Crucible*, pp. 65–70. Needham, pt 3, pp. 29–32. In vol. 5, pt 5 Needham deals at length with what he calls 'physiological alchemy' intended to achieve physical changes leading to protracted longevity. Marshall, *The Philosopher's Stone*, pp. 27–30. The dualistic doctrine of *yang-yin* seems to have appeared in China in the third century BC. Davis, 'The Chinese beginnings of alchemy', p. 156. Wu Lu-ch'iang and Davis, 'An ancient Chinese treatise', pp. 216–18. On the relationship between *yang* and *yin*, alchemy, and the *I Ching*, see Robinet, 'Le monde à l'envers dans l'alchimie intérieure Taoïste', pp. 243–5. Waley, 'Notes on Chinese alchemy', p. 5. Sivin, 'Chinese alchemy and the manipulation of time', pp. 521–2. See further ibid., pp. 518–20 as an example of the regulation of combustion and time. On the ritual aspects of the alchemical process, see Pregadio, 'I due aspetti del rituale nell'alchimia cinese', pp. 135–49.

15   For a survey of the important periods of Chinese alchemy, see Needham, pt 3, pp. 117–208. Read, 'Chinese alchemy', pp. 877–8. On Wei Po-Yang, Needham, *op.cit.*, pp. 50–75. Wu Lu'ch'iang and Davis, 'An ancient Chinese treatise', pp. 213–15. Marshall, *The Philosopher's Stone*, pp. 36–41.

16   On Ge Hong, see Tortchinov, 'Science and magic', (1998), at *www.levity.com/alchemy/gehong.html*. On Ko Hung, see Needham pt 3, pp. 75–113. Forke, 'Ko Hung, der Philosoph und Alchimist', pp. 115–26. Marshall, *The Philosopher's Stone*, pp. 42–9. White, *The Alchemical Body*, p. 64. Holmyard, *Alchemy*, p. 41. Davis, 'The Chinese beginnings of alchemy', p. 160.

17   M. Strickmann 'On the alchemy of T'ao Hung-ching', pp. 123–92. Cooper, *Chinese Alchemy*, p. 63. Needham, pt 3, pp. 169–71.

18   Schafer, 'Orpiment and realgar in Chinese technology and tradition', p. 85. Marshall, *The Philosopher's Stone*, p. 29. Needham, pt 4, pp. 276–7, 463–5; pt 3, pp. 86–7, 285, 218. Cf. Ch'en Shao-Wei in his eighth-century monograph on the alchemical preparation of cinnabar, 'If lustrous cinnabar is further taken in the sevenfold-recycled or ninefold-cyclically-transformed state, etc.' quoted in Sivin, 'Chinese alchemy and the manipulation of time', p. 516.

19   Schafer, *art.cit.* supra, pp. 86, 76. Davis and Chao Yün-Ts'ung, 'An alchemical poem by Kao Hsiang-Hsien', pp. 237, 239. Sivin, *art.cit.* supra, p. 522, n. 14. On semi-open language see Spooner and Wang, 'The divine nine turn Tan Sha method', pp. 235–42.

20   Cooper, *Chinese Alchemy*, p. 144. Cooper also points out the further associations alchemists made with these two. *Yang* represented solution, sulphur and gold, the sun and the heavens, heating and hardness. *Yin* represented coagulation, the moon and the earth, cooling, softness, quicksilver and silver. Needham, pt 3, p. 70. ibid., pt 5, p. 186. Wu Lu-Ch'iang and Davis, 'An ancient Chinese treatise on alchemy', p. 253. Robinet, 'Le monde à l'envers dans l'alchimie intérieure Taoïste', pp. 245–6. Marshall, *The Philosopher's Stone*, pp. 64–9.

21   Quoted in Needham, pt 3, p. 185.

22 Needham, pt 2, p. 11; pt 3, p. 117. Diagram: ibid., p. 121. Quotations: ibid., p. 171; pt 5, p. 189; pt 3, p. 185. See also Chikashige, *Alchemy*, pp. 39–54.

23 Needham, pt 3, pp. 212–15, 250. Marshall, *The Philosopher's Stone*, pp. 71, 79.

Notes to Chapter 2: India: The Way of Tantra and Mercury

1 Quotation from Needham, pt 4, pp. 411–12. Contacts: ibid., pp. 197–8; pt 3, pp. 160–5, 139.

2 Nāgārjuna: Needham, pt 3, pp. 161–4. White, *The Alchemical Body*, pp. 66–77. Tantra: Marshall, *The Philosopher's Stone*, pp. 108–16. Ray, *History of Chemistry*, pp. 113, 61, 62, 126, 114. Bogar: White, *op.cit.*, pp. 87, 376–7, note 60. Quotations: Needham, *op.cit.*, p.161. Eliade, *The Forge and the Crucible*, p. 131. White, *op.cit.*, p. 54. White suggests that Indian interest in alchemy probably arose out of early contacts with China, ibid., p. 53. Marshall dates the most important period of practical alchemy in India to between c. AD 700 and c.1300, *op.cit.*, p. 97.

3 Govinda, *Foundations of Tibetan Mysticism*, p. 55. Needham, pt 3, p. 162. Quotation: White, *The Alchemical Body*, p. 315. Marshall, *The Philosopher's Stone*, p. 97.

4 Needham, pt 2, p. 243. Ray, *History of Chemistry*, pp. 129–31, 134. Needham, pt 5, p. 277. Eliade, *The Forge and the Crucible*, pp. 132–4. White, *The Alchemical Body*, pp. 186–9. Walter, *The Role of Alchemy*, p. 77, n. 61.

5 Quotations: Marshall, *The Philosopher's Stone*, p. 136. White, *The Alchemical Body*, pp. 336–7.

6 White, *The Alchemical Body*, pp. 49, 55. Marshall, *The Philosopher's Stone*, p. 188. Tantrism: S. Gupta *et al.*, *Hindu Tantrism*. White, *op.cit.*, pp. 143, 197. Needham, pt 5, pp. 259–61, 277.

7 Needham, pt 5, pp. 261–3. 'Hathayoga set about the alchemical aim of forging and re-casting an "incorruptible diamond body"', ibid., p. 276. Eliade, *The Forge and the Crucible*, pp. 128–9. Magical alchemy talks of transmutation and bodily immortality as prizes to be won via a struggle with the gods. Tantric alchemy aims at immortality, invincibility and transcendence of the human condition. Siddha alchemy combines mercurial preparations and *hatha* yoga to attain immortality. White, *The Alchemical Body*, pp. 53, 55, 76, 209–10. White also observes, 'The Mediaeval Siddhas of India were self-styled imitators of divine and semidivine Siddhas who, through their conjoined practice of alchemy, hatha yoga, and tantric ritual . . . sought to join the ranks of the latter at the end of their practice or at the end of their lives', ibid., p. 335. *Siddha* means 'someone who has been perfected', and is thus close to the Chinese term *hsien*. Marshall remarks that the traditions of Ayurveda (medicinal) and Siddha (religious, connected with Śiva) draw on the practical aspects of alchemy, while Tantra is connected with its spiritual aspects.

8 Ray, *History of Chemistry*, p. 128. White, *The Alchemical Body*, pp. 144–69. Vyali: Govinda, *Foundations of Tibetan Mysticism*, pp. 56–7. White, *op.cit.*, pp. 258, 259, 245, 176–7, 162, 172–3. Distillation equipment has been found at Taxila in the Vale of Peshawar: Needham, pt 4, pp. 86–7. Pictures of Indian alchemical apparatus can be seen on the alchemy website, www.levity.com/alchemy/in_app_1.html and www.levity.com/alchemy/in_app_2.html.

9 As Mircea Eliade observed, 'As far as the Indian alchemist is concerned, operations on min-

eral substances were not, and *could not be*, simple chemical experiments. On the contrary, they involved his karmic situation; in other words, they had decisive spiritual consequences,' *The Forge and the Crucible*, p. 141 (Eliade's italics).

10   Walter, *The Role of Alchemy and Medicine in Indo-Tibetan Alchemy*, p. 138. See also ibid., p. 8, note 10, p. 77, note 61.

11   Thus, for example, a yogic text may use alchemical terms of purification, desiccation, reduction and oxidation in describing techniques for purifying the body. Walter, *op.cit.* supra, p. 70, n. 23.

12   Walter, *op.cit.*, pp. 36–45, 169–71. Needham, pt 3, p. 36. According to the fourteenth-century *Rasaratnasamucchaya* by Vāgbhatta II, urines from the elephant, the female buffalo, the ass and the horse are to be used during certain types of calcinations: Ray, *History of Chemistry*, pp. 191–2. *Philosophia Maturata*, London 1662, p. 15. The dung in this case was used as a surrounding warming agent rather than a constituent ingredient of the elixir, but a fifteenth-century miniature from *Aurora consurgens* shows a man defecating *into* a crucible.

13   Mercury: White, *The Alchemical Body*, pp. 55, 65, 48–9. Aung, 'Alchemy and alchemists in Burma', pp. 346–54. Quotation from p. 349. Japan: Needham, pt 3, pp. 174–80.

Notes to Chapter 3: Roman Egypt: The White and the Yellow Arising from Blackness

1   Needham, pt 4, pp. 346–55. Quotation, p. 355. Lindsay, *The Origins of Alchemy*, pp. 68–9. See also W. Gundel, 'Alchemie', in *Reallexicon für Antike und Christentum*, Stuttgart: Hiersemann Verlags-GMBH, vol. 1, 1950, pp. 240–1.

2   Read, *Prelude to Chemistry*, p. 8. Plato, *Timaeus* 32c, 49b–c. Aristotle, *Meteorologica* 1.3 (339a.33–35), 4.1 (378b.10–14). Needham, pt 2, pp. 21–2.

3   Needham, pt 2, pp. 189, 220, 247–8. Jacobson, 'Corinthian bronze', pp. 60–4. Quotations: Cyril Stanley Smith in Needham, pt 2, pp. 25–6. *Leiden Papyrus* 38 in Halleux, *Alchimistes grecs*, p. 94. Cf. Needham, *op.cit.*, pp. 252–4. Von Lippmann, *Entstehung und Ausbreitung der Alchemie*, pp. 4–10. *Papyrus Holmiensis* 18 in Halleux, *op.cit.*, p. 116. Von Lippmann, *op.cit.*, pp. 10–24.

4   Suidas, *Lexicon* s.v.'khemeia'. See also Needham, pt 2, pp. 28–9.

5   Berthelot, *Alchimistes grecs*, Greek text, p. 44. Needham, pt 4, pp. 325–7. De Pascalis, *Alchemy*, pp. 26–30. De Pascalis elides Pseudo-Demokritos with Bolos of Mendes, an identification which is by no means certain. Quotation: Berthelot, *op.cit.*, pp. 46–7. Hershbell, 'Democritus and the beginning of Greek alchemy', pp. 14–33. Lindsay, *The Origins of Alchemy*, pp. 90–124.

6   Quoted by Patai, *The Jewish Alchemists*, pp. 61–2. See also Hopkins, 'A study of the keratokis process', pp. 329–34. Lindsay, *The Origins of Alchemy*, pp. 240–52.

7   Quotation: Patai, *The Jewish Alchemists*, p. 65. See also Read, *Prelude to Chemistry*, pp. 14–15, 145–8. Needham, pt 5, p. 11. Kleopatra quotation: Linden, *The Alchemy Reader*, p. 45. Roberts, *Mirror of Alchemy*, p. 57. Lindsay, *The Origins of Alchemy*, pp. 240–77.

8   Patai, *op.cit.* supra, pp. 65–9, 74–6. Von Lippmann, *Entstehung und Ausbreitung der Alchemie*, pp. 46–50. Pattison Muir, *The Alchemical Essence*, pp. 34–5. Moses had alchemical knowledge attributed to him in a dialogue, *The Good Work and Good Fortune of the Creator and the*

Success of Toil and Length of Life, Berthelot, *Alchimistes grecs*, Greek text, pp. 300–15. The first imam of Shia Islam, Ali ibn Abi-Talib, is said to have called alchemy 'the sister of prophecy', Marshall, *The Philosopher's Stone*, p. 219.

9   Isis fragment: Berthelot, *Alchimistes grecs*, Greek text, pp. 28–35. The manuscript is found in the Codex Marcianus, an eleventh-century collection, but its subject-matter and style suggest it originated in c. first century AD. Marshall, *The Philosopher's Stone*, pp. 179–80. 1 Enoch 6.13; 7.12; 8.1–4, trans. R.H. Charles, *Apocrypha and Pseudepigrapha of the Old Testament*, Oxford: Clarendon Press, 1913. My italics.

10   Charron, 'The Apocryphon of John', pp. 442, 444–7. The 'philosophers' of the dialogue could equally well be translated as 'learned men' or 'men interested in the natural sciences'. De Pascalis, *Alchemy*, pp. 31–4. Lindsay, *The Origins of Alchemy*, pp. 253–77. On the difficulties of providing a meaningful definition of 'Gnosticism', see K.L. King, *What is Gnosticism?* Cambridge, MA: Harvard University Press, 2003, pp. 5–19.

11   Sheppard, 'Gnosticism and alchemy', pp. 86–101; 'The redemption theme and Hellenistic alchemy', pp. 42–6. Charron, *op.cit.* supra, p. 455. Fowden, *The Egyptian Hermes*, p.118. Quotation: ibid., pp. 89–90. It is worth noting that Maria wanted to impart colour changes to metals – black, white, yellow, 'violet' – because these represented *inner* changes undergone by the metals during successive laboratory operations, and while it is possible to interpret this as a reference purely to physical changes, it is equally possible to see it in purely spiritual terms.

12   Mertens, *Zosime de Panopolis*, pp. xi–xix. Marshall, *The Philosopher's Stone*, pp. 204–9. Needham, pt 4, pp. 125–6. Hopkins, 'A study of the kerotakis process', pp. 326–43. Holmyard, *Alchemy*, p. 28. Mertens, *op.cit.*, pp. cxvi–xix. Read, *Prelude to Chemistry*, pp. 40–1, 154.

13   Fowden, *The Egyptian Hermes*, pp. 120–6. Lindsay, *The Origins of Alchemy*, pp.323–57. Text of dream: Mertens, *Zosime de Panopolis*, pp.35–8. M.L. von Franz, 'Die alchemistische Makrokosmos-Mikrokosmos-Idee im Lichte der Junschen Psychologie', *Symbolos* 1 (1960), pp. 27–38.

14   Lindsay, *The Origins of Alchemy*, pp. 323–57. Synesios, *De insomniis* in *Patrologia Graeca*, vol. 66, cols. 1297–1300. See also P. Cox Miller, *Dreams in Late Antiquity: Studies in the Imagination of a Culture*, Princeton: Princeton University Press, 1994. Marshall, *The Philosopher's Stone*, p. 194. Gilchrist, *The Elements of Alchemy*, pp. 23–34. Needham, pt 4, p. 386. Fowden, *The Egyptian Hermes*, pp. 125–6. Sherwood Taylor, 'The visions of Zosimos', *Ambix* 1 (1937), pp. 88–92.

15   De Pascalis, *Alchemy*, pp. 41–2. Arkelaos in Holmyard, *Alchemy*, pp. 31–2. Marshall, *The Philosopher's Stone*, pp. 210–11. Browne, 'Rhetorical and religious aspects of Greek alchemy', pp. 129–37. Quotation from Arkelaos given in Browne's translation. Von Lippmann, *Entstehung und Ausbreitung der Alchemie*, pp. 98–102, 103–5, 109. M. Papathanassiou, 'Stephanus of Alexandria', pp. 121–33. Needham, pt 4, p. 401.

16   Olympiodoros in Berthelot, *Alchimistes grecs*, Greek text, p. 70. Browne, 'The poem of the philosopher Theophrastos upon the sacred art', *Scientific Monthly* 11 (September 1920), p. 212. Stephanos in Holmyard, *Alchemy*, p. 31.

Notes to Chapter 4: The Islamic World: Balance and Magic Numbers

1   Nasr, *Islamic Science*, pp. 197–9. Ullmann, 'Al-Kîmiyâ', p. 111. Marshall, *The Philosopher's Stone*, pp. 215, 252. Holmyard, *Alchemy*, pp. 97–100 (translation by R. Steele and D.W. Singer). Needham, pt 4, pp. 368–72. De Pascalis, *Alchemy*, pp. 50, 52. Plessner, 'Hirmes', pp. 463–5.

2   Needham, pt 4, pp. 374–8. Carusi, 'Il sole e la sua ombra', pp. 257–73. Theophrastos: Linden, *The Alchemy Reader*, p. 65. Ullmann, 'Al-Kīmiyā', p. 111. Is there a misprint in this passage? Ullmann seems to equate *al-ajsād* with Greek *sōmata* (bodies), but a more direct equivalent would be *ajsām* meaning 'bodies'. Forbes, *Studies in Ancient Technology*, vol.1, pp. 142–3.

3   De Pascalis, *Alchemy*, pp. 43–5. Needham, pt 4, pp. 409–11, 426–7. Nasr, *An Introduction to Islamic Cosmological Doctrines*, pp. 3–5. The Harranians had inherited their notion of correlation between divinities, metals, plants and planets from their Sumerian and Akkadian forebears. See Forbes, *Studies in Ancient Technology*, vol.1, p. 132. Quotation: Burnett, 'The astrologer's assay of the alchemists', p. 105.

4   On Khālid ibn Yazīd, see Marshall, *The Philosopher's Stone*, pp. 217–18. Needham, pt 4, pp. 389–90. Hopkins, 'A study of the kerotakis process', pp. 345–6. Needham, pt 4, pp. 389, 196, 391–3, 459–61. Corbin, 'Le livre du glorieux', pp. 75–81. On Jābir as an historical or legendary figure, see Hill, 'The literature of Arabic alchemy', pp. 333–4. Nasr, *Islamic Science*, p. 195. Needham, *op.cit.*, p. 394. Nasr, *Introduction to Islamic Cosmological Doctrines*, p. 49. Marshall, *The Philosopher's Stone*, pp. 221–2. Holmyard, *Alchemy*, pp. 68–82, esp. pp. 76–8, but note that he mistakenly accepts the identification of Jābir with Geber. Wilson, 'Jabirian numbers', pp. 1–13. See also Nasr, *Introduction*, p. 50 and cf. Patai, *The Jewish Alchemists*, p. 374.

5   Needham, pt 4, pp. 395–6. Holmyard, *Alchemy*, pp. 73, 79–80. Von Lippmann, *Entstehung und Ausbreitung der Alchemie*, pp. 363–9. Needham, pt 4, p. 393; pt 2, p. 15.

6   Goodman, 'Al-Rāzī', pp. 474–7. Nasr, *Islamic Science*, pp. 200, 270–1. Needham, pt 4, p. 398. Marshall, *The Philosopher's Stone*, pp. 227–30. Ullmann, 'Al-Kīmiyā', p. 112. Von Lippmann, *Entstehung und Ausbreitung der Alchemie*, pp. 400–1. Partington, 'The chemistry of Rāzī', pp. 192–6. Heym, 'Al-Rāzī and alchemy', pp. 184–91. Holmyard, *Alchemy*, pp. 86–92.

7   Needham, pt 4, pp. 397–8, 401–2, 404–8. Ullmann, 'Al-Kīmiyā', pp. 113–14. Al-Masūdī, *Meadows of Gold and Mines of Gems*, pp. 358–9. De Blois, 'Al-Tughrā'ī', pp. 599–600. Al-Tughrā'ī preserved a detailed summary of one of Zosimos's texts, and many quotations from the original, translated into Arabic. See El Khadem, 'A translation of a Zosimos text', pp. 168–78. Pellat, 'Al-Djāhiz', pp. 385–7. Nasr, *Islamic Science*, p. 197.

8   Hill, 'The literature of Arabic alchemy', p. 338. Needham, pt 2, p. 31. Meyerhof, 'Alī al-Bayhaqī's Tatimmat Siwān al-Hikma', pp. 149–50. Nasr, *Introduction to Islamic Cosmological Doctrines*, pp. 177–96. Holmyard, *Alchemy*, pp. 92–7. Quotation: ibid., p. 95. Linden, *The Alchemy Reader*, pp. 95–8. Von Lippmann, *Entstehung und Ausbreitung der Alchemie*, pp. 405–7.

9   Marshall, *The Philosopher's Stone*, pp. 248–50. Needham, pt 4, pp. 398–401. Patai, *The Jewish Alchemists*, pp. 35–6. Holmyard, *Alchemy*, pp. 82–6. Von Lippmann, *Entstehung und Ausbreitung der Alchemie*, pp. 483–4. Plessner, 'The place of the Turba Philosophorum in

the development of alchemy', pp. 335, 337. Quotation: www.levity.com/alchemy/turba.html (adapted).

Notes to Chapter 5: Mediaeval Europe: Translations, Debates and Symbols

1   Marshall, *The Philosopher's Stone*, pp. 258, 259. Read, *Prelude to Chemistry*, pp. 42–3. Holmyard, *Alchemy*, pp. 105–10. De Pascalis, *Alchemy*, pp. 54–5. Needham, pt 4, p. 403. Glick, *Islamic and Christian Spain*, pp. 307–8. Thorndike, *History of Magic*, vol. 2, ch. 38.

2   Needham, pt 4, pp. 389–90, 484. Thorndike, *History of Magic*, vol. 2, pp. 214–17. Von Lippmann, 'an Leere, Unklarheit, und albernem Gefasel', *Entstehung und Ausbreitung der Alchemie*, p. 319.

3   Thorndike, *History of Magic*, vol.2, pp. 567–73. Newman, 'Technology and alchemical debate', pp. 423–6, 431–3. Crisciani, 'Alchemy and Mediaeval universities', p. 2. Bacon quotation: *Opus Tertium*, pp. 39–41. Needham, pt 4, pp. 492–8, (quotation from p. 494). Paravicini Bagliani, 'Ruggero Bacone e l'alchimia di lunga vita', pp. 33–54. De Pascalis, *Alchemy*, pp. 62–3

4   Moran, *Distilling Knowledge*, pp. 23–4. Bacon, *Opus Minus*, pp. 370–5. Newman, 'The philosophers' egg', pp. 77–9, 80–93. Bacon, *Secretum Secretorum*, text given in Newman, *op.cit.*, p. 80, n. 1. Crisciani, *op.cit.* supra, pp. 2, 3. Barthélemy, 'Les liens entre alchimie et médecine', pp. 119–20.

5   Ortulanus in Maxwell-Stuart, *The Occult in Mediaeval Europe*, p. 219. Newman, 'Technology and alchemical debate', pp. 433–9. See also Camilli, 'Scientia mineralis e prolongatio vitae', pp. 211–25. Roberts, *The Mirror of Alchemy*, p. 33. Note that these disagreements do not seem to have been part of the rivalry between Dominicans and Franciscans, since members of both orders appeared on both sides of the argument. Hughes, *Arthurian Myths and Alchemy*, pp. 16, 103. Multhauf, 'John of Rupescissa', pp. 364–5. Pietro d'Abano in Maxwell-Stuart, *op.cit.*, pp. 200–1. See also Crisciani, 'The conception of alchemy', pp. 165–81.

6   Text of *Liber Lucis* in Multhauf, 'John of Rupescissa', p. 361, n. 6. Lydgate, Maxwell-Stuart, *op.cit.* supra, p. 218. Karpenko, 'Alchemy as *donum Dei*', p. 68. Schummer, 'The notion of nature in chemistry', pp. 708–11. See also Ulrich, 'Christliche Theologie und versokratische Ledren in der Turba Philosophorum', pp. 97–123. Crisciani, *Il papa e l'alchimia*, pp. 45–50.

7   Ruland, *Lexicon* s.v. 'materia prima', (pp. 322–6). Maxwell-Stuart, *The Occult in Mediaeval Europe*, pp. 229–30, 223–5, 226–8. Patai, *The Jewish Alchemists*, pp. 258–60, 236. De Pascalis, *Alchemy*, pp. 65–6, 69–70.

8   Arnald of Bruxella: Maxwell-Stuart, *The Occult in Mediaeval Europe*, pp. 211–12. Ripley's vision: Ashmole, *Theatrum Chemicum Britannicum*, p. 374. See also Prinke, 'Hunting the blacke toade', 78–90. Dastin quotation: Holmyard, *Alchemy*, pp. 151–2. Marshall, *The Philosopher's Stone*, pp. 321–2. Josten, 'The text of John Dastin's letter to Pope John XXII', pp. 34–51. 'Dastin's Dream' in Ashmole, *op.cit*, pp.257–68. De Pascalis, *Alchemy*, pp.77–82. John of Rupescissa: Maxwell-Stuart, *op.cit*, p. 216. Hughes, *Arthurian Myths*, pp. 62–3, 89, 213–14, 229–32.

9   Needham, pt 4, p. 373 note g. Marshall, *The Philosopher's Stone*, pp. 268–9. Voss, 'The hierosgamos theme', *www.istanbul-yes-istanbul.co.uk/alchemy/Rosariumfinal.htm*. Abraham,

Dictionary of Alchemical Imagery, pp. 106–7. Ashmole, *Theatrum Chemicum Britannicum*, 'This lion maketh the sun sith soon/To be joined to his sister the moon', p. 279. Nicoll, *The Chemical Theatre*, pp. 138–41. Masson, 'Queer copulation', pp. 37–48. Colours: 'Magnesia is the smelted ore of iron. When the mixture is still black it is called the Black Raven. As it turns white, it is named the Virgin's Milk, or the Bone of the Whale. In its red stage, it is the Red Lion. When it is blue, it is called the Blue Lion. When it is all colours, the sages name it Rainbow. But the number of such names is legion: and I can mention only these few', *The Testament of Cremer*, 159. Abraham, *op.cit.*, pp. 44–5. Read, *Prelude to Chemistry*, pp. 146–7. Roberts, *The Mirror of Alchemy*, pp. 55–6. Nicoll, *op.cit.*, pp. 39–40, 99–100. Dastin quotation: M. Pereira, *L'Oro dei Filosofi*, Spoleto: Centro italiano di Studi sull' Alto Medioevo 1992, p. 142 note 55. Obrist, 'Visualisation in Mediaeval alchemy', p. 131. Constantine of Pisa quotation: Obrist, 'Cosmology and alchemy', p. 135.

10 Ronca, 'Religious symbolism in Mediaeval Islamic and Christian alchemy', p. 110. *Aureum Vellus* quotation: Patai, *The Jewish Alchemists*, pp. 268–9. ibid., pp. 141–3, 234–6, 293–7 (quotation from p. 295), 300–13 (pseudo-Maimonides quotation from p. 306). Al-Jildakī: Needham, pt 4, p. 483. Cf. Anon, *The Sacred and Divine Art of Gold-Making*, pp. 174–5. Suler, 'Alchemy, col. 547.

11 Text of the petition to Henry VI in Pereira, 'Mater medicinarum', p. 41, n. 4, my translation. Pereira, 'Alchemy and the use of the vernacular languages', pp. 339–48. Karpenko, 'The oldest alchemical manuscript in the Czech language', pp. 61–73. A survey of pseudo Arnaldian texts in Catalan is given by L. Cifuentes, 'Les obres alquimíques "Arnaldianes" en Català a finals de l'edat mitjana', in J. Perarnau (ed.), *Actes de la II Trobada Internacional d'Estudis sobre Arnau de Vilanova*, Barcelona: Institut d'Estudis Catalans, 2005, pp. 129–50. Suler, 'Alchemy', cols. 542–4. Calvet, 'L'alchimie médiévale, est-elle une science chrétienne?' pp. 4–7. On the Khunrath engraving, see further Forshaw, 'Alchemy in the amphitheatre', pp.154–76.

Notes to Chapter 6: The Sixteenth and Seventeenth Centuries: Pretension, Fraud and Redeeming the World

1 Climate: B. Fagan, *The Little Ice Age: How Climate Made History*, New York: Basic Books, 2000, pp. 90, 91. W. Behringer, *Witches and Witch-Hunts*, English trans. Cambridge: Polity Press, 2004, pp. 88–9. *Fama*, pp. 29–30. *Confessio*, pp. 50–1. Webster, *From Paracelsus to Newton*, p. 10. G. Meynell, 'The French Academy of Sciences, 1666–91', *www.haven.u-net.com/6text_7B2.htm*

2 Luther: Maxwell-Stuart, *The Occult in Early Modern Europe*, p. 202. Greiner, *Les métamorphoses d'Hermès*, pp. 363–93. Mackay, *Memoirs of Extraordinary Delusions and the Madness of Crowds*, London 1841, reprint Ware: Wordsworth Editions Ltd, 1995, p. 153. Thorndike, *History of Magic and Experimental Science* vol. 5, pp. 534–5, 537–40. Crisciani, *Il papa e l'alchimia*, p. 54. Paracelsus: Ball, *The Devil's Doctor*, pp. 243, 142, 166–7, 190, 261–8. Paracelsus on alchemists: Christie, 'The Paracelsian body', p. 289. Growing gold: Maxwell-Stuart, *op.cit.*, p. 206. Weeks, *Paracelsus*, pp. 106–9. Holmyard, *Alchemy*, pp. 165–76. Koyré, *Mystiques, spirituels, alchimistes*, p. 70, his italics. For a critical voice, see Vickers, 'Analogy versus identity', pp. 126–49. Moran, *Distilling Knowledge*, pp. 70–9. Thorndike, *op.cit.*, pp. 381, 658.

3 Maxwell-Stuart, *op.cit.* supra, pp. 214–19. Davis, *The Autobiography of Denis Zachaire*, pp. 3–13.

4 Platters: E. Le Roy Ladurie, *The Beggar and the Professor*, English trans., Chicago and London: University of Chicago Press, 1997, pp. 49, 69–70. Åkerman, *Queen Christina of Sweden*, pp. 269–83. J. Strype, *Annals of the Reformation and Establishment of Religion*, Oxford: Clarendon Press, 1824, vol. 2, pt 1, pp. 520–3; vol. 2, pt 2, pp. 554–8. On 29 July 1570, John Bulkeley, a student at Oxford, and William Bedo, a stationer, were examined in the Tower on charges of using alchemy to diminish and lessen the coin of the realm, *Calendar of State Papers, Domestic*. Del Rio, *Disquisitiones Magicae*, Leiden 1608, book 1, chapter 5, question 1, section 4. Ridolfi, *Maghi, streghe e alchimisti*, pp. 115–34. Nummedal, 'Alchemical reproduction', pp. 56–68. Smith, 'Alchemy as a language of mediation', pp. 2–3.

5 Shackelford, 'Tycho Brahe', pp. 219, 227. Christianson, *On Tycho's Island*, pp. 91–2, 227, 102–3. Smith, *op.cit.* supra, p. 7. Evans, *Rudolf II and his World*, pp. 214–15. Thorndike, *History of Magic and Experimental Science*, vol. 7, pp. 273–5. On holy Paracelsianism, see Gilly, 'Theophrastia Sancta', pp. 151–85. Craven, *Doctor Heinrich Khunrath*, pp. 2, 3, 6. Forshaw, 'The occult works of Heinrich Khunrath', pp. 110–18. Libavius, *Exercitatio alia de abominabili impietate magiae Paracelsicae per Oswaldum Crollium aucta* in *Examen Philosophiae Novae*, Frankfurt am Main 1615, pp. 66, 72. Bianchi, 'G. Naudé, critique des alchimistes', p. 413.

6 On Hartmann: Thorndike, *History of Magic and Experimental Science* Vol.8, pp. 116–17. Moran, *Distilling Knowledge*, pp. 109–11. Hartmann attributed the recipe for this potable gold to the English alchemist Francis Anthony, on whom see further Linden, *The Alchemy Reader*, pp. 170–3. Evans, *Rudolf II and his World*, pp. 206–7. G. Naudé, *op.cit.* supra, pp. 310–11 note 9. Libavius on Hartmann, *De philosophia vivente seu vitali Paracelsi iuxta P. Severinum Danum ex repetitione I. Hartmanni chymiatri Marburgensis*, in *Examen Philosophiae Novae*, Frankfurt am Main 1615, pp. 181, 168, 249, 253. Marshall, *Theatre of the World*, pp. 129–31. Quotation from Croll: Maxwell-Stuart, *The Occult in Early Modern Europe*, pp. 127–8. Gilly, 'Paracelsianism brings forth a fine Hermetical treatise', pp. 194, 197.

7 Anna Zieglerin's interpretation of alchemy is a good example of this individualism. Her version of some of the processes was peculiar to herself, and deeply personal, and we cannot take her as representative of other contemporary alchemists, other than as a reminder that many of them had views sufficiently individual to render them suspect in the eyes of orthodox authorities, and therefore liable to professional or religious harassment. Alchemical Mass: Coudert, *Alchemy*, pp. 90–1. Neagu, 'The Processus sub Forma Missae', pp. 105–17.

Notes to Chapter 7: The Rosicrucian Episode and its Aftermath

1 Hollandius: Maxwell-Stuart, *The Occult in Early Modern Europe*, pp. 223–4. Galileo, quoted in *Astronomy Now* (October 2004), p. 12.

2 Dickson, *The Tessera of Antilia*, pp. 66–71. Yates, *The Rosicrucian Enlightenment*, pp. 41–58. My translation of the title of the *Fama* differs somewhat from the one she gives. McIntosh, *The Rosicrucians*, pp. 50, 32–40. On Moritz, see further Moran, *The Alchemical World of the German Court*. *Fama* and *Confessio* translation of Thomas Vaughan, 1652, modified.

'Theophilus Schweighardt' (a pseudonym), published a detailed engraving of the mother-house of the Rosicrucian Fraternity in his *Speculum Sophicum Rhodo-Stauroticum*, 1618. See further A. McLean, 'A Rosicrucian emblem', *The Hermetic Journal* 39 (September 1988), pp. 19–22.

3   On Andreae and the Rosicrucian manifestos: Vanloo, *L'Utopie Rose-Croix*, pp. 77–81. Edighoffer, *Les Rose-Croix*, pp. 35–50, 99–121. McIntosh, *The Rosicrucians*, pp. 43–6. Dickson, *op.cit.* supra, pp. 30–48. Andreae's circle of acquaintances is examined further by Ron Heisler, 'Rosicrucianism: the first blooming in Britain', *The Hermetic Journal* (1989), pp. 30–61.

4   Sediwój: Szydło, *Water Which Does Not Wet Hands*, pp. 27–42, 127–42. Szydło, 'Michael Sendivogius and the Statuts des Philosophes Inconnus', pp. 72–89. Prinke, 'Michael Sendivogius and Christian Rosencreutz', pp. 72–98. Prinke, 'The twelfth adept', pp. 156–89. Maier: Yates, *The Rosicrucian Enlightenment*, pp. 80–90. Vanloo, *L'Utopie Rose-Croix*, pp. 172–7. Thorndike, *History of Magic and Experimental Science*, vol. 7, pp. 172–3. De Jong, *Michael Maier's Atalanta Fugiens*, pp. 39–48, 9–15. Read, *Prelude to Chemistry*, pp. 236–54, 281–9. Godwin, 'A context for Michael Maier's Atalanta Fugiens', pp. 4–10.

5   U. Szulakowska, 'The apocalyptic eucharist and religious dissidence in Stefan Michelspacher's Cabala, Spiegel der Kunst und Natur', *Aries* 3 (2003), pp. 200–23. G. Kirbeg, 'An early Rosicrucian text', *The Hermetic Journal* 20 (Summer 1983), pp. 19–25. Read, *Prelude to Chemistry*, pp. 260–7. A. McLean, 'The Hermetic garden of Daniel Stolcius', *The Hermetic Journal* 10 (Winter 1980), pp. 21–6. 'Flamel', *Exposition of the Hieroglyphicall Figures*, xviii–xxiv, xli–xliii. Linden, *Darke Hieroglyphicks*, pp. 208–11.

6   Monteverdi, *Letters*, nos 83 and 84. O. Morris, *The Chymick Bookes of Sir Owen Wynne of Gwydir*, Arizona: Arizona Centre for Mediaeval and Renaissance Studies, 1997, pp. 1–13. Winthrop: Newman, *Gehennical Fire*, pp. 39–50. Thorndike, *History of Magic and Experimental Science*, vol. 7, pp. 178–202, 54–5.

7   Dixon and ten-Doesschate Chu, 'An iconographic riddle', pp. 615–25. McLean, 'A Kabbalistic-alchemical altarpiece', pp. 21–6; 'A Rosicrucian/alchemical mystery centre in Scotland', pp. 11–13, quotation from p. 13; 'An alchemical gate in Rome', pp. 30–4.

8   Linden, *op.cit.* supra, pp. 118–31. On an alchemical interpretation of Shakespeare's *King Lear*, see Nicoll, *The Chemical Theatre*, pp. 136–239. Linden, *The Alchemy Reader*, pp. 199–207. Greiner, *Les métamorphoses d'Hermès*, pp. 497–529, 542–5. Larue, 'Théâtre et alchimie', pp. 261–73. MacDonald, 'Descartes, the lost episodes', pp. 438–48. Matton, 'Cartésianisme et alchimie', pp. 115, 121, 123–8, 133–4, 150–72; quotation from p. 154. On alchemy-chemistry, see Mandosio, 'Quelques aspects de l'alchimie dans les classifications des sciences et des arts au xviie siècle', pp. 19–61.

9   Clericuzio, *Elements, Principles, and Corpuscles*, ch. 1. Newman, *Atoms and Alchemy*, ch. 3. Cavendish quotation: E. Graham, H. Hinds, E. Hobby, H. Wilcox (eds), *Her Own Life: Autobiographical Writings by Seventeenth-Century Englishwomen*, London and New York: Routledge, 1989, p. 93. Moran, *Distilling Knowledge*, pp. 119–20.

Notes to Chapter 8: Theology Wearing a Mask of Science: The Later Seventeenth Century

1 Van Helmont: Debus, *The French Paracelsians*, pp. 110–11. De Paschalis, *Alchemy*, pp. 125–6. Moran, *Distilling Knowledge*, pp. 139–42. Thorndike, *History of Magic and Experimental Science*, vol. 7, pp. 218–40. Schweitzer: De Paschalis, *op.cit.*, pp. 126–7. Thorndike, *op.cit.*, vol. 8, pp. 361–2. Holmyard, *Alchemy*, pp. 259–67. Principe, *The Aspiring Adept*, pp. 104–5. Busardier and Richthausen: Holmyard, *op.cit.*, pp. 128–32. Seyler: Principe, *op.cit.*, pp. 95–6. Fabre, *Alchymista Christianus*, ch. 25. Quotation from *L'abrégé*: Debus, *op.cit.*, pp. 75.

2 Mendelsohn, 'Alchemy and politics', pp. 30, 34–50 (quotation from p. 38), pp. 70–8, (quotation from p. 71). Webster, *The Great Instauration*, pp. 384–402. Young, *Faith, Medical Alchemy, and Natural Philosophy*, pp. 81–98, 152–81 (quotation p. 174).

3 Dream: quoted in Newman, *Gehennical Fire*, p. 65. Newman and Principe, *Alchemy Tried in the Fire*, pp. 197–204 (quotation p. 203). Alkahest: Newman's translation in *op.cit.*, p. 146. College and death: Newman, *op.cit.*, pp. 201–5.

4 Moran, *Distilling Knowledge*, pp. 137–47. Principe, *The Aspiring Adept*, pp. 30–58, quotations pp. 32, 219.

5 Principe, *op.cit.* supra, pp. 188–213. Dobbs, *The Foundations of Newton's Alchemy*, pp. 198, 134–46, quotation pp. 145–6. Webster, *The Great Instauration*, p. xv. Humphrey Newton: quoted in Dobbs, *op.cit.*, pp. 7–8. Dobbs, *The Janus Faces of Genius*, pp. 37–42. Philalethes, *The Mirror of Alchemy*, vv. 271–6. P.H. Reill, *Vitalising Nature in the Enlightenment*, Berkeley, Los Angeles, London: University of California Press, 2005, p. 79. Castillejo, *The Expanding Force in Newton's Cosmos*, pp. 108–13.

Notes to Chapter 9: Alchemy in an Age of Self-Absorption: The Eighteenth and Nineteenth Centuries

1 De Paschalis, *Alchemy*, p. 147. Debus, 'Alchemy in the age of reason', pp. 231–3. Overton Fuller, *The Comte de Saint-Germain*, pp. 225, 114 (quotation), 230, 167–8, 178. De Paschalis, *op.cit.*, p. 152. Gervaso, *Cagliostro*, pp. 44, 68–9, 89–90. McCalman, *The Seven Ordeals of Count Cagliostro*, pp. 12, 23, 45. Fictuld: A. Faivre, *Access to Western Esotericism*, Albany: State University of New York Press, 1994, pp. 178–86. Karpenko, 'Alchemy as *donum Dei*', pp. 9–10; 'Die Edelgeborne Jungfer Alchymia', pp. 50–3, 54–5, 59 (quotation p. 59).

2 De Pascalis, *Alchemy*, pp. 152–60. Read, *Prelude to Chemistry*, pp. 245–6. M. Howard, *The Occult Conspiracy*, London: Rider, 1989, pp. 61–4. Collis, 'Alchemical interest at the Petrine Court', pp. 3, 8–10, 4–8, 10–14. Debus, *The French Paracelsians*, pp. 190–5. Metzger, *Newton, Stahl, Boerhaave*, pp. 191–9. McLean, 'General Rainsford', pp. 129–34. Holmyard, *Alchemy*, pp. 267–70. 'James Price', *Dictionary of National Biography*. Cf. the case of Johann Semler, Professor of Theology at the University of Halle, who thought he had caused metallic transmutation into gold while he was conducting certain iatrochemical experiments, only to discover during a remarkably public demonstration that his servant had been fiddling the previous results. Holmyard, *op.cit.*, pp. 270–2.

3   Quen, 'Dr Eneas Munson (1734–1826)', p. 317. Butler, *Awash in a Sea of Faith*, p. 77. Versluis, *The Esoteric Origins of the American Renaissance*, pp. 35–6. Diderot, 'Cours de chimie de Rouelle', *Oeuvres complètes*, vol. 9, Paris: Hermann, 1981, p. 214. Debus, *The French Paracelsians*, pp. 195–8. Metzger, *Newton, Stahl, Boerhaave*, pp. 113–16. De Pascalis, *Alchemy*, pp. 161–2. McLean, 'Alchemical agriculture', *The Hermetic Journal* (1991), pp. 140–4.

4   Hitchcock: Versluis, *op.cit.* supra, pp. 54–71. Barrett, *The Magus*, reprint of 1801 edition, Bath: Bath Press, 1989, pp. 51–70. Brooke, *The Refiner's Fire*, pp. 159–62, 258 ('Mormon celestial marriage replicated alchemical marriage'), 274, 276.

5   McLean, 'Bacstrom's Rosicrucian Society', pp. 25–9, quotation p. 25. Principe and Newman, 'Some problems with the historiography of alchemy', pp. 389–91. Godwin, 'A Behemist circle in Victorian England', pp. 53–7. Mary Ann South, *A Suggestive Inquiry*, part 1, chapter 2.

6   Lévi, *Transcendental Magic*, pp. 113, 287, 357–8; *Key of the Mysteries*, p. 147. Principe and Newman, *op.cit.* supra, pp. 392–3. Khunrath: Szulakowska, *The Alchemy of Light*, pp. 91–2. I. Regardie, *The Complete Golden Dawn System of Magic*, Phoenix, AZ: Falcon Press, 1984, vol. 6, pp. 48–52, quotations, pp. 48, 52. Ayton: quoted in Howe, *The Magicians of the Golden Dawn*, p. 63. A. Crowley, *Confessions*, London: Arkana, 1979, p. 807. Owen, *The Place of Enchantment*, pp. 124–5.

Notes to Chapter 10: A Child of Earlier Times: The Twentieth Century

1   Westcott quotation from F. King (ed.), *Astral Projection, Ritual Magic, and Alchemy*, Wellingborough: Aquarian Press, 1987, p. 191. Kauffmann, 'The mystery of Stephen H. Emmens', pp. 79, 67, 72–4, 80. Figuier, *L'alchimie et les alchimistes*, pp. 335–64. Jung, *Memories, Dreams, Reflections*, pp. 193–4; 'Religious ideas in alchemy', p. 231. Principe and Newman, 'Some problems with the historiography of alchemy', pp. 401–8. Gibbons, *Spirituality and the Occult*, pp. 107–11.

2   Stavish, 'The history of alchemy in America, Part 3', www.alchemylab.com/AJ4-2.htm. De Pascalis, *Alchemy*, pp. 165–7. 'Fulcanelli', *Le Mystère des cathédrales*, pp. 36, 70. De Pascalis, perhaps by a *lapsus calami*, dates de Montluisant to the eighteenth century, but the *Dictionnaire Nationale de Biographie* is quite clear that he was an early seventeenth-century figure. Böke and Koopmans, 'Fulcanelli's most likely identity', parts 1 & 2. Walter Lang, preface to 'Fulcanelli', *op.cit.*, pp. 29–30.

3   McGill, *August Strindberg*, pp. 341–2, 348–9 (quotation p. 350), 354, 362–3. Strindberg, *Inferno* and *From an Occult Diary*, English trans., London: Penguin, 1979, p. 42. Russell, 'Transformation of mercury into gold', p. 312. Anon., 'The present position of the transmutation controversy', pp. 758–60 (quotation p. 760). Garrett, 'Experiments upon the reported transmutation of mercury into gold', pp. 391–406. See also *Scientific American*, December 1924, March and November 1925, April and August 1926, March 1928. At the same time as Tausend was being put on trial, a Polish engineer, Zbigniew Dunikowski, was in similar trouble for somewhat similar claims and exploits. He attracted the interest of Mussolini, but when the Second World War broke out interest ceased and Dunikowski disappeared. Marshall, *The Philosopher's Stone*, p. 419.

4 Tahil, 'Archibald Cockren: modern alchemist', pp.35–9. Cockren, *Alchemy Rediscovered and Restored*, pp.114–15, 122–3, 126–7, 119. Gilchrist, *Alchemy*, pp.138–9. Marshall, *The Philosopher's Stone*, pp.419–20. Barbault: Gilchrist, *op.cit.*, pp.139–42. Marshall, *op.cit.*, pp.421–2. Barbault, *Gold of a Thousand Mornings*, pp.47, 29, 37–9, 113–21. McLean, *A Commentary on the Mutus Liber*, pp.39–60. McLean, 'Capillary dynamolysis', *The Hermetic Journal* 8 (Summer 1980), pp.28–32. M. Theroux, 'Lunar influence on the electrochemical production of colloidal silver', *www.borderlands.com/journal/lunar.htm* Dubuis: Marshall, *op.cit.*, pp.444–52. White, *The Alchemical Body*, pp.336–9. D'Espagnet, *Enchyridion Physicae Restitutae*, English trans., London 1651, aphorism 146.

Select Bibliography

Abraham, L., *A Dictionary of Alchemical Imagery* (Cambridge: Cambridge University Press, 1998).

Abrahams, H.J., 'Al-Jawbari on false alchemists', *Ambix* 31 (July 1984), pp. 84–7.

Åkerman, S., *Queen Christina of Sweden and Her Circle: The Transformation of a Philosophical Libertine* (Leiden: Brill, 1991).

——*Red Cross over the Baltic: The Spread of Rosicrucianism in Northern Europe* (Leiden: Brill, 1998).

'Albertus', *The Alchemist's Handbook: Manual for Practical Laboratory Alchemy* (revised ed. Maine: Samuel Weiser Inc., 1974).

al-Masūdī, *Meadows of Gold and Mines of Gems*, English trans. P. Lunde and C. Stone (London and New York: Kegan Paul International, 1989).

Anon., *Collectanea Chemica* (London: Vincent Stuart Ltd, 1963; reprint of 1893 ed.).

——'The present position of the transmutation controversy', *Nature* 117 (29 May 1926), pp. 758–60.

——*The Book of Lambspring and the Golden Tripod* (Lampeter: Llanerch Enterprises, 1987).

——*The Sacred and Divine Art of Gold-Making*, ed. A. Colinet = *Les Alchimistes Grecs*, vol. 10 (Paris: Les Belles Lettres, 2000).

Adams, A. and S.J. Linden, (eds), *Emblems and Alchemy = Glasgow Emblem Studies*, vol. 3 (Glasgow: University of Glasgow, 1998).

Ashmole, E., *Theatrum Chemicum Britannicum* (London: Grismond, 1652).

Aung, M. Htin, 'Alchemy and alchemists in Burma', *Folklore* 44 (December 1933), pp. 346–54.

Bacon, R. 'Opus Minus', in J.S. Brewer (ed.) *Opera quaedam hactenus inedita* vol. 1, (London: Longman, Green, Longman and Roberts, 1859).

——'Opus Tertium' in J.S. Brewer (ed.) *Opera quaedam hactenus inedita* vol. 1, (London: Longman, Green, Longman & Roberts, 1859).

Ball, P., *The Devil's Doctor: Paracelsus and the World of Renaissance Magic and Science* (London: William Heinemann, 2006).

Barbault, A., *Gold of a Thousand Mornings*, English trans. (London: Neville Spearman, 1975).

Barthélemy, 'Les liens entre alchimie et médecine. L'example de Guillaume
    Sedacer', *Alchimia e Medicina nel Medioevo = Micrologus* 9 (Firenze: Edizioni
    del Galluzzo, 2003), pp. 109–34.

Bayer, P., 'Lady Margaret Clifford's alchemical receipt book and the John Dee
    circle', *Ambix* 52 (November 2005), pp. 271–84.

Bernoulli, R., 'Seelische Entwicklung im Spiegel der Alchemie und
    verwandtner Disziplinen', *Eranos-Jahrbuch* 3 (1935), pp. 231–87.

Berthelot, M., *Collections des anciens alchimistes grecs*, 3 vols (Paris, 1888).

Bianchi, L., 'G. Naudé, critique des alchimistes', in J.-C. Margolin and
    S. Matton, *Alchimie et Philosophie à la Renaissance* (Paris: Librairie
    Philosophique J. Vrin, 1993), pp. 405–21.

Brill 2000), pp.599–60.

Böke, C. and J. Koopmans, 'Fulcanelli's most likely identity', pt 1, www.
    alchemylab.com/AJ7-2.htm; pt 2, www.alchemylab.com/AJ7-3.htm.

Brann, N.L., 'Alchemy and melancholy in Mediaeval and Renaissance thought:
    a query into the mystical basis of their relationship', *Ambix* 32 (November
    1985), pp. 127–47.

Brehm, E., 'Roger Bacon's place in the history of alchemy', *Ambix* 23
    (March 1976), pp. 53–8.

Brooke, J.L., *The Refiner's Fire: The Making of the Mormon Cosmology,
    1644–1844* (Cambridge: Cambridge University Press, 1996).

Browne, C.A., 'Rhetorical and religious aspects of Greek alchemy', *Ambix* 2
    (December 1946), pp. 129–37.

Burnett, C., 'The astrologer's assay of the alchemist', *Ambix* 39 (1992), pp. 103–9.

Butler, J., *Awash in a Sea of Faith* (Cambridge & London: Harvard University
    Press, 1990).

Calvet, A., 'Une pratique de l'or potable au xvie siècle: le Traité du Grand
    Oeuvre de Philippe Rouillac', in S. Matton, *Documents oubliés sur l'alchimie*
    (Geneva: Librairie Droz, 2001), pp. 131–60.

——'L'alchimie médiévale, est-elle une science chrétienne?' in *Les dossiers du
    Grihl, Libertinage, athéisme, irreligion. Essais et Bibliographie 2007.*
    http://dossiersgrihl.revues.org/document321.html

Camilli, G., 'Scientia mineralis e prolongatio vitae nel Rosarius
    Philosophorum', *Le crisi dell'alchimia = Micrologus* (Brepols, 1995).

Carusi, P., 'Il sole e la sua ombra. Nodi lunari e rappresentazioni dell'eclisse
    nell'alchimia islamica', *Natura, scienza e società medievali = Micrologus* 12
    (Firenze: Edizioni del Galluzzo, 2004), pp. 257–73.

Castillejo, D.C., *The Expanding Force in Newton's Cosmos* (Madrid: Ediciones
    de Arte y Bibliofilia, 1981).

Cavarra, B., 'Alchimia e medicina nei testi byzantini', *Alchimia e medicina nel
    Medioevo = Micrologus* 9 (2003), pp. 1–17.

Charron, R., 'The Apocryphon of John (NHC II,1) and the Graeco-Egyptian alchemical literature', *Vigiliae Christianae* 58 (2005), pp. 438–56.

Chikashige, M., *Alchemy and Other Chemical Achievements of the Ancient Orient* (Tokyo: Rokakuho Uchida, 1936).

Christianson, J.R., *On Tycho's Island: Tycho Brahe and His Assistants, 1570–1601* (Cambridge: Cambridge University Press, 2000).

Christie, J.R.R., 'The Paracelsian body', in Grell, *Paracelsus* (Leiden: Brill, 1998), pp. 269–91.

Clericuzio, A., *Elements, Principles, and Corpuscles: A Study of Atomism and Chemistry in the Seventeenth Century* (Dordrecht: Kluer Academic Publishers, 2000).

Clulee, N.H., 'The Monas Hieroglyphica and the alchemical thread of John Dee's career', *Ambix* 52 (November 2005), pp. 197–216.

Cockren, A., *Alchemy Rediscovered and Restored* (London: Rider & Co., 1940).

Colinet, A., *Les Alchimistes Grecs*, vol. 10: *L'anonyme de Zuretti* (Paris: Les Belles Lettres, 2000).

Collis, R., 'Alchemical interest at the Petrine Court', www.esoteric.msu.edu/VolumeVII/Russian alchemy.htm.

Cooper, J.C., *Chinese Alchemy: The Taoist Quest for Immortality* (Wellingborough: Aquarian Press, 1984).

Corbin, H., 'Le livre du glorieux de Jābir ibn Hayyān', *Eranos-Jahrbuch* 18 (1950), pp. 47–114.

Coudert, A., *Alchemy: The Philosopher's Stone* (London: Wildwood House, 1980).

Craven, J.B., *Count Michael Mayer* (Kirkwall: William Peace & Son, 1910).

——*Doctor Heinrich Khunrath: A Study in Mystical Alchemy* (Glasgow: Hermetic Studies no. 1 (1997)).

Cremer, *Testament*, in Anon., *The Book of Lambspring and the Golden Tripod* (Lampeter: Llanerch Enterprises, 1987), pp. 152–60.

Crisciani, C., 'The conception of alchemy as expressed in the Pretiosa Margarita Novella of Petrus Bonus of Ferrara', *Ambix* 20 (November 1973), pp. 165–81.

——'From the laboratory to the library: alchemy according to Guglielmo Fabri', in A. Grafton and N. Siraisi (eds), *Natural Particulars: Nature and the Disciplines in Renaissance Europe* (Cambridge, MA: MIT Press, 1999), pp. 295–319.

——*Il papa e l'alchimia: Felice V, Guglielmo Fabri e l'elixir* (Rome: Viella, 2002).

——'Alchemy and Mediaeval universities. Some proposals for research', www.cis.unibo.it/NewsLetter/101997Nw/cresci.htm.

Crisciani, C. and A.P. Bagliani (eds), *Alchimia e Medicina nel Medioevo* (Firenze: Edizioni del Galluzzo, 2003).

Croll, O., *Alchemomedizinische Briefe, 1585 bis 1597*, ed. W. Kühlmann and
    J. Telle (Stuttgart: Franz Steiner Verlag, 1998).
Davis, T.L., 'The Chinese beginnings of alchemy', *Endeavour* 2 (1943),
    pp. 154–60.
——*The Autobiography of Denis Zachaire* (London: Holmes Publishing Group,
    2001).
Davis, T.L. and Chao Yün-Ts'ung, 'An alchemical poem by Kao Hsiang-Hsien',
    Isis 30 (1939), pp. 236–40.
Debus, A.G., 'Alchemy in an age of reason: the chemical philosophers in early
    eighteenth-century France', in I. Merkel and A.D. Debus (eds), *Hermeticism
    and the Renaissance: Intellectual History and the Occult in Early Modern
    Europe* (Cranbury, NJ: Associated University Presses, 1988), pp. 231–50.
——*The French Paracelsians: The Chemical Challenge to Medical and Scientific
    Tradition in Early Modern France* (Cambridge: Cambridge University Press,
    1991).
——(ed.), *Alchemy and Early Modern Chemistry: Papers from Ambix* (London:
    Jeremy Mills Publications for the Society for the History of Alchemy and
    Chemistry, 2004).
de Blois, F. C., 'Al-Tughrā'ī', in *Encyclopaedia of Islam*, 2nd ed., vol.10 (Leiden:
De Jong, H.M.E., *Michael Maier's Atalanta Fugiens: Sources of an Alchemical
    Book of Emblems* (Leiden: Brill, 1969).
De Pascalis, A., *Alchemy: The Golden Art*, English trans. (Rome: Gremese
    International, 1995).
Dickson, D.R., *The Tessera of Antilia: Utopian Brotherhoods and Secret Societies
    in the Early Seventeenth Century* (Leiden: Brill, 1998).
Dixon, L.S., *Alchemical Imagery in Bosch's Garden of Delights* (Ann Arbor:
    UMI Research Press 1981).
Dixon, L.S. and ten Doesschate Chu, 'An iconographic riddle: Gerbrandt van
    den Eeckhout's Royal Repart in the Liechtenstein Princely collections', *Art
    Bulletin* 71 (December 1989), pp. 610–27.
Dobbs, B.J.T., *The Foundation of Newton's Alchemy, or, The Hunting of the
    Greene Lyon* (Cambridge: Cambridge University Press, 1975).
——*The Janus Faces of Genius: The Role of Alchemy in Newton's Thought*
    (Cambridge: Cambridge University Press, 1991).
DuBruck, E.E., 'Theophrastus Bombastus von Hohenheim, called Paracelsus:
    highways and byways of a wandering physician (1493–1541)', *Fifteenth-
    Century Studies* 25 (1999), pp. 1–10.
Dubs, H.H., 'The beginnings of alchemy', *Isis* 38 (1947–8), pp. 62–86.
Edighoffer, R., *Les Rose-Croix et la Crise de la Conscience européenne au xviie
    siècle* (Paris: Éditions Dervy, 1998).
Eliade, M., *The Forge and the Crucible: The Origins and Structures of Alchemy*,

English trans. 2nd ed. (Chicago and London: University of Chicago Press, 1978).

El Khadem, H.S., 'A lost text by Zosimos, reproduced in an old alchemy book', *Journal of Chemical Education* 72 (1995), pp. 774–5.

——'A translation of a Zosimos text in an Arabic alchemy book', *Journal of the Washington Academy of Sciences* 84 (September 1996), pp. 168–78.

'Eugenius Philalethes', *The Fame and Confession of the Fraternity of the R.C., commonly, of the Rosie Cross* (London, 1652).

Evans, R.J.W., *Rudolf II and his World: A Study in Intellectual History, 1576–1612* (Oxford: Clarendon Press, 1973).

Fabre, P.J., *L'alchimiste chrétien (Alchymista Christianus)*, ed. F. Greiner (Paris and Milan: SÉHA & ARCHÈ, 2001).

Fara, P., *Newton, The Making of a Genius* (London: Macmillan, 2002).

Figuier, L., *L'alchimie et les alchimistes* (Paris, 1854).

'Flamel, N.', *Exposition of the Hieroglyphicall Figures* (1624), ed. L. Dixon (New York and London: Garland Publishing, 1994).

Forbes, R.J., *Studies in Ancient Technology*, 2nd ed., vol. 1 (Leiden: Brill, 1964).

Forke, A., 'Ko Hung, der Philosoph und Alchimist', *Archiv für Geschichte der Philosophie* 41 (1932), pp. 115–26.

Forshaw, P., 'Alchemy in the amphitheatre: some consideration of the alchemical content of the engravings in Heinrich Khunrath's Amphitheatre of Eternal Wisdom (1609)', in J. Wamberg (ed.), *Art and Alchemy* (Copenhagen: Museum Tusculanum Press, 2006), pp. 154–76.

——'Curious knowledge and wonder-working wisdom in the occult works of Heinrich Khunrath', in R.J.W. Evans and A. Marr (eds), *Curiosity and Wonder from the Renaissance to the Enlightenment* (Aldershot: Ashgate, 2006).

Fowden, G., *The Egyptian Hermes: An Historical Approach to the Late Pagan Mind* (Princeton: Princeton University Press, 1993).

'Fulcanelli', *Le Mystère des cathédrales*, English trans., 2nd ed. (Sudbury: Neville Spearman Ltd, 1971).

Gabriele, M., 'Le Caravage et les quatre éléments', in F. Greiner, *Aspects de la tradition alchimique au xviie siècle* (Paris: S.É.H.A., 1998), pp. 287–94.

García Font, J., *Historia de la Alquimía en España* (Madrid: Editora Nacional, 1976).

Garrett, M.W., 'Experiments upon the reported transmutation of mercury into gold', *Proceedings of the Royal Society of London*, Series A (1926), pp. 391–406.

Gervaso, R., *Cagliostro*, English trans. (London: Victor Gollancz Ltd, 1974).

Gibbons, B.J., *Spirituality and the Occult: From the Renaissance to the Modern Age* (London and New York: Routledge, 2001).

Gilbert, R.A., *A.E. Waite: Magician of Many Parts* (Wellingborough: Crucible, 1987).

Gilchrist, C., *The Elements of Alchemy* (Longmead: Element Books, 1991).

Gilly, C., *Adam Haselmayer: Der erste Erkunder der Manifeste der Rosencreutzer* (Amsterdam: In de Pelikaan, 1995).

——'Theophrastia Sancta. Paracelsianism as a religion in conflict with the established Churches', in *Transformation of Paracelsism 1500–1800: Alchemy, Chemistry and Medicine (Glasgow Symposium 15–19 September 1993)* (Leiden: Brill, 1998), pp. 151–85.

——'Paracelsianism brings forth a fine Hermetical treatise: Suchten's De tribus facultatibus', in C. Gilly and C. van Heertum (eds), *Magia, Alchimia, Scienza dal 400 al 700: L'influsso di Ermete Trismegisto*, vol.1 (Venezia and Amsterdam: Centro Di, 2002), pp. 192–8.

——'L'Amphitheatrum Sapientiae Aeternae di Heinrich Khunrath', in C. Gilly and C. van Heertum (eds), *Magia, Alchimia, Scienza dal 400 al 700: L'influsso di Ermete Trismegisto*, vol.1 (Venezia and Amsterdam: Centro Di, 2002), pp. 325–50.

Glick, T.F., *Islamic and Christian Spain in the Early Middle Ages* 2nd ed., (Leiden: Brill, 2005).

Godwin, J., 'A Behemist circle in Victorian England', *The Hermetic Journal* 46 (1992), pp.48–71.

—— 'The deepest of the Rosicrucians: Michael Maier', in R. White, *The Rosicrucian Enlightenment Revisited* (Hudson, New York: Lindisfarne Books 1999), pp. 101–23.

Goodman, L.E., 'Al-Rāzī', *Encyclopaedia of Islam* new ed., (Leiden: Brill, 1995), pp. 474–7.

Goodrick-Clarke, N., *Paracelsus: Essential Readings* (Wellingborough: Crucible, 1990).

Govinda, A., *Foundations of Tibetan Mysticism* (London: Rider, 1960).

Greiner, F. (ed.), *Aspects de la tradition alchimique au xviie siècle* (Paris: S.É.H.A., 1998).

——'Art du feu, art du secret: obscurité et ésotérisme dans les textes alchimiques de l'âge baroque', in F. Greiner, *Aspects de la tradition alchimique au xviie siècle* (Paris: S.É.H.A., 1998), pp. 207–31.

——*Les métamorphoses d'Hermès: Tradition alchimique et ésthetique littéraire dans la France de l'âge baroque (1583–1646)* (Paris: Honoré Champion, 2000).

Grell, O.P., *Paracelsus: The Man and his Reputation, his Ideas and their Transformation* (Leiden: Brill, 1998).

Gupta, S., Goudriaan, T. and Hoens, D.J., *Hindu Tantrism* (Leiden: Brill, 1979).

Haage, B.D., *Alchemie im Mittelalter* (Zurich: Artemis & Winkler, 1996).

Halleux, R. (ed.), *Les Alchimistes Grecs*, vol. 1: *Papyrus de Leyde, Papyrus de Stockholm, Fragments de Recettes* (Paris: Les Belles Lettres, 1981).

——'Albert le Grand et l'alchimie', *Revue des sciences philosophiques et théologiques* 66 (1982), pp. 57–80.

Hamarneh, S.K., 'Arabic-Islamic alchemy: three intertwined stages', *Ambix* 29 (July 1982), pp. 74–87.

Hannaway, O., *The Chemists and the Word: The Didactic Origins of Chemistry* (Baltimore: Johns Hopkins University Press, 1975).

Haskell, Y., 'Round and round we go: the alchemical Opus Circulatorium of Giovanni Aurelio Augurello', *Bibliothèque d'Humanisme et Renaissance* 59 (1997), pp. 583–606.

Heisler, R., 'John Dee and the secret societies', *The Hermetic Journal* 46 (1992), pp. 12–24.

Hereward, T., *The Quest for the Phoenix: Spiritual Alchemy and Rosicrucianism in the World of Michael Maier (1569–1622)* (Leiden: Walter de Gruyter & Co., 2003).

Hershbell, J.P., 'Democritus and the beginning of Greek alchemy', *Ambix* 45 (1998), pp. 14–33.

Heym, G., 'Al-Rāzī and alchemy', *Ambix* 1 (1938), pp. 184–91.

Hill, D.R., 'The literature of Arabic alchemy', in M.J.L. Young, J.D. Latham, R.B. Serjeant (eds), *Religion, Learning and Science in the 'Abassid Period* (Cambridge: Cambridge University Press, 1990), pp. 328–41.

Holmyard, E.J., *Alchemy* (New York: Dover Publications, 1990; reprint of 1957 edition).

Hopkins, A.J., 'A study of the kerotakis process as given by Zosimus and later alchemical writers', *Isis* 29 (1938), pp. 326–54.

Howe, E., *The Magicians of the Golden Dawn: A Documentary History of a Magical Order, 1887–1923* (Wellingborough: The Aquarian Press, 1985).

Hughes, J., *Arthurian Myths and Alchemy: The Kingship of Edward IV* (Stroud: Sutton, 2002).

Jacobson, D.M., 'Corinthian bronze and the gold of the alchemists', *Gold Bulletin* 33 (2000), pp. 60–6.

Jones, B., *Lithochymicus*, ed. R.M. Schuler, *Alchemical Poetry, 1575–1700* (New York and London: Garland Publishing, 1995), pp. 210–428.

Josten, C.H., 'The text of John Dastin's letter to Pope John XXII', *Ambix* 4 (December 1949), pp. 34–51.

Jung, C.G., 'Religious ideas in alchemy', *Collected Works*, English trans., vol.12, *Psychology and Alchemy* (London: Routledge & Kegan Paul, 1953), pp. 215–463.

——*Memories, Dreams, Reflections*, English trans. (London: Collins and Routledge & Kegan Paul, 1963).

——'The visions of Zosimos', *Collected Works*, English trans., vol. 13, *Alchemical Studies* (London and Henley: Routledge & Kegan Paul, 1967), pp. 57–108.

Kahn, D., 'Alchimie et architecture: de la pyramide à l'église alchimique', in
F. Greiner, *Aspects de la tradition alchimique au xviie siècle* (Paris: S.É.H.A.,
1998), pp. 295–335.

Karpenko, V., 'The oldest alchemical manuscript in the Czech language', *Ambix*
37 (July 1990), pp. 61–73.

——'Christoph Bergne: the last Prague alchemist', *Ambix* 37 (November 1990),
pp. 121–33.

——'Alchemy as *donum Dei*', *HYLE – International Journal for the Philosophy
of Chemistry* 4 (1998), pp. 63–80.

——'Die Edelgeborne Jungfer Alchymia: the final stage of European alchemy',
Bulletin of the History of Chemistry 25 (2000), pp. 50–63.

Kauffman, G.B., 'The mystery of Stephen H. Emmens: successful alchemist or
ingenious swindler?' *Ambix* 30 (July 1983), pp. 65–88.

Kibre, P., 'Albertus Magnus on alchemy', in J.A. Weisheipl (ed.), *Albertus Magnus
and the Sciences* (Toronto: Pontifical Institute of Mediaeval Studies, 1980).

Kiss, F.G., B., Lang, and C.,Popa-Gorjanu, 'The alchemical Mass of Nicholas
Melchior Cibinensis: text, identity, and speculations', *Ambix* 53 (July 2006),
pp. 143–79.

Koyré, A., *Mystiques, spirituels, alchimistes du xvie siècle allemande* (Paris:
A. Colin, 1955).

Larue, A., 'Théâtre et alchimie', in F. Greiner, *Aspects de la tradition alchimique
au xviie siècle* (Paris: S.É.H.A., 1998), pp. 261–73.

Laurant, J.-P., 'L'Alchymie du Maçon de François-Nicolas Noël', in S. Matton,
Documents oubliés sur l'alchimie (Geneva: Librairie Droz 2001), pp. 439–55.

Lévi, E., *Transcendental Magic*, English trans. (London: Rider, 1984).

——*The Key of the Mysteries*, English trans. (London: Rider, 1984).

Linden, S.J., *Darke Hierogliphicks: Alchemy in English Literature from Chaucer
to the Renaissance* (Lexington: University Press of Kentucky, 1966).

——(ed.), *The Alchemy Reader: From Hermes Trismegistus to Isaac Newton*
(Cambridge: Cambridge University Press, 2003).

Lindsay, J., *The Origins of Alchemy in Graeco-Roman Egypt* (London: Muller,
1970).

Lu-Ch'iang, Wu, and T.L. Davis, 'An ancient Chinese treatise on alchemy
entitled Ts'an T'ung Ch'i', *Isis* 18 (1932), pp. 210–89.

MacDonald, P.S., 'Descartes, the lost episodes', *Journal of the History of
Philosophy* 40 (2002), pp. 437–60.

MacDonald Ross, G., 'Leibniz and the Nuremberg Alchemical Society', *Studia
Leibnitiana* 6 (1974), pp. 222–48.

Maillard, J.-F., 'Descartes et l'alchimie: une tentation conjurée?' in F. Greiner,
Aspects de la tradition alchimique au xviie siècle (Paris: S.É.H.A., 1998),
pp. 95–109.

Mandosio, J.-M., 'Quelques aspects de l'alchimie dans les classifications des sciences et des arts au xviie siècle', in F. Greiner, *Aspects de la tradition alchimique au xviie siècle* (Paris: S.É.H.A., 1998), pp. 19–61.

Mann, C., 'Queer copulation and the pursuit of divine conjunction in two Middle English alchemical poems', in S.M. Chewning (ed.), *Intersections of Sexuality and the Divine in Mediaeval Culture: The Word Made Flesh* (Aldershot: Ashgate, 2005), pp. 37–48.

Margolin, J.-C. and S. Matton, (eds), *Alchimie et Philosophie à la Renaissance* (Paris: Librairie Philosophique J. Vrin, 1993).

Marshall, P., *The Philosopher's Stone* (London: Macmillan, 2002).

——*The Theatre of the World: Alchemy, Astrology and Magic in Renaissance Prague* (London: Harvill Secker, 2006).

Masson, C., 'Queer copulation and the pursuit of divine conjunction in two Middle English alchemical poems', in S.M. Chewning (ed.), *Intersections of Sexuality and the Divine in Mediaeval Culture* (Aldershot: Ashgate, 2005).

Matton, S., 'Cartésianisme et alchimie: à propos d'un témoignage ignoré sur les travaux alchimiques de Descartes', in F. Greiner, *Aspects de la tradition alchimique au xviie siècle* (Paris: S.É.H.A., 1998), pp. 111–84.

——(ed.), *Documents oubliés sur l'alchimie, la kabbale et Guillaume Postel* (Geneva: Librairie Droz, 2001).

Maxwell-Stuart, P.G., *The Occult in Early Modern Europe* (Basingstoke: Macmillan, 1999).

——*The Occult in Mediaeval Europe* (Basingstoke: Palgrave, 2005).

Mazzeo, J.A., 'Notes on John Donne's alchemical imagery', *Isis* 48 (1957), pp. 103–23.

McCalman, I., *The Seven Ordeals of Count Cagliostro* (London: Century, 2003).

McGill, V.J., *August Strindberg, the Bedevilled Viking* (New York: Brentano's, 1930).

McIntosh, C., *The Rosicrucians: The History and Mythology of an Occult Order*, revised ed. (Wellingborough: Crucible, 1987).

McLean, A., 'A Rosicrucian/alchemical mystery centre in Scotland', *The Hermetic Journal* 4 (Summer 1979), pp. 10–13.

——'Bacstrom's Rosicrucian Society', *The Hermetic Journal* 6 (Winter 1979), pp. 25–9.

——'A Kabbalistic/alchemical altarpiece', *The Hermetic Journal* 12 (Summer 1981), pp. 21–6.

——*A Commentary on the Mutus Liber* (Tysoe: Hermetic Research Trust, 1982).

——'An alchemical gate in Rome', *The Hermetic Journal* 21 (Autumn 1983), pp. 30–4.

'General Rainsford: an alchemical and Rosicrucian enthusiast', *The Hermetic Journal* 44 (1990), pp. 129–34.

Mendelsohn, J.A., 'Alchemy and politics in England, 1649–1665', *Past and Present* 135 (May 1992), pp. 30–78.

Mertens, M., *Les Alchimistes Grecs*, vol. 4: *Zosime de Panopolis* (Paris: Les Belles Lettres, 1995).

Metzger, H., *Newton, Stahl, Boerhaave, et la Doctrine Chimique* (Paris: Librairie Félix Alcan, 1930).

Meyerhof, M., 'Alī al-Bayhaqī's Tatimmat Siwān al-Hikma', *Osiris* 8 (1948), pp. 122–216.

Moran, B.T., 'Privilege, communication, and chemistry: the Hermetic-alchemical circle of Moritz of Hessen-Kassel', *Ambix* 32 (November 1985), pp. 110–26.

——*The Alchemical World of the German Court: Occult Philosophy and Chemical Medicine in the Circle of Moritz of Hessen* (Stuttgart: Franz Steiner Verlag, 1991).

——*Distilling Knowledge: Alchemy, Chemistry, and the Scientific Revolution* (Cambridge, MA: Harvard University Press, 2005).

Multhauf, R.P., 'John of Rupescissa and the origin of medical chemistry', *Isis* 45 (December 1954), pp. 359–67.

Nagoaka, H., 'Preliminary note on the transmutation of mercury into gold', *Nature* 116 (18 July 1925), pp. 95–6.

Nasr S.H., *An Introduction to Islamic Cosmological Doctrines* (Cambridge, MA: Harvard University Press, 1964).

——*Islamic Science: An Illustrated Study* (World of Islam Publishing Company Ltd, 1976).

Neagu, C., 'The Processus sub Forma Missae: Christian alchemy, identity, and identification', *Archaeus* 4 (2000), pp. 105–17.

Needham, J. and Wang Ling, *Science and Civilisation in China*, vol. 3, *Mathematics and the Sciences of the Heavens and the Earth* (Cambridge: Cambridge University Press, 1959).

——*Science and Civilisation in China*, vol. 4, *Physics and Physical Technology*, part 1, *Physics* (Cambridge: Cambridge University Press, 1962).

Needham, J. and Lu, Gwei-Djen, *Science and Civilisation in China*, vol. 5, *Chemistry and Chemical Technology*, pt 2, *Spagyrical Discovery and Invention: Magisteries of Gold and Immortality* (Cambridge: Cambridge University Press, 1974).

Needham, J., Ho Ping-Yü and Lu Gwei-Djen, *Science and Civilisation in China*, pt 5, *Chemistry and Chemical Technology*, pt 3, *Spagyrical Discovery and Invention: Historical Survey from Cinnabar Elixirs to Synthetic Insulin* (Cambridge: Cambridge University Press, 1976).

Needham, J. and Lu Gwei-Djen, *Science and Civilisation in China*, vol. 5, *Chemistry and Chemical Technology*, pt 5, *Spagyrical Discovery and Invention: Physiological Alchemy* (Cambridge: Cambridge University Press, 1983).

Newman, W.R., 'Technology and alchemical debate in the late Middle Ages', *Isis* 80 (September 1989), pp. 423–45.

——*Gehennical Fire: The Lives of George Starkey, an American Alchemist in the Scientific Revolution* (Cambridge, MA: Harvard University Press, 1994).

——'The philosophers' egg: theory and practice in the alchemy of Roger Bacon', in *Le crisi dell'alchimia = Micrologus* 3 (1995), pp. 37–48, 75–101.

——*Atoms and Alchemy: Chymistry and the Experimental Origins of the Scientific Revolution* (Chicago and London: University of Chicago Press, 2006).

Newman, W.R. and A. Grafton, (eds), *Secrets of Nature: Astrology and Alchemy in Early Modern Europe* (Cambridge, MA: MIT Press, 2001).

Newman, W.R. and L.M. Principe, *Alchemy Tried in the Fire: Starkey, Boyle, and the Fate of Helmontian Chemistry* (Chicago and London: University of Chicago Press, 2002).

Nicoll, C., *The Chemical Theatre* (London: Routledge & Kegan Paul, 1980).

Nierenstein, M. and P.F. Chapman, 'Enquiry into the authorship of the Ordinall of Alchemy', *Isis* 18 (1932), pp. 290–321.

Norton, T., *The Ordinall of Alchimy* (London: Edward Arnold, 1928).

Nummedal, T.E., 'Alchemical reproduction and the career of Anna Maria Zieglerin', *Ambix* 48 (July 2001), pp. 56–68.

Obrist, B., *Les débuts de l'imagerie alchimique (xive–xve siècles)* (Paris: Le Sycomore, 1982).

——'Cosmology and alchemy in an illustrated thirteenth-century alchemical tract: Constantine of Pisa, The Book of Secrets of Alchemy', *I discorsi dei corpi = Micrologus* 1 (1993), pp. 115–60.

——'Visualisation in Mediaeval alchemy', *HYLE – International Journal for the Philosophy of Chemistry* 9 (2003), pp. 131–70.

——'Alchimie et allégorie scripturaire au Moyen Age', in G. Dahan and R. Goulet (eds), *Allégorie des Poetes, Allégorie des Philosophes: Études sur la Poétique et l'Herméneutique de l'Allégorie de l'Antiquité à la Réforme* (Paris: Vrin, 2005), pp. 245–65.

Overton Fuller, J., *The Comte de Saint-Germain: Last Scion of the House of Rákóczy* (London and The Hague: East-West Publications, 1988).

Owen, A., *The Place of Enchantment: British Occultism and the Culture of the Modern* (Chicago and London: University of Chicago Press, 2004).

Papathanassiou, M., 'Stephanus of Alexandria: Pharmaceutical notions and cosmology in his alchemical work', *Ambix* 37 (November 1990), pp. 121–33.

Paravicini Bagliani, A., 'Ruggero Bacone e l'alchimia di lunga vita. Riflessioni sui testi', *Alchimia e Medicina nel Medioevo = Micrologus* 9 (Firenze: Edizioni del Galluzzo, 2003), pp. 33–54.

Partington, J.R., 'The relationship between Chinese and Arabic alchemy', *Nature* 120 (30 July 1927), p. 158.

——'The chemistry of Rāzī', *Ambix* 1 (1938), pp. 192–6.

Patai, R., 'Raymund de Tarrega: Marrano, heretic, alchemist', *Ambix* 35 (March 1988), pp. 1–13.

——*The Jewish Alchemists* (Princeton: Princeton University Press, 1994).

Pattison Muir, M.M., *The Alchemical Essence and the Chemical Element* (London: Longman, Green & Co., 1894).

Pellat, Ch., 'Al-Djāhiz', in *Encyclopaedia of Islam*, 2nd ed. vol. 2 (Leiden: Brill 1965), pp.385–7.

Pereira, M., *The Alchemical Corpus attributed to Raymond Lull = Warburg Institute Surveys and Texts* 18 (London: Warburg Institute, 1989).

——'Mater medicinarum: English physicians and the alchemical elixir in the fifteenth century', in R. French, J. Arrizabalaga, A. Cunningham, L. García-Ballester (eds), *Medicine from the Black Death to the French Disease* (Aldershot: Ashgate, 1998), pp. 26–52.

——'Alchemy and the use of vernacular languages in the late Middle Ages', *Speculum* 74 (1999), pp. 336–56.

Plessner, M., 'Hermes Trismegistus and Arab science', *Studia Islamica* 2 (1954), pp. 45–59.

——'The place of the Turba Philosophorum in the development of alchemy', *Isis* 45 (December 1954), pp. 331–8.

Pregadio, F., 'I due aspetti del rituale nell'alchimia cinese', *Atti del Convegno sul tema 'Scienze tradizionali in Asia: Principi e Applicazioni'*, ed. L. Lanciotti and B. Melasecchi (Perugia: Fornari, 1996), pp. 135–49.

Principe, L.M., *The Aspiring Adept: Robert Boyle and his Alchemical Quest* (Princeton: Princeton University Press, 1998).

Principe, L.M. and W.R. Newman, 'Some problems with the historiography of alchemy', in W.R. Newman and A. Grafton (eds), *Secrets of Nature* (Cambridge, MA: MIT Press, 2001), pp. 385–431.

Prinke, R.T., 'The occult centre in Cracovia', *The Hermetic Journal* 38 (1987), pp. 12–19.

——Michael Sendivogius and Christian Rosenkreutz: the unexpected possibilities', *The Hermetic Journal* 44 (1990), pp. 72–98.

——'Hunting the blacke toade', *The Hermetic Journal* 45 (1991), pp. 78–90.

——'The twelfth adept: Michael Sendivogius in Rudolfine Prague', in R. White, *The Rosicrucian Enlightenment Revisited* (Hudson, New York: Lindisfarne Books, 1999), pp. 143–92.

Quen, J.M., 'Dr Eneas Munson (1734–1826)', *Journal of the History of Medicine* 31 (July 1976), pp. 307–19.

Ray, Prafulla Chandra, *History of Chemistry in Ancient and Mediaeval India* (Calcutta: Indian Chemical Society, 1956).

Read, B.E., 'Chinese alchemy', *Nature* 120 (17 December 1927), pp. 877–8.

Read, J., *Prelude to Chemistry* (London: G. Bell & Son, 1936).

Ridolfi, M.A.C., *Maghi, streghe e alchimisti a Siena e nel suo territorio (1458–1571)* (Siena: Edizioni il Leccio, 1999).

Roberts, G., *The Mirror of Alchemy* (London: The British Library, 1994).

Robinet, I., 'Le monde à l'envers dans l'alchimie intérieure Taoïste', *Revue de l'Histoire des Religions* 209 (1992), pp. 239–57.

Ronca, I., 'Religious symbolism in Mediaeval Islamic and Christian alchemy', in A. Faivre and W.J. Hanegraaff (eds.), *Western Esotericism and the Science of Religion* (Leuven: Peeters 1998), pp.95–117.

Ruland, M., *Lexicon alchemiae sive dictionarium alchemisticum* (Frankfurt am Main, 1612).

Ruska, J., *Arabische Alchemisten*, 2 parts (Heidelberg, 1924).

Russell, A.S., 'Transformation of mercury into gold', *Nature* 116 (29 August 1925), p. 312.

Ryan, W.F., 'Alchemy, magic, poisons, and the virtues of stones in Old Russian Secretum Secretorum', *Ambix* 37 (1990), pp. 46–53.

Ryding, K.C., 'Islamic alchemy according to al-Khwarizmi', *Ambix* 41 (November 1994), pp. 121–34.

Schafer, E.H., 'Orpiment and realgar in Chinese technology and tradition', *Journal of the American Oriental Society* 75 (1955), pp. 73–89.

Schuler, R.M., 'Some spiritual alchemies of seventeenth-century England', *Journal of the History of Ideas* 41 (1980), pp. 293–318.

Schummer, J., 'The notion of nature in chemistry', *Studies in the History and Philosophy of Science* 34 (2003), pp. 705–36.

Segonds, A.P., 'Tycho Brahe et alchimie', in J.-C. Margolin and S. Matton, *Alchimie et Philosophie à la Renaissance* (Paris: Librairie Philosophique J. Vrin, 1993), pp. 365–78.

Shackelford, J., 'Tycho Brahe, laboratory design, and the aim of science', *Isis* 84 (1993), pp. 211–30.

Sheppard, H.J., 'Gnosticism and alchemy', *Ambix* 6 (1957), pp. 86–101.

——'The redemption theme and Hellenistic alchemy', *Ambix* 7 (1959), pp. 42–6.

Sherwood Taylor, F., 'The visions of Zosimos', *Ambix* 1 (1937), pp. 88–92.

Sivin, N., *Chinese Alchemy: Preliminary Studies* (Cambridge, MA: Harvard University Press, 1968).

——'Chinese alchemy and the manipulation of time', *Isis* 67 (1976), pp. 513–26.

Smith, P.H., 'Alchemy as a language of mediation at the Habsburg Court', *Isis* 85 (1994), pp. 1–25.

——*The Business of Alchemy: Science and Culture in the Holy Roman Empire* (Princeton: Princeton University Press, 1994).

Soddy, F., 'The reported transmutation of mercury into gold', *Nature* 114
(16 August 1924), pp. 244–5.

South, Mary Ann, *A Suggestive Inquiry into the Hermetic Mystery* (Belfast:
William Tait 1918).

Spooner, R.C. and C.H. Wang, 'The divine nine turn Tan Sha method, a
Chinese alchemical recipe', *Isis* 38 (1947–8), pp. 235–42.

Stevens, D. (trans.), *The Letters of Claudio Monteverdi* (London: Faber, 1980).

Strickman, M., 'On the alchemy of T'ao Hung-ching', in H. Welch and A. Seidel
(eds), *Facets of Taoism: Essays in Chinese Religion* (New Haven and London:
Yale University Press, 1981), pp. 123–92.

Stryz, J., 'The alchemy of the voice at Ephrata Cloister', www.esoteric.msu.
edu/Alchemy.html.

Suler, B., 'Alchemy', *Encyclopaedia Judaica*, vol. 2 (Jerusalem: Keter Publishing
House, 1971), cols. 542–9.

Szulakowska, U., 'The tree of Aristotle: images of the Philosophers' Stone',
Ambix 33 (July/November, 1986), pp. 53–77.

——*The Alchemy of Light: Geometry and Optics in Late Renaissance Alchemical
Illustration* (Leiden: Brill, 2000).

——*The Sacrificial Body and the Day of Doom: Alchemy and Apocalyptic
Discourse in the Protestant Reformation* (Leiden: Brill, 2006).

Szydło, Z., 'Michael Sendivogius and the Statuts des Philosophes Inconnus',
The Hermetic Journal 46 (1992), pp. 72–91.

——*Water Which Does Not Wet Hands: The Alchemy of Michael Sendivogius*
(Warsaw: Polish Academy of Sciences, 1994).

Tahil, P., 'Archibald Cockren: modern alchemist', *The Hermetic Journal* 13
(Autumn 1981), pp. 35–9.

Tenney Davis, L., 'Count Michael Maier's use of the symbolism of alchemy',
Journal of Chemical Education 15 (September 1938), pp. 403–10.

Thompson, C.J.S., *Alchemy and Alchemists* (Toronto: Dover Publications,
reprint 2002).

Thorndike, L., *A History of Magic and Experimental Science*, 8 vols (New York:
Columbia University Press, 1923–58).

Tilton, H., 'Of ether and colloidal gold: the making of a philosopher's stone',
www.esoteric.msu.edu/Volume VII/Ether (old).htm.

——*The Quest for the Phoenix: Spiritual Alchemy and Rosicrucianism in
the Work of Michael Maier* (1569–1622) (Berlin and New York: Walter de
Gruyter & Co., 2003).

Trismosin, S., *Splendor Solis*, trans. J. Godwin (Grand Rapids: Phanes Press,
1991).

Ullmann, M., 'Al-Kīmiyā', *Encyclopaedia of Islam*, new ed., vol. 5 (Leiden: Brill,
1986), pp. 110–15.

Ulrich, R., 'Christliche Theologie und vorsokratische Lehren in der Turba Philosophorum', *Oriens* 32 (1990), pp. 97–123.

Van Lennep, J., *Alchimie: contribution à l'histoire de l'art alchimique* (Brussels: Crédit communal de Belgique, 1985).

Vanloo, R., *L'Utopie Rose-Croix du xviie siècle à nos jours* (Paris: Editions Dervy, 2001).

Versluis, A., *The Esoteric Origins of the American Renaissance* (Oxford: Oxford University Press, 2001).

Vickers, B., 'Analogy versus identity: the rejection of occult symbolism, 1580–1680', in B. Vickers (ed.), *Occult and Scientific Mentalities in the Renaissance* (Cambridge: Cambridge University Press, 1984), pp. 95–163.

Von Lippmann, E.O., *Entstehung und Ausbreitung der Alchemie* (Berlin: Julius Springer, 1919).

Voss, K.-C., 'The hierosgamos theme in the images of the Rosarium Philosophorum', in Z.R.W.M. von Martels (ed.), *Alchemy Revisited: Proceedings of the International Conference on the History of Alchemy at the University of Groningen, 17–19 April 1989* (Leiden: Brill, 1990).

Waite, A.E., *Lives of the Alchemical Philosophers* (London: George Redway, 1888).

Waley, A., 'Notes on Chinese alchemy', *Bulletin of the School of Oriental Studies* 6 (1930–32), pp. 1–24.

Walter, M.L., *The Role of Alchemy and Medicine in Indo-Tibetan Alchemy* (unpublished PhD thesis, Indiana University, 1980).

Watanabe-O'Kelly, H., *Court Culture in Dresden: From Renaissance to Baroque* (Basingstoke: Palgrave, 2002).

Webster, C., *The Great Instauration: Science, Medicine and Reform, 1626–1660* (London: Duckworth, 1975).

——*From Paracelsus to Newton* (Cambridge: Cambridge University Press, 1982).

Weeks, A., *Paracelsus: Speculative Theory and the Crisis of the Early Reformation* (Albany: State University of New York Press, 1997).

Westfall, R.S., 'Newton and alchemy', in B. Vickers (ed.), *Occult and Scientific Mentalities in the Renaissance* (Cambridge: Cambridge University Press, 1984), pp. 315–35.

White, D.G., *The Alchemical Body: Siddha Traditions in Modern India* (Chicago: University of Chicago Press, 1998).

White, M., *Isaac Newton: The Last Sorcerer* (London: Fourth Estate, 1997).

White, R. (ed.), *The Rosicrucian Enlightenment Revisited* (Hudson, New York: Lindisfarne Books, 1999).

Wilkinson, R.S., 'New England's last alchemists', *Ambix* 10 (February 1962), pp. 128–38.

Wilson, C.A., 'Jabirian numbers, Pythagorean numbers, and Plato's Timaeus', *Ambix* 35 (March 1988), pp. 1–13.

——'Pythagorean theory and Dionysian practice: the cultic and practical background to chemical experimentation in Hellenistic Egypt', *Ambix* 45 (March 1998), pp. 14–32.

Wilson, W.J., 'An alchemical manuscript by Arnaldus de Bruxella', *Osiris* 2 (1936), pp. 220–405.

Woolley, B., *The Queen's Conjuror: The Science and Magic of Dr Dee* (London: HarperCollins, 2001).

Wujastyk, D., 'An alchemical ghost', *Ambix* 31 (July 1984), pp. 70–83.

Yates, F.A., *The Rosicrucian Enlightenment* (London: Ark Paperbacks, 1986).

Young, J.T., *Faith, Medical Alchemy and Natural Philosophy: Johann Moriaen, Reformed Intelligencer and the Hartlib Circle* (Aldershot: Ashgate, 1998).

Yu, Ying-shi, 'Life and immortality in the mind of Han China', *Harvard Journal of Asiatic Studies* 25 (1964–5), pp.80–122

Index